My Mad World of
OPERA

My Mad World of
OPERA

Harold Rosenthal

WEIDENFELD AND NICOLSON
LONDON

to George without whom it all would have been impossible

Contents

———

Acknowledgements

———

To Herbert von Thal who suggested to me that I had a story to tell and convinced Weidenfeld and Nicolson that they should ask me to write it. To Deidre Tilley, my personal assistant on *Opera* who deciphered my untidy manuscript and typed it before it went to Sarah Chandor, who produced the finished text. To my associate editor, Rodney Milnes, who put in a lot of extra time in the *Opera* office in order to allow the editor enough time to write this book. To Francesca George for her help and advice and judicious editing of the finished text; and to the many people who have given me permission to quote from letters they have written to me.

Illustrations

———

Introduction

——

As each issue of *Opera* magazine appears I am still amazed that such a publication should have been born and should continue to survive in England, a country that has only really established an operatic tradition of its own during the last thirty or so years. As I look back over more than half-a-century of opera-going and thirty years of *Opera*, all but the first three of them as editor, I feel rather as Captain Vere must have felt at the end of Britten's *Billy Budd*, when he remembered that 'far-away summer of seventeen hundred and ninety-seven, long ago now, years ago, centuries ago ...'. Unlike Captain Vere, however, I do not have to add that 'I am an old man now!' But that autumn of 1930 when I was first taken to an opera seems to belong to another world, and the autumn of 1949, when *Opera* magazine was conceived, really does seem many years, if not actually centuries ago.

It was in October 1949 that three young men, Lord Harewood, Richard Buckle (then editor of *Ballet and Opera*), and myself, sat down to plan a new magazine to be devoted entirely to opera because the operatic section of *Ballet and Opera* was getting out of hand and becoming far too large for its editor and for most ballet-omanes. I do not suppose that any of us really believed that the new magazine was going to survive very long, though, of course, we hoped it would, or that it would become the best and most influential operatic publication in the world devoted to opera, for that is what I am often told that it is. Because many singers, conductors, producers and others involved in the extraordinary business of putting on opera appear to take the magazine quite seriously, I have, over the years, grown more and more conscious of the responsibilities of helping to shape both operatic policy and public taste; arrogant though that might sound.

To have spent all those years in the crazy world of opera has been both rewarding and frustrating. Rewarding, because it has brought me into personal contact with some of the finest artists in the world of opera, some of whom I can still, despite being a critic, count as close personal friends; and frustrating, because, although I enjoy being an editor and critic, I still regret that I have never been involved in operatic administration. There was a period during the 1960s when I might have been tempted to produce (or as they say in the straight theatre, direct) opera, had I been asked; and I believe I could have done so, though how successfully is of course conjecture. Never having been able to do more than croak since my voice broke, the question of my becoming a singer never arose; but even had I possessed the vocal potential I doubt whether I possessed the singleness of purpose or self-discipline to have been able to pursue the life of a singer.

Thoughts like those, however, were certainly not in my mind when I heard my first opera, *Madam Butterfly* (in English) in that far off autumn of 1930 at the Streatham Hill Theatre in south London; by the mid-1930s I had been well and truly bitten by the opera bug and had become infected with what today is called 'operamania'. How that all began and developed, and how what started as a teenage passion and hobby eventually became the means of earning my living and my mad world of both opera and *Opera*, I will try to relate in the ensuing pages.

I
Early Years

—

I was born at West Norwood, a suburb of south London, not far from the old Crystal Palace, during an air-raid in 1917. Both my parents were teachers and had met working in the same school, where my father was assistant headmaster and my mother the headmistress. It was a charitable institution for Jewish orphans, and my family and those of my parents' colleagues formed a very enclosed community. Until I was eleven years old, my friends were entirely drawn from the children at the orphanage and from the families of the teachers. Although the institution was run on orthodox Jewish lines, my parents were never strictly orthodox, and I was never conscious of having religion rammed down my throat.

My childhood was generally a happy one. There was always music at home, my mother played the piano; my father who had a rather beautiful baritone voice, sang. He had once thought of training to become a Jewish minister of religion, and because he was a considerable Hebrew scholar, one of his functions at Norwood was to conduct the service in the orphanage Synagogue on Sabbaths and Jewish holy days. Surprisingly, it was in the Synagogue that I heard my first operatic aria, for one of my father's delights was to incorporate classical melodies into the Jewish liturgical music, especially in the New Year and Day of Atonement services. I remember vividly hearing my father sing a very beautiful tune which was quite new to me one *Yom Kippur* service. I asked him after the service what it was: 'It comes from an opera by Verdi' he replied (I was about ten years old at the time) but did not go into any more detail. Some time later I discovered it was the Count of Luna's aria, 'Il balen', from *Il trovatore*. I asked Father whether I could hear some other music from the same opera, and as a result I was introduced to the pleasures of the gramophone. This was not in our own home but in a spacious room called the Committee Room, of the orphanage, where there was a large gramophone with an enormous horn, such as one still sees on EMI record labels with the little white dog gazing up into it; and there was a fine selection of old 78s by Caruso, Tetrazzini, Battistini, John McCormack and other singers with similar exotic names, who, as I got older, became well known to me.

There were several quite accomplished musicians on the staff of the school, including one Philip Bogod, who sang duets with my father at school concerts – I still remember their performances of the Gendarmes' duet from Offenbach's *Geneviève de Brabant* to which they added additional couplets with words of their own, naming, to the delight of their youthful audience, the two most troublesome pupils whom they 'would run in'! Then there was the gifted Solomon Taylor, who produced and conducted the annual Gilbert and Sullivan operetta; and so I heard my first *Trial by Jury* and *Pirates of Penzance* performed by young Jewish orphans accompanied by two pianos!

The next step was obviously a visit to a D'Oyly Carte Opera; it was *The Mikado* at the Streatham Hill Theatre, where I heard the great Henry Lytton as Ko-Ko. Yet somehow I sensed that it was not the real thing, and so I pestered my parents to be allowed to go to a real opera. I was promised that this would happen when I had celebrated my Barmitzvah, the Jewish boy's confirmation service, when he reaches the age of thirteen. I still had to wait two years for that event and by way of compensation I was given a gramophone of my own and a few records, including Galli-Curci singing 'Ah fors'è lui' from *La traviata* and Caruso singing 'Vesti la giubba'. I began to save a few pence each week from my pocket money, so I could go and buy my own records at the local HMV shop. My first purchase was, not unnaturally, 'Il balen' sung by Giuseppe De Luca, followed a little later by a ten-inch red-label disc of Lucrezia Bori singing the Gavotte from *Mignon* on one side and 'Connais-tu le pays?' from the same opera on the reverse; that was not because I knew anything about either Ambroise Thomas or his *Mignon*, but because we had learned the Gavotte as a class song the previous year – it began with the ridiculous words 'Softly tripping to and fro'!

As my thirteenth birthday approached the prospect of my first visit to a 'real' opera occupied my thoughts. Where would it be?

What would it be? By that time I knew of the existence of Covent
Garden, for my parents had a subscription for what was known as
the 'Grand Season': two seats in row six or seven, I cannot remember
which, in the amphitheatre, for one night a week – ten performances
in all, for the season only lasted ten weeks at the total cost of £3 5s
– that worked out at 6s 6d a performance, which was 1s less than a
seat in the dress circle for the Lyceum pantomime, a yearly childhood
treat. So I pleaded for a visit to Covent Garden; but as the season
lasted from the end of April until early July, and as my birthday was
at the end of September, I was obviously going to have to wait until
the summer of 1931 before that could take place, for a Barmitzvah
present could not be given in advance! However, I was taken yet
again to the Streatham Hill Theatre during the Christmas holidays
of 1930 to hear the Covent Garden Opera Company 'direct from
the Royal Opera House, Covent Garden', in *Madame* (*sic*) *Butterfly*,
sung in English. It was the last day of the company's autumn tour,
the date 20 December 1930, and a matinée – the evening was to be
Die Fledermaus, which I would hear in more august surroundings
the following summer. Our seats in row N of the Grand Circle cost
3s 6d, and the cast was headed by Maggie Teyte as Cio-Cio-
San, with Francis Russell as Pinkerton, Constance Willis as Suzuki,
Frank Sale (later to become a tenor) as Sharpless, and conducted
by John Barbirolli. In case you are wondering how I remember
all those details, it is because ever since that first opera visit I have
kept my programme and ticket stubs. I did not begin to make
written comments, either on the programme or in an operatic
diary until five years later, when I started to go to the opera on
my own and was able to choose what I wanted to see, rather than
being taken by my parents and having my operatic diet prescribed
by them.

Perhaps a few words about London operatic life in the 1930s might
be of interest. There was the annual 'Grand Season' at the Royal
Opera House lasting ten weeks, soon to be dramatically curtailed in
length because of the economic slump that followed the Wall Street
crash; then there were three opera performances a week at the Old
Vic, alternating with Shakespeare, and in January 1931, when Sadler's
Wells Theatre opened and the Vic-Wells Opera was formed, these
were increased to five, plus an evening of ballet. And, except for an

annual visit by the Carl Rosa Opera, either to the Lyceum Theatre or to one of the many suburban theatres, that was all. The Covent Garden English Company, which had been formed in 1929 when the British National Opera Company had been forced into liquidation, only survived until the autumn of 1931. In 1933 some of the members of that company were to form themselves into another short-lived organization, The Metropolitan Opera Company, which gave Wagner seasons at the Streatham Hill and Golders Green theatres in London; and it was this company which was to provide me with my first experience of Wagner in the theatre.

2

The Bug Begins to Bite

—

My parents' subscription night at Covent Garden was Tuesday, and so on 5 May 1931, the second night of the season, I climbed the steps to the amphitheatre and entered the magic world of the Royal Opera House for the first time. The amphitheatre, or, to give it the name by which it was known in the 1930s, the amphitheatre stalls, was the only part of the house other than the gallery, which in those days was separated from the amphitheatre, in which full evening dress was not *de rigueur*. The sight below me of stalls and boxes filled with men in white tie and tails and ladies in splendid evening dresses, many wearing long white gloves, and tiaras, and to me looking like people from another world (even the programme sellers, mostly men, were attired in tail coats), made an indelible impression on me. Perhaps the seeds of another of my strongly held attitudes about opera were also planted on that occasion: namely that opera was, and to some extent still is, an élitist entertainment. I also remember being shocked by the fact that in the lower parts of the house, people arrived late and left early – as they still do at the Metropolitan Opera in New York.

Die Fledermaus was a revival of the previous season's production, and had only been added to the repertory despite much opposition from the board after special pleading by Bruno Walter. Most of the board had thought it far too light-hearted an affair for the 'Grand Season', or indeed for Covent Garden at all; and there were many Covent Garden regulars who were appalled at the prospect of seeing and hearing their favourite Sieglinde and Marschallin (Lotte Lehmann), Sophie and Zerlina (Elisabeth Schumann), Fricka and Brangaene (Maria Olczewska), and Alberich and Beckmesser (Eduard Habich) as Rosalinda, Adele, Orlofsky and Frosch.

The first performance of the 1931 *Fledermaus* was dogged by illness among the principal singers; Lehmann had to omit the 'Czardas' in the second act because of a throat infection and Olczewska was replaced as Orlofsky by one Gabriele Joachim; but as I knew very little of the *Fledermaus* score I was not unduly perturbed. I enjoyed most of what I heard and laughed at the antics of Frosch and Dr Blind, played by Habich and Heinrich Tessmer; however, the interminable dialogue in Act III, spoken of course in German, was meaningless to me, and I suspect also to a large percentage of the audience. When I asked why we could not hear the opera in English, I was told that no one would come to Covent Garden if the operas were sung in that language, and, in any case, great international opera singers could not be expected to sing their rôles in English – something I have been told countless times since. Perhaps that *Fledermaus* helped sow the seeds of another of those heretical views I hold, that opera audiences should, on the whole, understand what is being sung on the stage.

La traviata was a rather different story. The simple programme synopsis was quite adequate, though my mother swore to me many years later that I asked her in a very loud voice, obviously to her embarrassment and the amusement of people sitting close by, 'Mummy, what is a *demi-mondaine*?' When I returned home that evening my father asked me who had been singing: 'Rosa Ponselle and Dino Borgioli' I duly informed him. 'My boy,' he replied, 'you should have heard Melba and Caruso.' I suppose I should have been impressed and remained silent, but being a precocious youth I countered with 'Oh, I suppose when you heard those singers your father told you that you should have heard Patti and De Reszke.' This was complete cheek on my part, for I had only just begun to delve into operatic folk-lore, and had no idea whether those two singers had ever appeared together in *La traviata*. In any case, as my grandparents only came to England from Poland in the late 1870s and had lived all their lives in Hull, I am certain they could never have heard opera at Covent Garden!

There followed three rather lean years as far as live opera performances were concerned. The 1932 Covent Garden season was reduced to a four-week Wagner Festival, and my parents were not avid Wagnerians; but even had they been, economic circumstances would have prevented them from renewing their subscription. However, I was slowly adding to my own record collection and discovering books about opera, including the 1925 edition of His Master's Voice *Opera at Home* and one of the early editions of Kobbé's *Complete Opera Book* which I found on the bookshelf of one of my adopted aunts; while the local lending library provided me with biographies of several composers.

On the other hand, my formal musical education progressed rather slowly; I was having piano lessons from my sister's piano teacher and struggling with elementary harmony and theory. The City of London School, which I attended from 1929–36, was sadly lacking at that time in any form of musical activity. Across John Carpenter Street, however, which ran down to the Embankment on the west side of the school, was the Guildhall School of Music from which one occasionally heard the voices of hopeful young students practising. One of the many teachers at the Guildhall was Lewis Cairns James; he had been there since 1904, and every Wednesday afternoon he crossed the street to the CLS to take two elocution classes. Elocution was an optional extra, and as I was fond of reciting and longed to act both in the school play and the annual Shakespearean extracts that were performed at a special prize day, called Beaufoy Day, I joined that class. It also had the added attraction of releasing me from organized games on Wednesday afternoon!

Cairns James was a great raconteur, and it was not long before he was regaling us with stories about his work as an operatic producer with the Beecham Opera Company – he was also responsible for the staging of the Guildhall School of Music's annual operatic performances until 1938. He was an avid Wagnerian and his graphic account of *The Mastersingers* whetted my appetite to hear that opera. This was partly assuaged by the broadcast of Act I from Covent Garden in the 1932 Wagner season; it was only after much pleading that I was allowed to listen to this, for the broadcast began at 6.55 p.m. and lasted until 8.30 p.m., the period during which I was supposed to be doing my homework. It was the first of many opera broadcasts that took precedence over Latin and Greek.

The chance to hear a live performance of *The Mastersingers* came the following year, again at the Streatham Hill Theatre, which was playing host to the grandly named if short-lived Metropolitan Opera Company. As well as *The Mastersingers* they were to perform the complete *Ring* and *Tristan and Isolde*, all in English, with singers such as Florence Austral, Miriam Licette, Walter Widdop, Parry Jones,

Browning Mummery, Norman Allin, Arthur Fear and Horace
Stevens in the casts; and the conductors were Albert Coates and
Aylmer Buesst. The season was announced in the local papers and
on hoardings in and around Streatham and Norwood. My father's
colleague, Sol Taylor, whose love of Wagner equalled his enthusiasm for Gilbert and Sullivan, offered to take me to one of the
performances, and I naturally opted for *The Mastersingers*. Before
the end of the evening I had been converted to Wagner, and to this
day his magic still casts a spell.

As 1934 was the year in which I took my School Certificate
examination, any idea of a visit to Covent Garden during the short
May and June season was quite out of the question; but there were
still broadcasts. By then I had discovered that in addition to the
Radio Times the BBC published another weekly paper, *World Radio*.
As its name implies, it listed, day-by-day and station-by-station, all
the important European broadcasts, and even included short-wave
broadcasts from America. It was published on Fridays, but our local
newsagent would let me have it late on Thursday evening, so I could
see what operatic treats were in store for the coming week.

With School Certificate over and a long summer holiday ahead,
I resumed my Wagnerian education every Monday night at the
Queen's Hall Promenade Concerts. Monday night was always Wagner night, and the programmes were made up of those 'bleeding
chunks' so derided today, but then a wonderful way in which to
learn one's Wagner.

My School Certificate results were good, seven passes, six with
credit, just missing the seventh in Greek. I chose to specialize in
history and joined a small select band in what was known as the
History Sixth, where I discovered three kindred spirits who shared
my tastes in opera. Higher School Certificate was two years away
and my parents now allowed me considerable freedom in choosing
how I could spend both my free time and my pocket money;
consequently visits to Sadler's Wells became more frequent during
the 1934-5 season. It was also in 1935 that I began to keep three
'music' diaries: the first an operatic diary of performances I attended;
the second, a diary of operatic broadcasts that I heard; and the third
a diary of concerts. At about the same time one of my new-found
friends in the History Sixth, Ray Farrar, showed me copies of two
American musical magazines that could be purchased on book stalls

in the Charing Cross Road area: *Musical America* and *Musical Courier*. These chronicled not only all operatic and concert performances in the United States but also those in Europe, and I began to spend part of my weekly allowance on those periodicals from which I cut out all the opera reviews and stuck them in a series of scrap-books, which I still have; this process continued well into the 1950s. Into those scrap-books also went cuttings from *World Radio*, including articles on famous European opera houses and singers.

Late in 1934 I made two further important discoveries; the existence of the excellent Saturday music pages in the *Daily Telegraph*, with its columns of concert and opera announcements, weekly articles, and musical news features, and of the monthly magazine *The Gramophone*. This latter magazine was eventually to change my life. My first attempts at writing about opera appeared in its pages and continued to do so during the early 1940s. One of my war-time letters, published in November 1943, was read by Lord Harewood, or Viscount Lascelles as he then was, and initiated a correspondence between us which resulted in our eventual meeting, eventual collaboration and friendship. But, in 1935, that was nearly ten years away.

In February 1935 I began what was to become a regular part of my operatic life for the next few years, Saturday matinées at Sadler's Wells Theatre. This had to be done with a certain amount of discretion on my part, for my father was shortly to assume the headship of the Norwood Jewish School, and it would not have seemed quite 'right' for the headmaster's son to be seen getting onto a bus or tram not far from the school gates, on a Sabbath afternoon. So, in order not to cause embarrassment I used to walk a couple of miles before boarding a number 33 tram, which took me all the way to Rosebery Avenue, via the old Kingsway subway, and deposited me outside the doors of Sadler's Wells Theatre in a little over forty minutes. Sometimes I played truant from Synagogue service and spent the morning at the Guildhall Museum in the City where I had learned from my history master that one could consult file copies of *The Times*; from these I laboriously began to copy the casts of all the Covent Garden seasons since 1924, thus laying the foundation of what was to become, some twenty years later, my official history of Covent Garden. The opera bug had bitten me badly.

On 23 February I saw my first *Marriage of Figaro* at Sadler's Wells;

it was also the first Mozart opera I had seen in the theatre and I immediately fell in love with it and its composer. Since then I have seen *Figaro* more than any other opera; nearly two hundred times including festival performances at Glyndebourne, Salzburg and Munich, performances by students in music schools, and by touring groups in makeshift theatres. I have heard it sung in French, German, Italian, in Americanized English and even in Swedish; but it is Edward J. Dent's still witty and eminently singable translation that I first heard in 1935 which remains in my memory to this day and I can quote pages of it by heart.

It was at that *Figaro* performance that I first became conscious of Joan Cross's outstanding gifts as a singer and an actress. She sang the Countess in a cast that included Percy Heming (Figaro), Arnold Matters (Count), and Winifred Lawson, a guest from the D'Oyly Carte Company (Susanna); Clive Carey was the producer, and Warwick Braithwaite the conductor. My programme reminds me that:

> '. . . the dance in Act 3 has been arranged by Ninette De Valois [and that] the management owe the new scenery to the generosity of Mr Rex Whistler . . . and they also wish to express their gratitude to the management of the Royal Opera House, Covent Garden, who have lent them dresses and stage furniture and granted them facilities for painting in the Royal Opera House.'

The relationship between the two London houses has not always been so cordial!

The Vic-Wells Opera Company at that time included Joan Cross, Edith Coates, Ruth Naylor, Rose Morris, Olive Dyer, Arthur Cox, Sumner Austin, Redvers Llewellyn, Arnold Matters, Powell Lloyd, Ronald Stear, and Henry Wendon; there were regular 'guest appearances' by Nora Gruhn, Miriam Licette, Heddle Nash and Gladys Parr; and among the conductors were Lawrance Collingwood, Warwick Braithwaite and, as a regular guest, John Barbirolli. As well as the staple operatic diet of Mozart, Verdi and Puccini, the repertory included *The Snow Maiden, Eugene Onegin, Fra Diavolo,* Stanford's *The Travelling Companion* and Collingwood's *Macbeth*. I managed to hear quite a few of these works during the next two years. My seat used to cost me 1s 3d or 1s 6d although I could have got into the back of the gallery for 6d, and my programme cost 3d.

It was, incidentally, the inclusion of Collingwood's opera *Macbeth* and the confusion that this caused among the regular Shakespearean audience of the Old Vic, many of whom crossed the river to Rosebery Avenue thinking that they were going to see Shakespeare's *Macbeth*, that finally persuaded the Vic-Wells Trustees to agree to making Sadler's Wells the home of the opera and ballet companies.

The end of January or early February was the customary time for Covent Garden to announce its plans for the 'Grand Opera Season', and so the delivery of the Saturday *Daily Telegraph* was more eagerly awaited than ever; then, one morning, there it was – 'A Wagner and Rossini Festival' to be 'Followed by Performances of other Operas, under the artistic direction of Sir Thomas Beecham, commencing on Monday, April 29th 1935'. I wanted to learn more, so I made my way to Covent Garden and timidly asked at the box office for a 'Preliminary prospectus', from which I learned that in addition to the usual Wagner there were to be performances of *La cenerentola*, *L'Italiana in Algeri* and *Il barbiere di Siviglia*, as well as an opera whose name was new to me, *Schwanda*, and *Prince Igor* by Borodine (*sic*). What was even more interesting was the announcement that 'negotiations are in progress for an Autumn Season of Italian Operas by Verdi, Puccini and Donizetti. Further details will be announced later.'

The Wagner-Rossini Festival signified a break with tradition, for instead of the German and Italian parts of the season being kept quite separate, Beecham had decided to alternate performances. However, there was more Wagner than Rossini each week, and when the audience at the first *La cenerentola* of the season, which was sandwiched between two *Tristan* performances conducted by Furtwängler, displayed what can only be described as a remarkable restraint and lack of enthusiasm, Beecham issued one of his pompous announcements to the effect that 'laughter and applause were permitted and even to be encouraged during the Rossini operas'.

My regular visits to Covent Garden now began in real earnest. As there was no likelihood of being able to afford a subscription to the amphitheatre stalls, I was initiated into the ritual of queuing up for the gallery. And it was a ritual; the enthusiasts began to form a queue from five or six o'clock in the morning – sometimes earlier, and sometimes overnight as was to happen for the performance of

La Bohème in which the American singer-cum-film star, Grace Moore, was to appear. To get to Covent Garden as soon as possible after six o'clock in the morning meant setting my alarm clock at 4.30 a.m. to catch an early train to Blackfriars, then walking along Fleet Street to Covent Garden to join the queue. Shortly before eight o'clock, the two stool-men, Haley and Gough, arrived with their supply of camp stools, generally rationed to two per person. One distributed the stools, the other tore off a cloak-room ticket from a little book, which we then pinned on our stool, keeping the counterfoil so we could stake our claim in the evening one hour or so before the doors opened. The stool cost 6d, the seat in the gallery 3s 6d; the programme 3d (6d, I was later to learn, in the lower parts of the house, where it was printed on thicker white paper). Having bought the stool I would go off to breakfast in a Lyons tea shop and be at school by ten-to-nine.

The debut of Lily Pons as Rosina in *Il barbiere* attracted a larger early morning queue than usual, and I was only able to get a seat in the slips; this gave me a new view of the auditorium, and enabled me to watch the orchestra. I wrote on my programme that 'Ezio Pinza as Don Basilio stole the honours of the evening' and that the baritone Giovanni Inghilleri, who sang Figaro, 'was too soft and ineffective'. At the opera's third performance on 31 May the great Giuseppe De Luca unexpectedly reappeared, after an absence from London of twenty-five years, to sing Figaro. When I came to write his obituary for the January 1951 issue of *Opera* I recalled:

'Who among those present on that occasion will ever forget it? I was still at school and De Luca was nothing more to me than a name in the HMV Celebrity catalogue. Then came the revelation. I began to learn what *bel canto* really was; the phrasing was classic, the style effortless, and the impersonation unforgettable.'

One of my closest school friends, not in the History Sixth, but a classicist and brilliant scholar, was John Jarvie. His godfather, J. Robertson, was a gourmet and a music lover and he introduced a few of John's friends, including myself, to the pleasures of good food and wine. I remember one week-end when, after an exhausting walk across the South Downs, and quite unsuitably dressed, he took us to have a splendid meal at the Royal Albion Hotel in Brighton, followed by a concert at the Dome, for which he had procured tickets. It was the opening night of the restored concert hall and Beecham was conducting the London Philharmonic Orchestra. The solo singer was to have been Conchita Supervia, but she was replaced by Eva Turner.

I was thrilled by Eva Turner's singing and obviously displayed my enthusiasm, for I was asked whether I would like to hear her at Covent Garden a fortnight later. She was to sing in the autumn season that had been announced in the Rossini–Wagner prospectus, and the opera was to be *Un ballo in maschera*. The performance was on 30 September, my eighteenth birthday, and when I mentioned this to our host, he said, 'Wonderful – dinner at the Savoy grill first!'

John Jarvie told me that our seats were to be in the stalls at Covent Garden, but as it was an autumn season full evening dress was not necessary – I breathed a sigh of relief for I certainly did not own tails, but had recently become the proud possessor of my first dinner jacket, which would serve for both the Savoy and the Opera House.

Curtain time for *Un ballo in maschera* at Covent Garden was eight o'clock, and, with only a few minutes to spare, we took our seats in row P of the orchestra stalls – the only time I was to sit in that part of the house until I became a critic thirteen years later. Of course, it was a wonderful experience to be downstairs instead of in the gods, but somehow it was just not as exciting as queuing up for a stool, running up the stone stairs to the gallery and staking one's claim for a seat in one of the rows that had backs to them (otherwise you had the knees of the person behind you in the small of the back!). The unfashionable season did not draw large audiences, and there is nothing so dispiriting as sitting in a half-filled auditorium.

Nonetheless I enjoyed hearing an opera that was new to me and was thrilled by Eva Turner's magnificent singing as Amelia. The rest of the cast included Dino Borgioli as Riccardo (no nonsense in those days about authentic Swedish characters and settings), Arthur Fear as Renato, Stella Andreva as Oscar, Constance Willis as Ulrica, and Aristide Baracchi and Vincenzo Bettoni as Samuele and Tomasso (*sic*). Clarence Raybould, who very rarely conducted opera, was Beecham's unlikely choice as conductor.

This short 'Grand Opera Festival', which lasted only a fortnight, was hardly what we had been promised in that announcement in the 'Wagner and Rossini Opera Festival' prospectus, which had talked of an 'Autumn Season of Italian Operas by Verdi, Puccini and Donizetti'! To be sure, there were three Italian operas, *Ballo*, *Il barbiere di Siviglia* and *La Bohème*, and in addition to the three Italian singers whom I heard in *Ballo*, a fourth one, a new Italian soprano called Lisa Perli, was to make her debut as Mimi. Lisa Perli became part of operatic lore, for she was certainly no Italian, nor indeed an operatic singer at all, but the English concert and oratorio soprano, Dora Labette. She and Beecham, with whom she was on very intimate terms, had between them hatched their little plot to hoax public and critics – she had chosen the name Perli because she had been born in Purley!

There were also performances of *Siegfried* and *Der Freischütz*, both in English, as well as Delius's *Koanga*, the first night of which I listened to on the radio, and during which Beecham stormed out of the pit and went up onto the stage to admonish the noisy scene shifters.

Listening to opera on the radio began to occupy more and more of my time. We had a new wireless set at home which could pick up dozens of European stations, and with the help of *World Radio* I began to plan my listening week. My Radio Diary for the last week of 1935 and first few days of 1936 reminds me that I heard Mascagni's *Iris* from the Rome Opera with Pia Tassinari and Gigli; *Lohengrin* with Maria Caniglia, Ebe Stignani, Ettore Parmeggiani, Carlo Tagliabue and Tancredi Pasero; *Ernani* with Gina Cigna, Francesco Merli, Armando Borgioli and Pasero; and *Il matrimonio segreto* with Mafalda Favero, Giulia Tess, Tito Schipa, Salvatore Baccaloni and Fernando Autori, all broadcast from La Scala, Milan. Then there was a *Fledermaus* on New Year's Eve from the Vienna State Opera, with Richard Tauber and Adele Kern in the cast, and part of *Tristan und Isolde* conducted by Furtwängler from Munich. No wonder my school work began to suffer and that I hardly distinguished myself in my Higher School Certificate examinations the following summer.

Opera had definitely taken over, and at school I organized lunch-time gramophone recitals in the library, playing records of Gigli, De Luca, Rethberg and others. I began to plan my ideal opera seasons, filling note-books with impossible repertories and even more impossible casts, and making mock-ups of prospectuses for the opera house I one day hoped to help run. Non-operatic music still played a part in my life, and our English master, an outstanding teacher, the Reverend C.J. Ellingham, used to spend a weekly period playing us records of music by the three 'Bs' and urging us to go to concerts.

During the spring term, I decided to enter for the Sixth Form Declamation Competition at school. I must have been the first boy ever to have chosen a famous singer for his subject, and my effort on Enrico Caruso won the prize. I still have a copy of what I wrote and spoke on that occasion, typed out very shakily on a borrowed typewriter with two fingers. It was very sentimental, starting as it did with the obligatory quotation: 'Music when soft voices die, vibrates in the memory' and ending thus:

'The song is ended; the singer has gone on his way and we shall hear him no more. The road that he travelled is finer for his music; the ears that listened to his music are more attuned to melody. In simplicity, honesty and devotion to his art, and in unflagging effort lay the secret of his success. He knew no short cut to perfection, no royal road to fame, no easy steps up the great ladder of life. In his art he kept alive the great tradition of beauty, when he died he was at the height of his triumph. He knew not the grief of departing glory nor the bitter taste of oblivion. God fastened wings to his shoulder and he flew fearlessly to the sun. So he would be remembered – so let us think of him singing jubilantly in some land beyond our dreams. In a land of olive groves and vineyards, a land of warm breezes and golden sunshine, a land of enchantment like his own native Italy.'

Oh dear, what a gilding of the lily; what hyperbole! How much, I wonder now, had I cribbed from elsewhere? My nearest rival in the competition spoke movingly of Father Damian and really deserved to have won.

There certainly was no Caruso, nor even a Gigli, in the 1936 Covent Garden season, but there was one of the most exciting Italian tenors I had, or indeed have, ever heard, Giacomo Lauri-Volpi. He was the Radames, and Duke of Mantua that season and, because he only sang one performance of *Tosca*, I did not hear his Cavaradossi. This was the second season in which the great Ezio Pinza delighted me; this time as Ramfis and Sparafucile – he certainly was not too grand to refuse to sing supporting rôles as so many of his present-day successors seem to be – and at the end of the season in *Les Contes d'Hoffmann*. It was also the first season during which I heard *Die Meistersinger von Nürnberg* in German, with a memorable cast that included Tiana Lemnitz as Eva, Rudolf Bockelmann as Sachs, Ludwig Weber as Pogner, Herbert Janssen as Kothner, and Heddle Nash as David. Beecham conducted.

During that season I began to cut out the opera reviews from *The Times*, *Daily Telegraph* and *Morning Post*, and paste them in a school exercise book. Ernest Newman's reviews and articles from the *Sunday Times* I kept separately, for some reason that I cannot now recall. For me, Newman's operatic criticisms from 1936 onwards rivalled those of Bernard Shaw in the 1880s and early 1890s for wit and style. Of the new production of *Les Contes d'Hoffmann* which Beecham put on at the end of the season he wrote a classic notice. Beecham in a long interview about the production had talked about setting the Venetian scene not on the Grand Canal but in 'an inconspicuous back-water because I do not think at any time in the history of Venice such a dubious establishment as that which is controlled by Giulietta would have been permitted to exist in other than an inconspicuous back-water'. Newman latched onto this and nearly half his very long review was about the Covent Garden publicity department which had led him to expect too much!

> 'We were gravely informed [he wrote] that Giulietta's confectionary establishment had been removed of set purpose to one of the side canals, it being improbable that the Venice authorities would have tolerated so hot a place on the Grand Canal. Even as to that I would not like to be too certain ... I had come to expect scenes so richly voluptuous that I would have risen from a sick bed to see the first performance, for fear that a second on the same lines might have been prohibited. But instead what did I see? A scene and a company so decorous that, so far from endorsing Giulietta's licence, any Town Council, after inspecting the premises on the urging of the local vigilance society, would have certificated them as a perfectly well-conducted massage establishment.'

In 1936 a 'massage parlour' did not have its present-day connotations!

Newman's comment on Dino Borgioli's Hoffmann is also worth

quoting: 'Mr Borgioli had precisely the same formulae for the Hoffmann of the Venetian act as for the other two. So far as my own limited experience of such matters goes, one does not address Delilah and the vicar's aunt in exactly the same accents.'

3

University Days

—

On the last night of the 1936 summer season at Covent Garden, Beecham had promised, in his curtain speech, three opera seasons. Exciting prospects indeed. So when, in the autumn, I began my studies at University College, London, I was not quite as disappointed as I might have been that I was not joining several of my friends at either Oxford or Cambridge. Despite my rather poor showing in the Higher School Certificate, the City of London School had awarded me a leaving scholarship which helped the family financially, and, by undertaking, albeit reluctantly, to follow in my parents' footsteps and take up a career in teaching, I was awarded a further grant by the London County Council. For the first time in my life I was virtually independent and able to organize my own finances. It was about this time that I began to collect old theatre programmes and playbills. I had seen an advertisement in *The Exchange and Mart* in the local library offering interesting opera and concert programmes and giving a telephone number in an outlying suburb in north London. That was how I met Colin Shreve, an avid record collector, who later was to open a second-hand record shop in Newport Court just off the Charing Cross Road.

My first purchase of programmes included several from Vienna, Dresden, Leipzig, Cologne, Munich and other German-speaking cities. I found them fascinating, and the idea of compiling records of performances that had taken place in the leading European opera houses, complete with casts, occurred to me. Shortly after this I became aware of the existence of the British Museum Newspaper Library at Colindale, where files of all the leading foreign newspapers were available. Once again opera took over, and hours that might have been, I will not say better spent, but perhaps more profitably spent from the academic point of view, were devoted to laboriously copying out casts of the Vienna State Opera, the three Berlin opera houses and La Scala, Milan. Having been a classicist my knowledge of Latin and French helped me to understand the gist of what I read in the Italian papers, but I knew no word of German nor was I particularly anxious to learn any at that time.

Like so many people I was becoming conscious of what was happening in Europe. My parents had helped set up a hostel for Jewish refugee children from Germany; I had taken part in protest marches to the German Embassy; and at College I had met a number of German-Jewish refugee undergraduates. One who came from Berlin, named Wieblemann, was a great opera enthusiast, and when the Dresden Opera's visit in the autumn of 1936 was announced, he asked me whether I planned to go to any of the performances. I saw no reason why not; and he said how glad he was that I felt that politics and music should be kept quite separate – this despite the fact that already Bruno Walter, Schnabel, Friedrich Schorr and many other artists had either left Germany or been prevented from continuing their careers there. My friend and I were of course wrong. My parents had no such illusions and my father pleaded with me not to go to any of the Dresden Opera performances. We quarrelled, and he refused to speak to me for several weeks. Not even reports that on the first night of the season the German Ambassador, who was sitting in the Royal Box with Strauss, had given the Nazi salute, made me change my mind. That Strauss himself was to conduct a single performance of his *Ariadne auf Naxos* proved stronger than any parental pleas or Nazi salutes, and so on 6 November, I heard the seventy-two-year-old composer conduct the superb Dresden Staatskapelle in my first *Ariadne*, with Marta Fuchs as Ariadne, Torsten Ralf as Bacchus, and Erna Sack, an amazing coloratura soprano, as Zerbinetta.

I also heard a *Figaro*, sung in German of course and, I assume, in the famous translation of Hermann Levi, though his name had been removed from the programme. The cast included Maria Cebotari as Susanna ('Most enchanting' I wrote on my programme), and Paul Schoeffler as Figaro: both these singers were to return to Covent Garden when the Vienna State Opera paid its first post-war visit to London in 1947. Another singer who more than forty years later was still making appearances was the bass Kurt Böhme; and his namesake, Karl Böhm, then no more than a respectable *Kappelmeister*, was the conductor. He had succeeded Fritz Busch as music director of the Dresden Opera three years previously. Busch was already known in England from his work at Glyndebourne; but it was not until the summer of 1939 that I was to become acquainted either with him or with Glyndebourne.

During the winter of 1936-7 I continued my radio listening, and it was in December that I heard for the first time one of the greatest operas ever written, Verdi's *Falstaff*. In fact, I heard it twice; once on 13 December from the Rome Opera, conducted by Tullio Serafin, and again on 26 December, for the opening of the season at La Scala, Milan, conducted by Victor De Sabata. On each occasion Falstaff was sung by Mariano Stabile, whose name I had heard mentioned in the gallery queue at Covent Garden and whose appearances at Glyndebourne as Figaro in Mozart's opera in the summer of 1936 had earned the highest praise from the critics. Other singers in the two *Falstaff*s included Maria Caniglia, Ebe Stignani, Mafalda Favero, Cloe Elmo, all names that I was to get to know better as time went by. They were also names that I was going to 'drop' in the letters I was beginning to write to *The Gramophone* and which were published in its pages, beginning in May 1937.

Beecham's own 'Winter Season of International Opera' promised well with its judicious mixture of the familiar: *Les Contes d'Hoffmann*, *Il barbiere di Siviglia*, *Un ballo in maschera*, *Die Fledermaus* and *Hänsel und Gretel* and in those days three rarely-performed pieces, at least as far as London was concerned, *Manon Lescaut*, *Salome* and *Elektra*. Beecham had announced that the two Strauss operas would be given on one evening; but after Karl Böhm had refused to conduct both works on a single evening because it was against his artistic principles and also because it was impossible to assemble a satisfactory *Elektra* cast at short notice, the idea was abandoned, and *Elektra* was replaced by Puccini's *Gianni Schicchi*. The great Hans Knappertsbusch made his only Covent Garden appearance conducting *Salome*; many years later I learned that attempts by Beecham to re-engage him were discouraged by the British Ambassador in Berlin, Sir Eric Phipps, as he (Knappertsbusch) was 'anathema to the Nazi party and has been dismissed from his Munich post by them for not being subservient enough to them'.

Unfortunately, I missed hearing the double bill and a few other performances because, like so many people that winter, I fell a victim to the influenza epidemic that was raging at the time and which played havoc not only with audiences but also with the casts of several operas. Before the *Hänsel und Gretel* on 30 December, Beecham came in front of the curtain and told the rather sparse audience that:

'The whole cast of this opera has been ill with influenza. Edith Furmedge who was to have sung the part of Gertrud was taken ill during the afternoon, and her understudy Linda Seymour is also ill; and so Miss Edith Coates, who belongs to another operatic organization of which I do not know the name is taking the part of Gertrud. Miss Irene Eisinger [Gretel] was ill until an hour ago. I prescribed champagne and am sure you will be satisfied with the result!'

Of course, Edith Coates was a member of Sadler's Wells Opera, a fact of which Beecham was certainly not ignorant. She had sung the same rôle at the matinée of *Hansel and Gretel* in Rosebery Avenue that afternoon, in English of course; and as the Covent Garden *Hänsel* was in German and Coates did not know the rôle in that language, she sang the part in English. This was certainly not the first time that Sadler's Wells Opera was to come to the rescue of Covent Garden. Many years later, the first night of the new production of *Die Meistersinger* conducted by Solti was saved in a like manner, when Norman Bailey, the Sadler's Wells Hans Sachs, took over at the eleventh hour from an indisposed Hurbert Hofmann. Bailey, however, was able to sing his role in German.

On 18 February I was lucky enough to get a ticket for one of Chaliapin's last concerts in London, given appropriately enough at Covent Garden. His programme included Leporello's 'Madamina' from *Don Giovanni* and Basilio's 'La calunnia' from *Il barbiere di Siviglia*, as well as the inevitable 'Song of the Flea' and 'Volga Boatman'. Chaliapin was then sixty-four, and he died little more than a year later. I suppose that those who had heard him in his great days found him only a shadow of what he had been, but for me it was an unforgettable experience.

Preliminary plans for Covent Garden's 1937 season, 'The Coronation Season of International Opera', had been announced by Beecham the previous September, and nuggets of information appeared in the press during the autumn and winter. By the end of January the repertory and first list of singers were announced and we learned that the season would open on 19 April with *Otello*, in which the great tenor, Giovanni Martinelli, would be heard again in London for the first time since 1919. I certainly did not intend to miss what promised to be a great event. Gallery stools for the opening night of the season were to be given out on the day before, the Sunday. Gallery regulars greeted one another, exchanged reminiscences, and cautiously welcomed newcomers to their ranks. Except for Martinelli, the opening *Otello* conducted by Beecham was not particularly distinguished vocally; Cesare Formichi, the Italian baritone, was a very loud and unsubtle Iago, and the soprano Fernanda Ciani a very nondescript Desdemona. When I went to work at Covent Garden as archivist in the 1950s and began to sift through the correspondence and other documents of the pre-war years, I discovered that Formichi had persuaded Beecham to allow him to arrange the Italian and French part of the season – with disastrous results. Ciani was one of his many friends whom he engaged, as was also the conductor Francesco Salfi, who hacked his way through the third evening's opera *Don Pasquale*.

I had recently got to know this delightful Donizetti opera through the famous plum-label HMV recording, with Tito Schipa, Ernesto Badini and Afro Poli, and I was to hear it performed incomparably at Glyndebourne two years later. The Covent Garden cast had Mafalda Favero as Norina providing the best singing of the evening, and Dino Borgioli was a stylish Ernesto. But Umberto Di Lelio as Pasquale and Piero Biasini as Malatesta gave performances that Newman described as 'alternately trembling on the brink of vulgarity and inanity and taking the fatal plunge'. Di Lelio's daughter, Loretta, became a small-part singer in the post-war period and then married Franco Corelli. When I met her at Covent Garden in 1966 and told her I had heard her sing small rôles shortly after the war, she hotly denied it, saying that she still was at school in the late 1940s!

During the 1937 season I heard my first *Fliegende Holländer* (Flagstad, Max Lorenz, Herbert Janssen and Ludwig Weber, conducted by Fritz Reiner) and also Lawrence Tibbett's London debut as Scarpia in a *Tosca* with Cigna and Martinelli, conducted by Barbirolli, at which I heard booing in the opera house for the first time. A few nights before the season ended there was a much improved

Otello, again with Martinelli, but with Tibbett as Iago and the lovely Norwegian soprano, Eidé Norena, as a most beautiful and moving Desdemona.

The last two Covent Garden seasons before the outbreak of the second world war were obviously influenced by political events in Europe. The 1938 season took place shortly after the Austrian *Anschluss*, and the casts of the German operas included several refugee singers. Some, like Lotte Lehmann, Richard Tauber and Herbert Janssen had chosen voluntary exile and had made no secret of their dislike of the Nazi régime. Others, like Anita Oberländer, who sang the First Lady in *Die Zauberflöte*, and Rose Pauly, who sang Elektra, were Jewish. Erich Kleiber, who was making his Covent Garden debut conducting *Der Rosenkavalier*, had left Germany in 1934; he had refused to conduct at La Scala, Milan, in 1938, when Mussolini, copying the Nazi racial laws, dismissed Vittore Veneziani, the famous La Scala chorus master, and refused to allow Jews to attend opera performances. The Covent Garden music staff included a number of musicians like Leo Würmser, who had been a *répétiteur* first in Dresden then in Vienna; and Beecham also engaged the conductor Fritz Zweig, Stefan Zweig's brother, who had to leave Prague, to conduct one of the *Rosenkavalier* performances.

But the German and Austrian singers also included some ardent Nazis like the famous bass-baritone Rudolf Bockelmann, who proudly displayed the watch given to him by Goering, while his wife kept the place on her wrist that had been kissed by Hitler covered! Then there was the lovely Tiana Lemnitz who, like some of her colleagues, was so beastly to Lehmann back-stage that, on the first night of *Rosenkavalier*, which was being broadcast, she collapsed during the first act and had to be replaced by Hilde Konetzni. Despite these unpleasant events there were some memorable evenings. The Beecham *Zauberflöte*, with Tiana Lemnitz, Erna Berger, Richard Tauber, Gerhard Hüsch and Wilhelm Strienz in the cast was subsequently recorded, though not, alas, with Tauber as Tamino. Despite its age it still remains the most magical of all *Magic Flutes* on disc, and proves that one's memories of those performances and voices after more than forty years have not become more rosy as time passed by.

Beecham also conducted a single performance of *Die Entführung aus dem Serail* – the first had to be cancelled because Tauber lost his voice. I can still remember the way Beecham turned a Mozart phrase and the sparkle that he brought to the score. Erna Berger, Irma Beilke, Tauber, Heddle Nash and Ludwig Weber were the singers in this, my first *Entführung*. There were only three Italian operas that season, *Rigoletto*, *La Bohème* and *Tosca*, and all had Gigli in the cast. They were conducted by that most cultured of Italian musicians, Vittorio Gui, whom I was to get to know quite well in his post-war Glyndebourne days.

That summer, an important milestone was passed as far as my future career was concerned: the publication in *The Gramophone* of my first article – the subject, 'Italian and French opera at Covent Garden, 1924–38'. I concluded it thus:

> 'I would appeal to all those who are desirous of seeing originality in next season's repertory at Covent Garden, and who desire the season to be truly "International" and not a German opera festival, to try their utmost to open the eyes of those gentlemen in charge there to this fact in whatever manner they think best.'

In August, accompanied by my sister, I went to Provence for the first time. On the way home we spent a few days in Paris, and I payed my first visit to both the Opéra and the Opéra-Comique. At the Opéra we heard *Rigoletto* sung in French; there, the Sparafucile had no problems about carrying the rather matronly Gilda, Solange Delmas, across the stage in a sack, for at that time it was customary at the Opéra, and indeed in many other theatres, to omit the final Gilda–Rigoletto duet, thus saving the Gilda (and the Sparafucile) from discomfort. At the Opéra-Comique we heard *Madama Butterfly* (also in French) in which Bernadette Delprat, who had sung Antonia and Giulietta in the 1936 Covent Garden *Les Contes d'Hoffmann*, was Cio-Cio-San. 'One fine day' was encored, and second time round she sang it in Italian. Sitting in front of us was a very vocal French-man who sang to himself most of Pinkerton's rôle – our French companion sighed and remarked loudly '*Ah! Un autre ténor!*'

Returning home at the end of August, we were plunged into the Czechoslovak crisis. Tension mounted and towards the end of September war seemed inevitable; then came the Munich conference and Chamberlain's return. The previous evening I spent with my old school friend, Ray Farrar, at the Streatham Hill Theatre where Sadler's Wells Opera was appearing, at a performance of *Aida*, believing it would be the last opera performance we would hear for a very long time. Ten days later a three-week autumn season of opera in English opened at Covent Garden, given by the newly-formed Covent Garden English Opera Company.

Plans for that autumn season had been announced in June, and towards the end of July an organization known as 'The Young People's Opera Circle' was launched. Among its privileges was a voucher instalment system which enabled the members to buy tickets by instalments. Vouchers cost 1s or 2s each and could be purchased in books of ten at a time, and eventually exchanged for their full value in seats. I joined this scheme and by becoming a member of the 'Circle' was able to attend a rehearsal of *Faust*. Thus the 'Opera Circle' foreshadowed by a quarter of a century the 'Friends of Covent Garden'. The leading British singers of the day took part in that season: Eva Turner, Maggie Teyte, Lisa Perli, Luella Paikin, Ruth Naylor, Constance Willis, Walter Widdop, Heddle Nash, Henry Wendon, Dennis Noble, Arthur Fear, Arnold Matters, Harold Williams, Norman Allin, Norman Walker and Oscar Natzka, as well as the conductors Albert Coates, Eugène Goossens and Stanford Robinson.

Between the end of October 1938 and the beginning of May 1939 my diary reveals that I only went to the opera twice; once to the People's Palace in the Mile End Road to hear the Carl Rosa Company in *A Masked Ball*, and once to Sadler's Wells to hear *Cavalleria rusticana* with Florence Austral as Santuzza and *Pagliacci* with Arthur Carron (formerly Cox) as Canio. My diary of opera broadcasts, however, shows that during those six months I heard no less than eighty-one broadcasts, mostly from Italy; but also several from Paris and even two from the Metropolitan Opera in New York, picked up on short wave: *Lucia di Lammermoor* with Lily Pons, Galliano Masini, Carlo Tagliabue and Pinza; and *Aida* with Milanov, Bruna Castagna and Gigli. At that time I was also attending many more concerts and had the good fortune to hear our leading orchestras conducted by Weingartner, Toscanini and Bruno Walter at the Queen's Hall.

The last Covent Garden season before the war was, like its immediate predecessor, overshadowed by political events. Beecham had promised us a visit by the Czech National Opera Company from Prague, to perform Dvořák's *Rusalka* and Smetana's *The Secret*, under the direction of Václav Talich. Hitler marched into Prague on 15 March and two weeks later Covent Garden announced that the proposed visit had been postponed 'probably until next season'! In the circumstances the choice of *The Bartered Bride* to open the season, sung in German by a cast that included, as one critic put it, 'Nazi, Jew, Teuton, Briton and Slav', was hardly an inspired choice on Beecham's part. Among the cast were Hilde Konetzni, Sabine Kalter, Tauber, Fritz Krenn, Heinrich Tessmer, Marko Rothmüller, Stella Andreva and Mary Jarred.

Because of the troubled political background, the box office support for German opera in 1938 had fallen substantially and, quite understandably, many of Covent Garden's financial backers, who included a number of Jewish businessmen, were not prepared to continue pouring money into an enterprise that was giving so much employment to German artists. As a result, there was only one *Ring* cycle in 1939, instead of the customary two; and much more emphasis was placed on the Italian repertory, which included *Il trovatore* with the young Jussi Bjoerling making his Covent Garden debut, about which I wrote the following comment on my programme: 'Jussi Bjoerling is still immature, his top notes were thin and reedy, but he sang a good final act. It was Stignani's evening – what a singer!'

Early in June, Beecham conducted *Don Giovanni* for the first time for many years. It had a star-studded cast: Elisabeth Rethberg, Hilde Konetzni, Mafalda Favero, Tauber, Pinza, Virgilio Lazzari, Baracchi and Norman Walker. I can still visualize the tall, handsome Pinza in white doublet and hose, plumed hat, and exuding sex appeal, storming his way through the part with great bravado. I am equally sure it was not the kind of Mozart singing we would accept today. Tauber, on the other hand, sang with extreme good taste and exhibited marvellous breath control.

Three weeks after that *Don Giovanni*, I heard another performance of the same opera at Glyndebourne. When I had learned in the spring that it was possible for students to apply for side seats at Glyndebourne at 10s a ticket, accordingly I wrote to John Christie asking if I could be put on the list. To my surprise and delight I was sent tickets for each of the five operas in the Glyndebourne repertory, and as a belated and additional twenty-first birthday present, my parents offered to pay half the cost.

As well as *Don Giovanni* I was able to hear *Figaro*, *Così fan tutte*, *Don Pasquale* and Verdi's *Macbeth*, each wonderful in its own way. I doubt whether *Don Pasquale* with that still unequalled pair of *buffo* artists, Salvatore Baccaloni and Mariano Stabile, and conducted by Busch, has ever been equalled. I have enjoyed countless *Figaro* performances since 1939, but the impact of that perfectly rehearsed ensemble, the result of the work of Busch and Ebert, left a lasting impression on me. However, it was the *Macbeth* that completely shattered me. 'Verdi sounded really thrilling as never before in England!' I wrote, 'Busch and the orchestra were admirable, and the chorus beyond praise.' And as if writing a school report, I noted that 'Valentino should develop into a great Verdi baritone' and that 'David Franklin was still improving'!

Encouraged by having had my first full-length article printed in *The Gramophone*, I took courage in both hands and wrote to the editor, asking him whether he would be prepared to accept a review of the 1939 Covent Garden and Glyndebourne season from me. To my great joy and surprise he agreed, and a two-page article appeared in the August *Gramophone* that year. I never learned what Beecham's reaction to this audacity on my part was; but John Christie, in the first of many letters that he was to send me until shortly before his death in 1962, was clearly not amused, despite the fact that I had been full of praise for the Glyndebourne performances. He commented that 'for someone who had described himself as a student when applying for cheap tickets to set himself up as an authority and write a review of the opera season in a reputable journal was a bit of a cheek'. And, in retrospect, I suppose it was.

My last visit to Glyndebourne in 1939 was also the last night of the season. War again threatened and so when John Christie came onto the stage after the dinner interval to report 'serious news', we all feared that the worst had happened. In fact, he appeared to announce that Eton had been soundly beaten by Harrow in their annual cricket match at Lord's for the first time since 1908! Despite all that Glyndebourne says, it did and does attract what can only be termed an élitist audience and, in recent years, my reaction to the typical Glyndebourne audience has often brought me into friendly conflict with George Christie.

I had originally planned a fortnight's holiday in Switzerland for August, to coincide with the new Lucerne Festival that Toscanini had established after the *Anschluss* had forced him to leave Salzburg. However, my parents vetoed this idea and suggested instead a short holiday in France. I was never able to understand the logic of their decision, unless it was the belief that, if war broke out, it would be easier to return home from a country that was an ally, than from one that was neutral.

On our way down to the south of France, we stayed a few days in Vichy to hear some music. Each summer the Vichy Casino used to play host to a number of distinguished musicians, who appeared in both opera and concert. So it was that in those last days of peace I was able to hear Bruno Walter conduct Brahms and Mozart, and a concert of selections from *Boris Godunov* with Alexander Kipnis as the Tsar. I never again heard Kipnis in the flesh, and had to wait until 1946 before Bruno Walter returned to Europe. In the intervening years Vichy became rather more than a French spa where one could hear distinguished artists, several of Jewish origin, perform. The Kipnis *Boris* was on 17 August. Five days later came the announcement of the Berlin–Moscow pact, and I hurried back to London to help with the evacuation of my father's school to 'somewhere in England'.

By the beginning of October I had completed arrangements to go to Aberystwyth on the Welsh coast which was to be University College's war-time home: there I would spend my final year at college and take my degree. My radio, gramophone and records naturally accompanied me, and, as in London, I continued to listen to opera broadcasts, especially from Italy. On 7 December I was joined by a few friends to listen to the opening night of La Scala's 1939–40 season; this was *Guglielmo Tell* with Alexander Sved, Gabriella Gatti and Teodor Mazaroff, conducted by Gino Marinuzzi. The following evening the first performance of the Rome season was broadcast – *Falstaff* with the incomparable Stabile and conducted by Tullio Serafin.

During the Christmas vacation I joined my parents in Worthing, where they and their school had been evacuated. They had taken a house, for quite naturally they thought they would be there 'for the duration', and like most people had no idea that before the end of the following summer the south coast would have to be evacuated because of the threat of invasion. Between 26 December and 9 January I heard eight operas on the radio, including my first *Vespri*

Siciliani from the Teatro Carlo Felice in Genoa, and my first *Quatro rusteghi* (by Wolf-Ferrari) from Rome, which I remember enjoying immensely and noting in my diary that perhaps one day it might be sung at Glyndebourne (in the event it came to Sadler's Wells shortly after the end of the war). I was unable to go to a live performance until the Easter vacation, when, on 14 March, I heard yet again my favourite opera, *The Marriage of Figaro*, at Sadler's Wells, with Joan Cross as the Countess.

During the five months that elapsed before my next visit to the Wells, much was to happen that overshadowed opera, music and university examinations. France fell on the day I was taking one of my Latin papers; my family and school were moved from Worthing to Hertford; and the Battle of Britain began. On 28 August I went to a performance of *Tosca* at the Wells. Although the blitz on London was not launched until 7 September, there were already regular air-raids, and one of these took place during *Tosca*; it was announced by a message flashed onto a small screen that had been erected in front of the footlights. As far as I can recall not a single person left the theatre. I cannot blame them for it was a fine performance, with the Canadian soprano, Jeanne Dusseau, a really magnificent Tosca (my notes in the programme read that she was the equal to Iva Pacetti and Gina Cigna), and Percy Heming an elegant and menacing Scarpia. During the following week I went to two of the last Promenade Concerts to be given at the Queen's Hall; the one on 2 September was a Wagner programme. German music was not unofficially banned as it had been during the 1914–18 war.

At the end of July I learned that I had got through my finals – just – and had become a fully-fledged Bachelor of Arts. I then had to await my call-up, which had been deferred until I had completed my studies. September and October passed by without my hearing anything from the authorities, and during those two months I brought my musical scrap-books up to date, for I was still able to buy American music magazines from the shop which I frequented in Leicester Square; and I also continued to make copious biographical notes on famous singers, gathering information from reference books in public libraries. It also occurred to me that my musical experiences of the previous twelve months might make the subject of an article; so I set to work, calling the piece 'August 1939–August 1940 – A University Student's Musical Experiences during the first year of the War', and sent it to *Musical Opinion*, the poor relation of the more august *Musical Times*. The article ended with my hopes for the future which I expressed in suitably portentous phrases:

> 'It is difficult to look ahead, and indeed dangerous to prophesy; but I hope the arts will survive these times. They *must* survive, and be placed on a more stable footing than hitherto. The enthusiasm for music among the young people I have met this last year is the most heartening thing I have experienced since the war began.'

The article was accepted, and appeared in the November issue of *Musical Opinion*. A few days after it was published, as if spurred on by hopes for the future, I decided not to wait until I was called up, but instead to volunteer for the army. My bad eyesight and flat feet resulted in my being graded 'B3', which meant that I was recommended for a desk job in the Royal Army Pay Corps. This had its advantages, for most of my time was spent in London apart from two short interludes in the winter and spring of 1943 when I was posted to an anti-aircraft unit on the east coast as preliminary training for a commission that I failed to get. I was lucky in getting myself billeted 'at home', first in Hertford from where I travelled up daily on a very early morning train to King's Cross, and then later in our old house in Norwood; so, for the next five years, I was able to enjoy London's war-time musical life.

4

The War Years

—

After the closure of Sadler's Wells Theatre early in September 1940, the opera company was about to be disbanded; but Tyrone Guthrie, the director of the Old Vic and Sadler's Wells, thought otherwise. He set up a small company of twenty, a chorus of four, two pianists (Lawrance Collingwood and Norman Feasey) and with a basic set toured *The Marriage of Figaro* and *La traviata*, performing in church halls and works canteens in northern industrial cities. Their success was enormous; and by February 1941, with the help of the newly-set up CEMA (Council for the Encouragement of Music and the Arts) and the Carnegie Trust, the company was enlarged to fourteen soloists, a chorus of nine and an orchestra of fifteen; and the singers acted as stage managers and wardrobe mistresses. The resuscitated Sadler's Wells Opera came back to London in February 1941 for a short season at the New Theatre in St Martin's Lane, where, together with the Sadler's Wells Ballet and the Old Vic Theatre Company, they appeared regularly for the next few years. As well as *Figaro* and *Traviata* the repertory for their first London season comprised *Madam Butterfly*, *Die Fledermaus* and *The Beggar's Opera*. I need hardly say that I chose *Figaro* as the first piece I wanted to hear after six months without opera.

Although there was little opera in London in 1941 there was a great deal of other music: the National Gallery lunch-time concerts; orchestral concerts at Queen's Hall, until it was destroyed by bombs; a series of nightly concerts at the Coliseum by the London Philharmonic Orchestra, and the first Promenade Concert season at the Royal Albert Hall. I took in as many of these events as I could, and during the Proms season heard several singers including Eva Turner, Joan Hammond, Richard Tauber, Dino Borgioli and Walter Widdop.

During the long winter evenings, made even drearier by the blackout, my thoughts often turned to how opera might be organized in post-war Britain; I put my ideas onto paper and eventually turned them into an article entitled 'A Plan for Post-War Opera' which I sent to *Musical Opinion*. Once again my piece was accepted and appeared in May 1941. In the article I suggested that there should be a British company at post-war Covent Garden which might include such singers as Joan Cross, Hella Toros, Marjorie Lawrence, Stella Andreva, Edith Coates, Arthur Carron, Heddle Nash, Dennis Noble, Norman Walker, David Franklin and several more. I also suggested that failing Beecham's return as music director, the choice might fall either on one of the refugee conductors then resident in England or America, or on one of the British conductors like Albert Coates, Eugène Goossens or John Barbirolli, all of whom were at that time working in the States. I discussed the possibility of state support and of forming a supporters' club rather like the Metropolitan Opera Guild in New York. I do not suppose that anything I wrote in that article influenced those who were responsible for setting up post-war Covent Garden, though, as it turned out, several of my rather obvious suggestions were followed. The article was obviously read by several people who had been connected with pre-war opera and they wrote to me. One was Charles Moor, who had been Covent Garden's stage director and later became Beecham's right-hand man; another was Eva Turner, who expressed great personal interest in both the article and its writer which resulted in a friendship that has lasted ever since; and a third was a wonderful gentleman called Arthur Notcutt, who was a tea merchant in the city and had been an opera-goer since the early years of the century. Notcutt wrote occasional articles for the musical press and from 1942, the year my father died, until his own death in 1956 became virtually a second father to me. He left me all his personal opera diaries as well as many programmes and press cuttings, going back to 1902.

In 1942 there was an increase in the amount of opera in London. As well as the Sadler's Wells seasons at the New Theatre, there was a series of performances of Mussorgsky's *Fair at Sorochints* first at the Savoy and then at the Adelphi Theatre, sung in Russian, with that wonderful artist Oda Slobodskaya and a young Czech refugee baritone, Otakar Kraus, who was to play so important a part in the operatic life of this country from 1950 onwards. At the Strand Theatre, an organization that called itself Albion Operas Limited mounted a strange production of *The Tales of Hoffmann*, which included excerpts from *La Belle Hélène* and additional dialogue by one Olive Moore. In the cast were Henry Wendon as Hoffmann – later in the run the young Peter Pears sang some of the performances; Percy Heming as Coppelius, Dapertutto and Dr Miracle, as well as Offenbach himself who had somehow been worked into this version; Ruth Naylor as Antonia; and a young unknown soprano, Victoria Sladen, as Helen in the *Belle Hélène* scenes. The actor Esmé Percy croaked his way through the character rôles of Cochenille, Pitichinaccio and Frantz. Several refugee musicians were listed in the programme: H. F. Redlich (*sic*) was assistant conductor to Walter Susskind, Alfred Kalmus, later to take over Universal Edition, was general manager, and among the singers were Ernst Urbach, who was to launch the London Opera Club and was one of Amy Shuard's teachers, George Israel and Hilde Zweig.

In April 1942, while I was on leave, I attended a matinée performance of *The Magic Flute* at the New Theatre; on returning home I learned that my father, who had suffered a heart attack some months earlier and had never really recovered, had died. My mother told me what time his death occurred, and it must have been while Sarastro was singing 'In diesen heil'gen Hallen'; and whenever I hear that aria it has a strangely moving effect on me. After my father's death my mother decided to return to teaching and this meant that our old house in Norwood became home once again. Not only did this make my daily journey to the Army Pay Office in Finsbury Circus in the city far easier than it had been when living in Hertford, but it also meant that I was able to hear more opera and other music than during the previous two years.

It would become boring merely to list with full casts the operas I heard during the next two years, but between April 1942 and April 1944 I went to nearly fifty opera performances, which averaged out at one a fortnight, which was not bad going in war-time conditions. Sadler's Wells' London seasons were still being given at the New Theatre, and the Carl Rosa Company's twice-a-year visits to London took place either at the old Winter Garden Theatre in Drury Lane, the Lyric Hammersmith or the Orpheum Cinema in Golders Green. During that time I heard seven performances of *The Marriage of Figaro*, six of *The Barber of Seville*, five of *The Magic Flute*, and an assortment of *Traviatas* and *Rigolettos* at the New Theatre, and several *Fausts*, *Trovatores* and *Merry Wives of Windsors* given by the Carl Rosa.

It was in 1943 that Tyrone Guthrie asked Joan Cross to take over the directorship of the Sadler's Wells Opera Company, a position she held until 1945. One cannot exaggerate the importance of this appointment in the operatic life of England. It was Joan Cross who auditioned and engaged Peter Pears as a soloist for the company in 1943, and this led to her meeting Benjamin Britten and the production of *Peter Grimes* at Sadler's Wells when the theatre reopened in June 1945; an event which changed the whole course of opera in Great Britain.

Pears's rôles with the Sadler's Wells Opera during the rest of the war included the Duke of Mantua, Alfredo in *La traviata*, a hilariously funny Count Almaviva in *The Barber of Seville*, Tamino, a most vulnerable Vašek in *The Bartered Bride*, and, surprisingly, Rodolfo in *La Bohème*. It was to see and hear this remarkable artist in those early days of his operatic career that I returned time and time again to the New Theatre. It was not only Peter Pears who made those Sadler's Wells Opera performances so enjoyable, for the company, under Joan Cross's guidance and with the help of its music director, Lawrance Collingwood, achieved an ensemble and spirit that was unique.

One of the outstanding productions of this period was Smetana's *The Bartered Bride*. Its success was due in no small measure to the help given by the exiled Czech Government in London, who released from the Czech forces Lance-Bombardier Sasha Machov, a leading Czech dancer and choreographer. He not only arranged the dances but also helped the producer, Eric Crozier, to capture an authentic Czech atmosphere. Machov, who joined Pamela May, a leading member of Sadler's Wells Ballet, and students of the Sadler's Wells Ballet School in the dances, returned to Prague in 1946 as director of ballet at the National Theatre, and five years later committed suicide. The Czech Government also advised on scenery and costumes, lending the designer, Reece Pemberton, books and photographs of country life in Czechoslovakia. Eric Crozier who was later to stage the first *Peter Grimes*, collaborated with Joan Cross in producing a new English translation.

The cast included Rose Hill, the company's talented Susanna and Gilda, as Mařenka; Edmund Donlevy, their Figaro and Papageno, as the bumbling marriage broker, Kecal; Arthur Servent as the romantic Jenik; Peter Pears as an incomparable Vašek; and another of Joan Cross's discoveries, the bass Owen Brannigan, who was to become the leading *buffo* performer in British opera, as Tobias Micha. Lawrance Collingwood's Slav musical training made him an ideal conductor. On the first night on 10 November 1943, Dr Beneš, the President of Czechoslovakia, and members of the late Council and Government in exile, were present. It was a truly memorable operatic event.

During the autumn of 1943 and winter of 1944 there was a great deal of orchestral activity in London. As well as the regular concerts by the London Symphony and Philharmonic Orchestras at the Albert Hall, a new orchestra was formed by Sidney Beer, a wealthy South African-born diamond merchant and race-horse owner, who had helped underwrite Beecham's last two Covent Garden seasons. Beer's London orchestra was called the National Symphony and was led by David McCallum; it numbered many distinguished players in its ranks and that ensured that, despite Mr Beer's lack of experience, the performances were never less than respectable. As well as giving regular Albert Hall concerts, it appeared every Sunday evening at the Orpheum Cinema in Golders Green. At its concert on 5 December 1943, Beer included in his programme the Marschallin's Monologue and Finale to Act I, the trio and closing duet from Act III of Strauss's *Der Rosenkavalier* with Joan Hammond as the Marschallin, Leonie Ziffado as Octavian and Irene Eisinger, Glyndebourne's pre-war Despina and Covent Garden's Gretel, as Sophie. The excerpts were sung in German and the audience included a goodly section of the Austrian and German refugee colony from north London.

All this musical activity inspired me with the idea of starting a music appreciation course in the Army Pay Office, a suggestion that the adjutant readily agreed to. And so with the help of a portable gramophone, a selection of 78 rpm records, and the use of a large notice board on which I would pin up the coming week's musical events in London, illustrated where possible with pictures, I began my lecturing career. Those lectures must have been a success, for one of the ATS officers asked me if I would do a series of similar lectures for her ATS girls. Whereas *my* lectures were voluntary affairs, the ATS lectures were compulsory, and nothing is as dispiriting as giving a talk on Mozart's operas to an audience half of whom looked, and indeed were, bored, some of whom fell asleep, and a goodly portion of whom produced their knitting! It did, however, prepare me for some of the talks I was to give many years later to women's luncheon clubs!

I have stressed the important contributions made to British musical life by the influx of refugees from Europe in the 1930s and later. One musician who played an important role in my own life was the German baritone, Walter Gruner (1905–1980). He was related to the conductor Hermann Grunenbaum, who was also the head of the opera class at the Royal Academy of Music and the ex-Covent Garden chorus master, and his cousin was the soprano Nora Gruhn. I first came across Walter Gruner's name in the chorus list of *The Fair at Sorochints*: within eighteen months I was attending a series of musical appreciation classes on opera that he was giving in a private house in south London. Those classes had been arranged by an old friend of my family, a German-born lady called Erna Josephs (the aunt of the composer Wilfred Josephs). She had come to England from Berlin before the 1914–18 war, but she had never lost her German accent. She was an active worker in the Jewish refugee organization, and not only arranged these Sunday morning lectures in her own house, but also helped Gruner get a regular teaching appointment at the City Literary Institute. In the post-war period Gruner was to become one of the most distinguished voice teachers in this country, holding an important position at the Guildhall School of Music and numbering among his pupils Jill Gomez and Benjamin Luxon.

Erna Joseph's large circle of friends included a family called Weiner. Lena Weiner (or Lesser as she was then) had been a teacher at my parents' school in 1912 and through them had met the Josephs. Now, more than forty years later, that family came again into contact with a Rosenthal through their daughter Phyllis, who had recently left Goldsmiths College and was embarking on a teaching career in London. She had been invited to come to Gruner's Sunday morning lectures. Phyllis and I found we had much in common, even if she was then more a ballet than opera enthusiast; I invited her to come with me to some Carl Rosa and Sadler's Wells performances, and we also attended the first performance of Tippett's *A Child of our Time* at the Adelphi Theatre on 19 March 1944; Walter Goehr was the conductor and Joan Cross and Peter Pears were among the soloists. A little more than three weeks later we went to a performance of *Figaro* at the New Theatre, after which I asked Phyllis to marry me. On 7 August 1981 we celebrated our thirty-seventh wedding anniversary.

In the autumn of 1943 *The Gramophone* began to publish a series of articles entitled 'When De Reszke Reigned'; these were written by P. G. Hurst, who for many years had contributed to that magazine notes on old vocal records for a feature known as 'Collectors' Corner'; he was also the first person to broadcast a programme on the BBC devoted to historical gramophone records. Hurst, like so many record collectors, held steadfastly to the belief that the art of great singing died in the early years of this century, if not earlier. On the other hand I have always believed that most of us only choose to remember the outstanding performers and performances we have heard; and just as distance lends enchantment to the view, so our aural memories are inclined to give us an exaggerated picture of what we ourselves actually heard at the time. I therefore decided to write a letter to *The Gramophone* on this subject, and at the same time say something about the task on which I had been engaged since schooldays in compiling details of operatic performances and biographies of singers. And so in the November issue of *The Gramophone* that year the following letter appeared:

'War-time Opera Stars
'While welcoming P. G. Hurst's new series of articles on 'The Golden Age' of opera as yet another sign of the small but growing increase of interest in what is, in this country at any rate, the most neglected branch of music, I would suggest that this love of dwelling in the past is a typical British weakness of which we could be well rid. What is happening at the present is just as interesting and, I feel, more important.

'Since about 1935 I have been working on records of operatic performances that have taken place at the most important operatic centres of the world, and been compiling brief biographies of singers who have appeared in opera since about 1919 ... Finally, if any readers have programmes, critiques, or casts of opera performances that have taken place in any part of the world since 1919, I would greatly appreciate the loan of these in order to continue my musical research, which has been greatly interrupted since the war, owing to the difficulty of contact with the Continent.'

I certainly hoped for a few replies and indeed I did receive several letters, two of which brought me into contact with two people who were instrumental in changing my life. One I met within a few weeks of that letter appearing: the other I was not to meet until the summer of 1945. The first letter came from an American soldier who was stationed in England at the time; his name was Curt Weiler and he had been a singer in pre-Nazi Germany. We arranged to meet in the tea room of Liverpool Street Station and in order to recognize one another each of us carried a copy of *The Gramophone*. Weiler knew Professor Edward J. Dent quite well and he arranged for me to meet him; he also introduced me to a magazine called *Opera News*, which was published weekly by the Metropolitan Opera Guild during the New York opera season. I cannot remember now how I actually managed to send money to America at that time in order to subscribe to that magazine – perhaps Curt Weiler arranged it for me. We continued to meet until shortly after D-Day; we continued to correspond, and Weiler eventually became the first New York correspondent of *Opera* magazine.

Opera magazine! I do not think any thought of such a publication had ever occurred to me, but possibly it had to the writer of the second letter, which arrived mid-April (1944) as its writer was serving with the Grenadier Guards in Italy, and had only got round to writing to me on 11 April. It consisted of eight pages in a firm, often illegible hand, that I was to get to know so well, and the signature at the bottom was 'Lascelles'. I make no apology for quoting extensively from it:

'Dear Mr Rosenthal,

'I have been meaning to write to you for some time, after reading your letter in the November 'Gramophone'. It says quite a number of things with which I entirely agree – Hurst in the 'Gramophone' is fairly interesting, but often irritatingly biased, and his exclusion of any (even remotely) contemporary effort is most tiresome. I once had some correspondence with him over a record (of De Luca) and happened to praise Amato in it. In his answer, he said that he had only one record of this v. fine baritone 'as he did not start recording before 1908'!

'Since coming to Italy I have managed to go to Naples several times and naturally visited the gramophone shops and also Ricordi's. There are a lot of good new records, though so many that have not yet appeared in England that I despair of even a tenth of them ever reaching our catalogues...

'Ricordi's had a number of back issues of a periodical called 'Musica d'Oggi' which I promptly bought (at 1d. each, they were the only cheap things in Naples, except opera seats at 7/6d!) and found them most interesting in spite of my very limited Italian. Perhaps you will fare better in this respect, and I am sending them under separate cover to the address you give in the 'Gramophone' in the hope that they may be of some interest to you...

'When I left England a year ago I had just been on two months sick leave, and then had the idea of laboriously compiling a history of modern opera – I mean really by this, putting the emphasis on post-1900 performances and personalities and also on the operas performed with some frequency in this era...

'I don't know whether you really have any confidence in an operatic revival in England. It has certainly taken place in America with a vengeance, but I am still strangely unpatriotic towards what to me is the most fascinating art form in the world...

'Sadler's Wells I admire enormously, but the standard of individual singing is not very high. Joan Cross is I think one of the finest singers in the world, but otherwise they have no soloists of outstanding merit. The ensemble is however very good indeed ... But why we don't have *Aida* with Turner, Coates, Widdop, Noble, Roderick Lloyd and Norman Walker I simply can't imagine.

'I hope this has not bored you. But I am most interested in your project.'

In addition to the actual letter the writer had enclosed two pages of casts that he had copied out from various sources – a task I was to perform for him in the future on many occasions. Lascelles, of course, was the elder son of the Princess Royal and the Earl of Harewood, and would himself succeed to that title in 1947. He was, and in a way is, a fundamentally shy person and so it was not until 1950 that we became on first-name terms.

I replied to him at length and within a few weeks received an answer, this time written in pencil and even more illegible than the first, asking for casts of the Dresden State Opera's 1936 season at Covent Garden and ending by saying that he was 'Looking forward to Rome and I hope Gigli, Caniglia, Bechi, Pagliughi and Pasero have stayed behind.' George never got to Rome, instead he spent the rest of the war at Colditz, and the letters I wrote to him while he was a prisoner there never reached him.

The first of my many meetings with Professor Dent was for afternoon tea not long after I had become engaged. I always enjoyed those conversations in his top-floor flat in South Kensington, though at first these were more monologues than dialogues. He was a wicked old man who made the most outrageous statements about establishment figures and told me of his hopes for opera in post-war Britain. Glyndebourne he could not abide, nor those starry inter-national casts at Covent Garden. I must have endeared myself to him with my enthusiasm for Sadler's Wells Opera and his translations of Mozart, Rossini and Verdi. On one occasion he sang, or rather croaked, to me some of his translation of Wolf-Ferrari's *I quatro rusteghi*, which he had called *The School for Fathers*, and which he had made for the 1939-40 season at Sadler's Wells; because of the war its production was postponed and it was eventually heard there in June 1946. It was largely at Dent's urging that I became the first post-war archivist of the Royal Opera House in 1951.

I had continued to add to my own operatic archives during the war years. I have already mentioned *Musical America* and *Musical Courier*, and I was, through Curt Weiler, receiving *Opera News*. As a result of a letter I wrote to that paper, early in 1945, which appeared under the heading 'From an English Fan', in which I said that 'I would be happy to hear from members of the Guild on operatic matters', I made several more useful contacts. As well as reports of all United States performances, all these three publications included reviews and news from South America, Sweden and Switzerland. As the allied armies advanced in Italy, articles from musicians and critics serving with the US Forces began to appear; those by Henry Pleasants and Robert Lawrence were particularly vivid and illumi-nating. Then, after the liberation of Paris, French newspapers reappeared on the bookstalls in Charing Cross Road, and these included in their pages reports of French operatic life. Strangely enough, even during the worst days of the U-Boat offensive, when millions of tons of allied shipping were being lost, American newspapers still arrived in London regularly, and so I had been able to add to my scrap-books cuttings from the *New York Times* and *Herald Tribune* reporting operatic happenings in the States.

At home, between 'D Day' (6 June 1944) and 'VE Day' (7 May 1945), the period of the Flying Bombs and Rockets in southern England, operatic life continued. In fact the Sadler's Wells Company's last two London war-time seasons were given in the larger Princes Theatre in Shaftesbury Avenue. It was there, in August 1944, shortly after we were married that Phyllis enjoyed her first *Così fan tutte* with an ensemble that seemed to us to be perfect, though obviously greater individual voices have been heard in the opera: Joan Cross, Margaret Ritchie, Rose Hill, Peter Pears, John Hargreaves and Owen Brannigan, conducted by Lawrance Collingwood. On the first night, during the Act I Finale, the belt that was holding up John Hargreaves's baggy trousers snapped, and the effect was hilarious.

In the concert hall there was a return to something like pre-war standards with Beecham, Barbirolli, Coates and then, after the liberation of France, Paul Paray and Roger Desormière conducting, and Menuhin, Neveu, and Yvonne Lefébure as instrumentalists. During the series of concerts by the London Philharmonic Orchestra at the Coliseum in April 1945 a new name appeared among the list of conductors, Karl Rankl. His appointment as the first music director of the new opera company that was to be formed at post-war Covent Garden was announced just over a year later.

5

The First Years of Peace

———

It was in June 1944 shortly after 'D Day' that we learned, through the press, that Boosey and Hawkes had leased Covent Garden and were planning 'All-the-year-round opera and ballet for 1945 if the "world situation" permits'. In the event it was not until mid-February 1946 that the Opera House re-opened and with ballet rather than opera. It was only in September 1946 that opera was heard there again, when the San Carlo Company from Naples began a seven-week season. Covent Garden's own infant opera company with Karl Rankl as music director began life the following year.

The two-and-a-half years that elapsed between Boosey and Hawkes's announcement and the first night of *Carmen* in January 1947 were marked by arguments, recriminations and rumours. John Christie was the first person to enter the fray. In a long article in *The Times* entitled 'Observations on the aims and conditions of success in opera', Christie made it perfectly clear that he wanted Glyndebourne to play an important part in the future of opera in London – indeed for a time Christie seriously entertained the idea of purchasing the freehold of Covent Garden himself. The name of Rudolf Bing, Glyndebourne's pre-war general manager, was put forward as a suitable candidate for a similar position at post-war Covent Garden; at the same time the Thomas Beecham lobby was canvassing its candidate for music director. The *Evening News*, reporting on the inaugural meeting of the council of management of the new organization, stated quite confidently that 'It is expected that Sir Thomas Beecham, who returns to this country in September, will take on the musical directorship.' I am quite sure that Beecham thought he would be invited to assume control of the Opera House once more; in fact, Lady Cunard told several interested people that she was certain Beecham would get the job, but what had actually happened at the time was rather different. Beecham had asked the impresario Harold Holt, who had joined the Boosey and Hawkes directorate, to check the availability of a number of international singers who were resident in America, with the view of engaging them for an old-fashioned international opera season at Covent Garden in the summer and autumn of 1945. This would have been a privately sponsored season, with Beecham taking the lease of the Opera House from Boosey and Hawkes; however, this plan never materialized; neither did the promised seasons by the Royal Opera in Stockholm or the Opéra-Comique from Paris; nor a visit by La Scala Milan Orchestra under Toscanini, who cancelled the visit for political reasons. I remember Professor Dent making some caustic comments on all these events, or rather non-events. While we were waiting for definite news from Covent Garden, a far more important operatic event with far-reaching effects took place at Sadler's Wells – it is amazing how often it has been Sadler's Wells Opera and its successor the English National Opera rather than Covent Garden that has been the catalyst in our operatic lives.

The news that the Sadler's Wells Opera was going to return to its home in Rosebery Avenue appeared in the press shortly after 'VE Day' (7 May 1945). That was exciting enough in itself, but the announcement that the theatre would reopen, not with *Faust* or *Il trovatore*, as obviously some of the public and, as we were later to learn, not a few of the company would have liked, but with a new opera by a British composer, *Peter Grimes* by Benjamin Britten, was, as *The Times* put it, 'an omen favourable for *Peter Grimes* and for English opera!' Britten's name was already known to many of us. His music had been widely heard during the war years and I recollect the enormous success of the 'Michelangelo Sonnets' which I heard for the first time at a Wigmore Hall concert in September 1942, sung by Peter Pears with Britten at the piano. Then, just over a year later, I heard the first performance of the 'Serenade for tenor solo, horn and strings' in the same hall, again with Peter Pears and with Dennis Brain playing the horn and Walter Goehr conducting. In February 1944 I read with great interest an interview with Britten that appeared in *Tempo*, the Boosey and Hawkes house magazine. In it the composer expressed in no uncertain terms his views on opera. He said:

43

'I am passionately interested in seeing a successful permanent national opera in existence – successful both artistically and materially. And it must be vital and contemporary too, and founded less on imported "stars" than on a first rate, young and fresh, permanent company. Sadler's Wells have made a good beginning.'

By that time Peter Pears was a member of the Sadler's Wells Company, and Joan Cross became more and more determined that *Peter Grimes* should be the opera chosen to mark her company's return to the Wells. At the request of Britten and Boosey and Hawkes, the conductor Serge Koussevitsky who had commissioned the opera from Britten for the Tanglewood Festival in the USA, readily waived the rights of the opera's first performance, happy to allow the composer's own country to enjoy that privilege. Britten dedicated *Peter Grimes* to the conductor's wife, Natalie.

Sadler's Wells itself had been derequisitioned in the autumn of 1944; but the opera company was still committed to its touring programme in the provinces and to its 1945 spring season in London at the Princes Theatre. Britten had completed the full score of *Peter Grimes* early in 1945, and Eric Crozier, who was to produce the opera, recalls that rehearsals began during the company's winter tour, first in a Methodist Hall in Sheffield, then in a gymnasium in Birmingham, and finally in the Civic Hall in Wolverhampton.

On 7 June 1945, exactly one month after 'VE Day', Sadler's Wells reopened. I do not think that anyone who was present that evening will ever forget the excitement and impact of the occasion. The audience included many young people in uniform, and somehow we sensed that this was the beginning of a new era. There had not been a great British-born operatic composer since Purcell and most of our singers had made their livings in oratorio, at seaside concert parties and in pantomime. Those few who had achieved distinction during the brief Covent Garden seasons and at the infant Glyndebourne rarely got foreign engagements. The success of *Grimes* was to change all that. Opera suddenly became a respectable art form, and British singers, conductors and composers lost their inferiority complexes.

Also present at that first night was George Lascelles, though it was to be another four weeks before we actually met. He had returned to England after his release from Colditz just before 'VE Day', and

I had written to him shortly afterwards, congratulating him on his safe return and returning the fascinating copies of *Musica d'Oggi* he had sent me from Italy the previous year. I did not receive a reply until 23 June; this time it was easy to read as it was typewritten. He commented on the performances he had heard since his return to England, including *Peter Grimes*, which he said he found most moving, and he expressed the hope that it would remain in the repertory for,

> 'It is time we had some serious opera as opposed to nothing but Puccini, whom I like very much, but who is hardly aiming at the highest things in music, or heavy Teutonism, against which at the moment I have a definite reaction; and *Grimes* was certainly serious without being heavy or pretentious.'

He ended his letter by saying that as he was more or less straight, he would be only too delighted to hear some operatic news and more about my own researches.

I replied to his letter, and a little more than a fortnight later I returned home to find a message to telephone 'Lord Lascelles' at a Trafalgar number which I soon discovered was Friary Court, St James's Palace. I duly called him, and, for the first time, heard a voice that was, like the handwriting of its owner, to become increasingly familiar. He invited me to a performance of *Così fan tutte* at Sadler's Wells on 19 July, 'if I'd like to come', and added 'I gather it will be Peter Pears and not Tom Culbert as Ferrando.'

We met in the foyer at Sadler's Wells where he introduced me to Joan Cross. After the performance we returned to the Haymarket on a 19 bus, and walked to St James's Palace, where we wandered up and down that short stretch of the Mall outside the Palace, discussing opera. Shortly after that George went to Canada as Aide-de-Camp to the Governor General, the Earl of Athlone, and when he returned to England a year later he went to King's College, Cambridge to read English. We continued to correspond rather spasmodically during those two years.

The summer of 1945 had been truly exhilarating; Labour won the General Election, and it was Clement Attlee who on 2 September announced the end of the war in the Far East. Exactly one month later I obtained what was known as a 'Class B' release from the army which enabled me to return to the university as a post-graduate student and to qualify as a teacher. I spent a happy year at the Institute of Education in London meeting several of my pre-war friends again and making new contacts. I continued my operatic researches at the British Museum Newspaper Library at Colindale, combing through the arts pages of papers from Italy, Germany, Austria and Argentina, and adding to my fast-growing collection of cast lists. These were augmented by information I received from two foreign contacts I had made through *The Gramophone*: Leo Riemens in The Hague and Roberto Bauer in Milan. Riemens proved to be a mine of information about singers and performances in Germany in the inter-war years and during the war; Bauer, who was eventually to become Rudolf Bing's European adviser on singers, provided information on the Italian scene and wrote devastatingly funny comments on the performances he had heard.

Phyllis was expecting her first baby towards the end of June 1946 and so we left the flat we were sharing with my mother and sister in Hampstead and returned to the old family house in Norwood, which was to become our home until the end of 1953. Phyllis gave up teaching at the end of the spring term of 1946 and although we continued to go to opera and concerts, we did so on a much reduced scale. Early in June Sadler's Wells mounted the first performance of Wolf-Ferrari's *The School for Fathers* from which Professor Dent had played me extracts two years previously; with Howell Glynne, David Franklin, Nora Gruhn, Rose Hill and Valetta Iacopi in the cast and staged by Dennis Arundell, his first operatic production at the Wells, it gave enormous pleasure; but despite several revivals failed to establish itself in the repertory.

Our son, Simon, was born on 25 June, so Phyllis was unable to accompany me on my first post-war visit to Glyndebourne. This was not for Mozart but for Britten's *The Rape of Lucretia*. The first news that Glyndebourne was to reopen came in a press announcement that appeared in the mid-summer of 1945, inviting those interested to write to Glyndebourne in order to be put on a new mailing list. Needless to say I quickly responded and received a card that informed me that 'Although present political and world conditions make cut and dried arrangements difficult, they [i.e. Glyndebourne Opera Festival Management] would like you to know that plans are being made and they hope before long to send you some definite statement of their future policy.' As both Beecham's and Christie's approaches to Covent Garden had been rejected, it seemed quite natural that those two operatic entrepreneurs should explore the possibilities of an alliance and, according to Glyndebourne's official historian, Spike Hughes, Beecham offered to conduct a 1946 Glyndebourne Festival season without a fee. Christie eagerly accepted Beecham's offer and plans went ahead for a month's festival in June 1946 to consist of *The Magic Flute* (sung in English), *La Bohème*, and possibly *Lucia di Lammermoor*. These last two works were soon discarded and *Carmen*, which Glyndebourne had planned for its 1940 season, was announced instead. But when Beecham learned that a young British singer who had never appeared in opera was to be his Carmen – her name was Kathleen Ferrier – he withdrew, but not before he had uttered some pretty uncomplimentary things about Glyndebourne's policy and the famous pre-war Glyndebourne Mozart recordings under Fritz Busch.

It seemed strange to many people at that time that Busch was not invited to return to Glyndebourne and rejoin his old colleagues Ebert and Bing; but in 1942 he had agreed to become music director of the short-lived New Opera Company in New York whose stagings of *Così fan tutte* and *Macbeth* were based on the Glyndebourne productions; this had upset both Ebert and the Christies. With the withdrawal of Beecham and the absence of Busch, Glyndebourne had to make other plans.

The decision to reopen Sadler's Wells, in June 1945, with the première of Britten's *Peter Grimes* had not been popular with certain members of the company; and by the end of the first post-war summer season there was an open split. The full facts of that unhappy situation were not revealed until twenty years later, when, in June 1965, I published an article in *Opera* written by Eric Crozier. In it he revealed that the 'insurgent group within the company', as he termed it, demanded the postponement of the complete recording of *Grimes* for the British Council as they had decided instead to go on a tour for ENSA. The governors of Sadler's Wells replied by threatening to close the theatre and form a new company, but they weakly signed agreements with those who went on the ENSA tour. Britten then asked for *Grimes* to be withdrawn from the repertory; this led to the resignation of those who believed in *Grimes* and the progressive policy they thought would follow from its success. Then, at the final performance of the opera, the iron safety curtain was lowered without warning, and what had been announced as Joan Cross's farewell performance after twenty-one years at the Old Vic and Sadler's Wells ended abruptly.

Britten, Crozier, Joan Cross, Peter Pears and a few others then began to explore the possibility of setting up a new company which could perform works that did not require a large chorus and orchestra; and in the early autumn of 1945 when Glyndebourne issued its first post-war prospectus, we read that,

> 'A new operatic venture is in process of formation and Glyndebourne has made itself responsible. The new company will start activities with the production of a new opera by Benjamin Britten, *The Rape of Lucretia*, libretto by Ronald Duncan ... It is hoped and intended that one or two new English works will be produced every year by the new company in collaboration with Glyndebourne ... It is hoped that the work of this new operatic company may become an annual addition to Glyndebourne's Opera Festival of Classical Masterpieces, which will be revived in 1947. Rudolf Bing, General Manager of Glyndebourne Opera.'

This long-term plan between the new company and Glyndebourne never came to fruition, for by 1947 the new company had become the English Opera Group which gave the first performance of Britten's next opera, *Albert Herring*, at Glyndebourne. In 1948 this new group became the official opera-giving company of the Aldeburgh Festival which Britten and his friends had started that year. In 1947, Rudolf Bing had launched the first Edinburgh Festival with Glyndebourne assuming responsibility for its operatic performances.

But to return to Glyndebourne of 1946 and *The Rape of Lucretia*; I payed 7s 6d for my seat in row twelve of the stalls that summer. The performance began at 6.15, and the train, with Pullman Car facilities in both directions, left Victoria at 3.45, returning from Lewes at 9.58, and the third-class fare was 11s 11d. Dinner was at the inclusive charge of 7s 6d, with wine extra. So my first post-war Glyndebourne visit cost me less than £2!

As Scott Goddard so aptly put it, 'It was difficult to judge the performance of Benjamin Britten's *The Rape of Lucretia* because of the emotions aroused of being at Glyndebourne again.' It was not until a few years later that I got to terms with the work, and not until Janet Baker sang Lucretia in 1969 that I was truly moved by it.

None the less, it is nostalgic to look again at my 1946 *Lucretia* programme, if only to read the names of the artists concerned: Kathleen Ferrier, Joan Cross, Margaret Ritchie, Anna Pollak, Peter Pears, Otakar Kraus, and Edmund Donlevy were the singers, and Ernest Ansermet and Reginald Goodall shared the conducting.

That Glyndebourne *Lucretia* was in mid-July; within the next eight weeks two events occurred which, I must confess, at the time, thrilled me more than Britten's new opera: the production of *Don Pasquale* at the Cambridge Theatre and the visit to Covent Garden of the San Carlo Opera from Naples. I have already mentioned the successful war-time production of *The Fair at Sorochints*, first at the Savoy and then the Adelphi Theatres; those seasons had been sponsored by the Music Art and Drama Society, a non-profit-making society founded in 1941 by the Russian-born impresario Jay Pomeroy. 'Pom', as he affectionately came to be known in operatic circles, had also taken the lease of the Cambridge Theatre for seasons of Russian ballet and a series of symphony concerts. In 1944 the 'MAD Society' – the most unfortunate set of initials, to say the least, ever to have been given to an opera-giving organization, appropriate though they might be – presented Johann Strauss's *A Night in Venice* at the Cambridge Theatre where it ran for over five hundred performances. That success, plus the fact that Pom's favourite soprano, Daria Bayan, who was also his mistress, had operatic ambitions, resulted in the foundation of the New London Opera Company in the summer of 1946 based on the Cambridge Theatre. Pom was astute enough to invite the Italian conductor, Alberto Erede, who had worked with Busch at pre-war Glyndebourne, to become the company's music director, and the tenor, Dino Borgioli, long resident in London, who was Bayan's voice teacher, to become artistic director. The company began operations with a production of *La Bohème* for which the legendary Alexandre Benois designed the scenery and in which Bayan was, of course, the Mimi, and an American tenor, Lester Ferguson, the Rodolfo. Neither was particularly memorable vocally, but they both looked youthful and acted quite nicely.

The original aim of the MAD Society was to give opera in English with British singers, and so *Bohème* was sung in that language. Rehearsals began for the second opera in the repertory, Donizetti's *Don Pasquale*, and Martin Lawrence, who was to sing Pasquale, and the

Scottish tenor Andrew MacPherson, who was to be Ernesto, started to learn their rôles in English. However, there were difficulties over who should sing Norina and Dr Malatesta; and it did not take Erede and Borgioli very long to persuade Pom that if *Pasquale* was to succeed, it would be best to sing it in Italian and to engage two Italian artists for those rôles. Erede recommended a young Trieste-born soprano with whom he had worked during the war, Alda Noni, for Norina, and Borgioli suggested his old Glyndebourne colleague, Mariano Stabile, for Malatesta. The success of *Pasquale* was ensured, Noni became a firm favourite and was later engaged by Glyndebourne; Lawrence was launched on what promised to be a distinguished career; but perhaps it was his left-wing political affiliations that resulted in his being unfairly treated by operatic managements in England. Stabile was lionized and held up both by critics and established singers alike as offering an object lesson in style to the younger generation.

The New London Opera Company continued to prosper artistically, if not financially, at the Cambridge Theatre until May 1948, by which time it had given 609 performances and lost some £120,000. It had expanded its repertory to include *Rigoletto* and *Falstaff*, both produced by Carl Ebert, *Don Giovanni* and *Tosca*. It brought to London Margherita Grandi, Glyndebourne's pre-war Lady Macbeth, and established Marko Rothmüller as one of the finest singing-actors of the day; it introduced to London a new generation of Italian singers which, in addition to Noni, included Antonio Salvarezza, Italo Tajo and Giuseppe Taddei; and it proved to be an invaluable training ground for several British artists like Murray and William Dickie and Ian Wallace. Unfortunately, few of the singers who appeared at the Cambridge Theatre went to Covent Garden (Murray Dickie, Rothmüller and Grandi were the exceptions), for there was little love lost between the new Covent Garden administration and Pomeroy, especially after the latter's bid for the forty-two-year lease on the Opera House in December 1949. So irrational was David Webster's antipathy to the whole Cambridge Theatre enterprise that, when the La Scala Milan company made its historic visit to Covent Garden in September 1950, he vetoed their choice of Stabile to sing the title-rôle in *Falstaff*, a part in which he had not been equalled since he first sang it under Toscanini at La Scala in 1921.

The choice of the Naples company to give the first post-war opera at Covent Garden might seem strange; but, since September 1943, the San Carlo Opera House in Naples had been visisted by thousands of allied soldiers, sailors and airmen. Indeed, it came to London as the CMF (Central Mediterranean Forces) Opera Company, and owed its existence to the efforts of several British and American army officers who saw in its establishment a chance of providing a rather different kind of entertainment for the troops in Italy at the time. According to Peter Francis, who was one of the officers concerned and who in recent years has run a successful travel agency in England specializing in opera tours, it gave more than seven hundred performances between 1943 and 1946 and was attended by more than four million members of the allied forces. It brought a popular repertory to London, twenty-six principal singers, a chorus of fifty, but used Covent Garden's own orchestra.

La traviata was chosen for the opening night (16 September) and Violetta was sung by Margherita Carosio, whom the publicity agents claimed was 'a glamorous young Italian soprano – not yet thirty', which would have made her about twelve years old when she appeared at Covent Garden as Musetta and Xenia in *Boris Godunov* with Chaliapin in 1928! In fact she was born in 1908. I was to learn later, when I began to compile biographical entries for the *Concise Oxford Dictionary of Opera* as well as for Grove's *Dictionary of Music and Musicians* that singers have very selective memories when it comes to revealing the year of their birth and the date of their debut.

I noted in my programme that 'Carosio was a fine Violetta, who sang and acted superbly' – I also noted she had blood-red fingernails! Carlo Tagliabue, who had last sung in London in 1938, was the Germont, and a tenor called Gustavo Gallo, who sang flat in the Act I love duet, as even Gigli was inclined to, was a silly-looking Alfredo. The scenery came from the Covent Garden warehouse and the singers brought their own costumes. Franco Capuana, a fiery little Neapolitan, who endeared himself to the orchestra and was later invited back to work with Covent Garden's own company, conducted. My seat in the fifth row of the amphitheatre cost me 5s.

In all I attended eight of the company's performances and heard three young singers who were to make names for themselves: the tenors Mario Del Monaco, who sang Cavaradossi and Canio, and

Luigi Infantino, who sang Rodolfo and the Duke of Mantua, and the baritone Paolo Silveri who sang nearly every leading baritone rôle during the season. He was called on to replace the veteran Benvenuto Franci, of whose Figaro *The Times* critic wrote:

> 'So far from this Figaro having the entry to every house in Seville, he would have been shown the door at his first call. His singing of the "Largo al factotum" was both slovenly and vulgar, and the audience perceived the incongruity of his shouting at the top of his resonant and indeed splendid voice, music that derives from aristocratic comedy.'

And of his Scarpia, Ernest Newman remarked that: 'His most original touch was to gobble away at a hearty supper while Tosca was battling with "Vissi d'arte" – never before had I realized what a grand eating part this is.'

It is not easy to describe the emotions I experienced when I climbed those stone stairs to the amphitheatre again; I recognized several old familiar faces from pre-war days, and settled down, if not comfortably then certainly excitedly, to hear opera again at Covent Garden. True, I had seen a few ballet performances there since the theatre had reopened the previous February, but that was not the same. Covent Garden meant, and still does mean to me, and I am sure to many people, opera; and to hear once again the human voice in that wonderful acoustic was something I had been waiting for since the summer of 1939.

The San Carlo's season was originally planned to last until 19 October, after which the company was to perform at the Davis Theatre in Croydon. Great excitement was aroused by an announcement in mid-October that it would return to London to give four additional performances with Gigli and his daughter Rina – two of *La Bohème* and two of the inseparable operatic twins *Cavalleria rusticana* and *Pagliacci*, with Gigli singing both Turiddu and Canio on the same evening. The box office for these performances and for the new Sadler's Wells Ballet season opened on the same morning, and chaos reigned outside the opera house, with two queues totalling more than a thousand people getting hopelessly mixed up. Tempers were not improved by the announcement that 'application may be made for only ONE of the four performances of Beniamino Gigli, when tickets will be restricted to a maximum of six a person'. Why

we were not allowed to spread those six tickets over two performances I was never able to puzzle out.

The gossip columnists had a field day, for Gigli had only recently
been cleared of charges of collaboration during the war. 'Giglis, two
by two' proclaimed one headline; 'More a tender father than dis-
traught lover' said another. There had been no extra rehearsals for
the Gigli performances and there was plenty of ham-acting; and an
encore was allowed for 'Vesti la giubba'. International opera was
back with a vengeance: 'instant opera' is what some of today's critics
would have called it.

As for Covent Garden's own infant opera company, it began
rehearsing early in October. Karl Rankl's appointment as music
director had been announced in mid-June, as had the Covent Garden
Opera Trust's declaration of intent:

> 'To establish at the Royal Opera House a resident opera company
> of the highest standard mainly of British artists ... in the belief
> that the development of opera in England – and, indeed the
> formation of a style of performance – depends to a large extent on
> the use of English. The performances of the resident company will
> therefore be given in English. The Trust intends to do everything
> in its power to secure a high standard of English translations where
> none exists at present, and to attempt, in collaboration, to secure
> the adoption of standard English versions by schools, teachers,
> and opera companies throughout the English-speaking world.'

Wonderful, unattainable ideals, that were perforce to be short-
lived. How often in the ensuing years would the management be
reminded, often to its embarrassment, of them; and how often
was I to clash with the administration, with members of the board,
and later, when Solti was appointed music director, with that re-
doubtable figure, when I confronted them with those words. The
opera company showed its paces and faces in a production of
Purcell's *The Fairy Queen* in which the Sadler's Wells Ballet participated and which was conducted by Constant Lambert. The
opera season proper opened five weeks later in mid-January with
Carmen conducted by Rankl. *The Times* review began with the
words 'The answers are in the affirmative'; but, 'This British *Carmen*
is all wrong' (*Evening News*) and 'Bricks without Straw' (Desmond
Shawe-Taylor in the *New Statesman*) were nearer the mark.

As so often in those days (and in the future) I and many others found much more to enjoy at Sadler's Wells Theatre and, for the next two years, at the Cambridge Theatre. Of course, there were a few compensations at Covent Garden, including Eva Turner's return as Turandot and the visit of the Vienna State Opera in September 1948, when we heard for the first time Ljuba Welitsch, Elisabeth Schwarzkopf, Irmgard Seefried, Sena Jurinac, Hilde Gueden, Hans Hotter and Erich Kunz. The Vienna company brought the Vienna Philharmonic Orchestra with them to play in the pit, and the Musicians Union made fools of themselves by picketing the opera house in protest.

At the performance of *Don Giovanni* on 27 September, sung incidentally in German, as were also *Così fan tutte* and *Figaro*, Richard Tauber, who had been a distinguished member of the Vienna State Opera until Hitler marched into Austria, sang Don Ottavio. He had renewed many old friendships during the first fortnight of the season, and to hear him again in opera and in that context proved to be a most moving experience. We did not know at the time that this would be his last appearance on any stage, for the day after the performance he entered a London nursing home and was operated on for lung cancer; he never left his sick bed and died the following January. Of his Don Ottavio I wrote in my programme: 'How wonderful to hear again after eight years that Mozart mastersinger and to see him with his old colleagues after those terrible years.'

6

'Ballet and Opera' into 'Opera'

It is one thing to record one's personal impressions of performances in a programme or a diary, quite another to have reviews and articles published regularly in the press. I did not have the slightest idea of how to go about achieving this, and although I still had the occasional letter or article published in *The Gramophone* and *Musical Opinion* I could see little prospect at that time of making my living as a writer. I had been teaching for a year, was in a relatively secure and pensionable job, and was told that I had the makings of a good teacher. I still corresponded with George Harewood, and I talked a lot to Arthur Notcutt about my ambitions. 'Why not write some articles for *Opera News* in New York?' he suggested; and so, using the material I had compiled from my researches at the British Museum Newspaper Library and the information I was receiving from German and Italian opera houses about their activities during the war years, which was supplemented by long letters from my two untiring European correspondents, Leo Riemens and Roberto Bauer, I submitted an article to *Opera News*. This chronicled the activities of several singers who had appeared at the Metropolitan and elsewhere in the United States before 1940, whose careers I felt certain would be of interest to American opera-goers. My efforts were rewarded, and I was asked by the editor of *Opera News*, a remarkable woman whom I was later to meet, called Mary-Ellis Peltz, to write a second piece about outstanding European singers who had so far not appeared in New York.

I also began to send Mrs Peltz short reviews of the performances at Covent Garden and Sadler's Wells, which duly appeared. The next obvious step seemed to be to offer myself as the magazine's regular London correspondent, and this suggestion was likewise accepted. After becoming the accredited correspondent of *Opera*

News I sent some copies of what had already appeared in print under my own name to the press offices of the two London opera houses, and asked, rather timidly, whether I could be put on their press lists. Sadler's Wells quickly agreed; Covent Garden was a little less forthcoming, saying they would send occasional tickets when possible.

Michael Wood, Covent Garden's press officer, was a wonderful man; he was an ex-guards officer, tall, with a fine military bearing, a very measured drawl and always impeccably dressed. His office, just off the balcony stalls at the Opera House, soon became well-known to me, and there Michael (and his Jack Russell terrier), always made me welcome. He was to become a sympathetic champion of my work and a dear friend. The Sadler's Wells press officer was an old Fleet Street 'pro' called John Carlsen; his knowledge of opera may not have been very profound, but he loved Sadler's Wells Theatre and was on good terms with everyone.

At about this time, I happened to pass a bookstall in Charing Cross Road, where my eye fell on a small magazine called *Ballet and Opera*. I bought the November issue, asked the bookseller whether he had a copy of the October issue, which he did, and devoured both issues, or rather their operatic sections, on my bus journey back to south London. The magazine cost 2s and had fifty-six pages, of which between eight and ten were devoted to opera. The title page informed me that its editor was Richard Buckle and its opera editor, the Earl of Harewood. He had, I learned later, been introduced to Buckle by Eric Walter White (later Assistant Secretary of the Arts Council). In 1960, Eric recalled how he felt that just as Richard Buckle had done so much for the art of the dance in his magazine *Ballet* so the same thing could be done for opera. But those were the days of paper rationing and it was impossible to launch a new magazine at that time; so Eric thought that if he could persuade the editor of *Ballet* to include a few articles on opera in each issue and the innovation proved a success then, when controls were relaxed, an independent magazine could, as he put it, be 'hived off'.

Eric's own account of how George was introduced to Dickie Buckle appeared in *Opera*'s tenth birthday issue in February 1960:

'At this point I began to think of an appropriate editor. Clearly this ought to be someone who belonged to the younger generation and who would be personally interested in the post-war revival of opera in England and English opera; and on reflection it seemed to me that the ideal person would be Lord Harewood. Accordingly on 30 July 1948, I arranged a luncheon party at a restaurant in Charlotte Street to which I invited Lord Harewood and Richard Buckle, and somewhat to my surprise and despite the sweltering heat of the day, the idea found immediate favour with both the persons concerned. The first number of the joint magazine *Ballet and Opera* appeared in October 1948; and fifteen months later *Opera* was launched in its own right.'

I doubt whether George Harewood or Dickie Buckle knew on that hot summer day in 1948 either when or, indeed whether, there would ever be a separate opera magazine. I certainly did not when I wrote to George Harewood early in December that year suggesting that I might contribute one or two articles on 'opera abroad' for *Ballet and Opera*. A few days after Christmas 1948 I received a letter from George in which he wrote:

'I am anxious to include an article on operatic activities abroad in the next number of *Ballet and Opera* which goes to press at the beginning of next month [that didn't leave me much time]. I imagine it would be too difficult to include anything about American doings as well as those of the continent in a single article [a remark I found distinctly encouraging]. Probably we should have a separate piece on what they are doing in the States in a later issue ... I am all for mentioning singers' names, as I think it stimulates curiosity, and if they come to Covent Garden, might encourage people to go and find out what they are like in real life ... It occurs to me that you might have some photographs of some continental productions. My editor takes a strongly balletic view of operatic photographs, but no doubt in time, and with the right material, can be persuaded of their value!'

I spent my Christmas holiday producing the first article covering the 1946–7 and 1947–8 seasons at La Scala, Milan; Teatro dell'Opera, Rome; La Fenice, Venice, and the Teatro Donizetti at Bergamo. This I sent to George on New Year's Eve. 'You have produced just the sort of thing we needed, I think', he commented in his note of acknowledgement. And so, in the January 1949 issue of *Ballet and Opera* my first contribution appeared entitled 'Opera on the

Continent', a feature which was to develop, when *Opera* was established, first into 'News from Abroad', and then 'Our Critics Abroad'.

On 30 January a brief telegram arrived asking, 'Can you manage another "Opera Abroad" by February 4th? Send to Buckle. Signed Harewood.' Once again that did not leave much time, but I promptly produced my second piece on the post-war seasons to date, in Vienna, Berlin and Dresden; this appeared in the March issue, together with a contribution from Professor Dent on 'Laughter at the Opera'. Visits to Friary Court to discuss future articles and hear about George's recent Italian trip and frequent letters from George marked the next few weeks, and then came a request to cover the revival of Boughton's *Immortal Hour* at the People's Palace in the Mile End Road during the first week of April. So my first real reviews, as opposed to a resumé of events overseas, appeared in the May 1949 issue of *Ballet and Opera*, which had twenty-one pages devoted to opera – things were, indeed, looking up.

The 1948-9 season certainly had its excitement; at Covent Garden Ljuba Welitsch sang the title-rôle in a new production of *Aida*, as well as Musetta in which it was obvious that she and Elisabeth Schwarzkopf, the Mimi, were hardly on speaking terms. Astrid Varnay made a great impression as Brünnhilde and Isolde in the short autumn Wagner season, in which Set Svanholm made his London debut as Siegfried and Tristan. Peter Brook, Covent Garden's director of productions, an appointment that had been made long before the London public and critics were ready to accept a stimulating man of the theatre in the opera house, was responsible for the staging of *Fidelio* and *Figaro*; in the latter opera, a young Welsh baritone, Geraint Evans, made his first appearance in a leading rôle, and in both operas the singing of the Australian soprano Sylvia Fisher, who had recently joined the company, was greatly admired.

The most important operatic event in London that season, however, was the first performance in England of Verdi's *Simon Boccanegra* at Sadler's Wells on 27 October 1948. Covent Garden had promised this opera as far back as 1919 but it had never materialized. Norman Tucker had not only translated the text into English but had also made a few modifications to the music and added a few bars of recitative in order to simplify some of the intricacies of the plot. It goes without saying that some voices were raised in objection; but on the whole, the edition and, more importantly, the work, was received with great enthusiasm. I recollect it as being a most exciting evening – the kind of Verdi performance that we might expect, but do not always get, in a major opera house, but which Sadler's Wells, with its dedication to the music, nearly always gave and, as the English National Opera, still gives us. The music establishment was there in force and Covent Garden's contingent included David Webster and Karl Rankl, who were making one of their rare excursions to hear opera in the rival house. The impact of this sombre but powerful Verdi work on the public was extraordinary, and each successive group of performances was sold out as soon as it was announced.

The opera was cast from the regular Sadler's Wells company, and with Arnold Matters as Boccanegra, James Johnston as Gabriele Adorno, Howell Glynne as Fiesco, and Frederick Sharpe as Paolo, was particularly strong on the male side. Those singers recorded a number of items from the opera for HMV and listening to them again I realized that it was not just the enthusiasm of the moment that led all the critics to write so enthusiastically about both the performers and the work at the time. In fact, when the Verdi Institute of Parma organized an international conference on *Boccanegra* in Chicago in 1974, and George played several extracts from those 1949 recordings, several Italian critics could not believe that Britain at that time possessed so Italianate a tenor as James Johnston. In his review of the production in *Ballet and Opera* George judged the production of *Boccanegra* as 'ranking next to *Peter Grimes* amongst post-war Sadler's Wells achievements'.

The announcement that Covent Garden was to perform two complete cycles of Wagner's *Ring des Nibelungen* in May 1949 for the first time since 1939 with a cast that would include Flagstad, Svanholm, Hotter, and Ludwig Weber was warmly welcomed. Covent Garden's publicity department claimed that this was the first complete cycle in Europe since the war; but as my newspaper cuttings and information from foreign houses showed, this was not so; for it had been regularly performed at the Royal Opera in Stockholm since 1945 under Leo Blech, and there had also been cycles in 1947-8 and 1948-9 in Bordeaux, Lyons, Marseilles and Toulouse, as well as two cycles early in 1949 in Lisbon performed by an ensemble from the Bavarian State Opera in Munich. I mentioned this to George at one of our now regular get-togethers at Friary Court, and he said he'd tell David Webster. In a letter to me (9 May) George wrote:

'He [Webster] still obstinately and determinedly sticks to his idea that the Covent Garden *Ring* is the first complete cycle since the war. I suggested it was not, but he said he would keep up his contention unless I would produce chapter and verse to refute it ... You are the only person who is likely to have accurate information on the subject, and if Covent Garden insists in making their propaganda out of bubble-gum they must expect to have the bubble pricked. I hope it can be.'

I accordingly wrote my first letter to *The Times* which appeared on 28 May under the heading of 'Wagner Since the War'. Two days later I wrote to Webster 'pricking the bubble' as George had suggested. By return of post I received a curt reply from him: 'Thank you for your letter of 30th May. There was no Covent Garden bubble to burst. We are very modest people here!!!!' I am convinced that this did little to endear me to Webster and the uneasy personal relationship with him that developed during the next fifteen years dates from that time. Webster did not like to be contradicted and was always suspicious of those people whose operatic knowledge he thought was wider than his own. It was about this time I began, I believe, to be dubbed as a Beckmesser!

By the end of the 1948-9 season I was not only contributing regular articles to *Ballet and Opera* on the post-war operatic scene abroad, but also reviews of those London performances that George himself was unable to attend, for he was then spending several weeks abroad listening to opera. It was also about that time that he became engaged to Marion Stein, daughter of Erwin Stein the Viennese musicologist and pupil of Schoenberg. My friendship with George was becoming more firmly established though we still addressed one another very formally as Lord Harewood and Mr Rosenthal; both of us, I suspect, were too shy at that time to make the first move to use first names.

At the end of June 1949, I invited George to lunch at a restaurant in Beak Street that had been a favourite haunt of mine since my university days; it was called 'Alberts', and its proprietor, Albert Pensione, was a great tennis and opera fan. George suggested I came first to Friary Court for a drink, and it was on that occasion that I met Rudolf Bing for the first time. Bing's appointment as general manager of the Metropolitan Opera in New York was shortly to become effective and I recollect that all three of us gossiped for about half-an-hour about Bing's plans for New York, and about singers he would or would not engage, and some he said he would *never* engage. He seemed to forget quite a few of those names during his régime!

For several years George had been a keen collector of gramophone records, and had already laid the foundations of his considerable collection of historical recordings. He had persuaded Dickie Buckle to allow him, from time to time, two or three pages in *Ballet and Opera* in which to review operatic discs – this was still the era of '78s' – and obviously this was one feature that George wanted to keep for himself. A chance meeting with one of my boyhood friends, John Amis, who used to live in the next road to us in Norwood, and with whom my sister and I shared the same piano teacher, resulted in my becoming a regular record reviewer for *The Musical Express*, a weekly paper that devoted more space to popular than classical music. Through John's good offices, Malcolm Rayment, its classical music editor, invited me to contribute a weekly column, and large boxes of records began to arrive regularly. My first two contributions were devoted to an HMV Special List recording of Verdi's *Un ballo in maschera*; this had been made in Rome towards the end of the war with a cast that included Gigli, Caniglia, Barbieri and Bechi, and was conducted by Tullio Serafin. It occupied thirty-three sides, and my review, which was published in two instalments, ran to nearly three thousand words!

I continued to contribute to *The Musical Express* for the next few years, and had my first experience of being confronted by an artist who had taken exception to something I had written. More often than not it has been the artist's husband, wife or over-zealous manager rather than the singer who would take the initiative. This first confrontation arose from what seemed to me to be quite an innocent remark in an otherwise excellent review (from the singer's point of view that is) of two Verdi arias recorded by Redvers Llewellyn. This Welsh baritone had been one of the outstanding members of the Sadler's Wells Opera during the 1930s, especially in the Verdi repertory; he was another example of a British artist who, if attitudes had been different in the pre-war years, would have made an international career. The record in question consisted of Ford's 'Vengeance' aria from *Falstaff* and Renato's 'Eri tu' from *Un ballo in maschera*. I commented about the 'excellent account of the Ford aria, put over with verve and understanding, and the English diction being masterly'; then, I continued, 'in "Eri tu" Llewellyn's voice shows signs of age' – and that is what he, or as I learned later his wife, had objected to. I received an irate telephone call from him and he asked me to go and see him in his flat just off Gower Street. I hardly had time to sit down and make a few polite comments before he fired at me the question 'And just how old do you think I am?' 'About fifty,' I managed to stammer – he was in fact forty-nine. 'Well that doesn't make me an old man does it?' After a little more verbal fencing we reached an understanding; as time went by, we became good friends and on several occasions during the 1960s he invited me to lunch at the Royal College of Music where he taught singing; one of his outstanding pupils was the baritone Thomas Allen. From then onwards I was very careful about referring to singers 'sounding their age'.

The opening night of the 1949–50 season at Covent Garden was the first performance of Arthur Bliss's *The Olympians*. This was the first première of a work by a British composer at the Opera House since Lloyd's quickly-forgotten *The Serf* in 1938. The date of the performance was 29 September, the day on which George Harewood and Marion Stein were married. I had already been asked to cover the first nights of the revivals that were to take place between 4 and 24 October while George and Marion were away on their honeymoon. Difficulties were raised, however, about the first night of *The Olympians* which George was unable to review for *Ballet and Opera*; the powers that be at the Opera House were obviously not going to send a valuable pair of press tickets to a virtually unknown substitute. However, they invited me to the dress rehearsal which began at 10.30 in the morning; but as I only dared ask my sympathetic headmistress for the afternoon off, I only saw half the rehearsal.

The problem of how *The Olympians* was to be reviewed in the November *Ballet and Opera* still had to be resolved; but as the first night was to be broadcast I was obviously going to be able to hear the whole work. So without saying in print that I was not at the first night, I began my two-and-a-half-page review in the magazine thus:

'It is an extremely difficult task to form a considered judgement on a new musical work of symphonic proportions after only one hearing, but it is well nigh impossible to offer more than one's fleeting impressions of a new opera of almost Wagnerian length on the strength of half a dress rehearsal and one performance, especially as no score is yet available . . . It may be as well therefore to confine myself to a few general observations of the work and its production, and then, after further hearings, a more detailed criticism can be given, to which may be added, I hope, the opinions of the Opera Editor who has been unable to witness any of the season's earlier performances.'

In retrospect I think that a nice compromise!

By the time my review appeared in print, plans were well ahead for that hiving off of the opera section of *Ballet and Opera* so that it could become that separate magazine that Eric White had envisaged. Whether the idea had formulated in George's mind while he was on his honeymoon or whether the fact that twenty-six of the fifty-six pages of the October issue of *Ballet and Opera* were devoted to opera and only twenty-four to ballet (the rest were advertisements) had so infuriated Dickie Buckle that he determined to propose the break when George returned to England in late October, none of us remembers clearly; but the decision was made in late October.

Before George went on his honeymoon he had also asked me to review for *Ballet and Opera* the revivals of *Le nozze di Figaro*, *Die Zauberflöte*, *La traviata*, *Aida*, *Fidelio* and *Il trovatore* at Covent Garden, and a production of Cimarosa's *Secret Marriage* at the Fortune Theatre, which had been put on by an organization called the London Opera Club, of which he was, incidentally, the President, and whose artistic director was Ernst Urbach. Reviews of the Cimarosa opera and *Figaro*, *Traviata* and *Zauberflöte* were despatched, on time, to Dickie Buckle who, in the absence of George, vetted them; and they duly appeared in the November issue. The new production of *Don Giovanni* at Sadler's Wells on 25 October had already been claimed by George as his first review of the season – it took place on the day (or day after, I cannot quite recollect) of George's return home. The first night was on a Tuesday, and on the following Sunday morning at about 11 o'clock my telephone rang and George, apologizing for the short notice, asked me if I could possibly come to Friary Court for lunch that day as he had something interesting he wanted to discuss with me.

I cannot say that Phyllis was exactly pleased to have Sunday lunch thus disrupted; but on returning home in the early evening I was able to tell her that George had asked me to become his assistant editor on a new magazine to be called *Opera* which would be launched in three months' time (i.e. early in February 1950). At that time there was no question of my leaving teaching to work with him full time, as the magazine was only going to be published on alternate months until it had established itself. In any case, neither George, Dickie nor myself could guarantee the success of the magazine, nor, indeed, could the publishers of *Ballet*, who although calling themselves 'Ballet Publications Limited', were part of an organization known as 'Sport-in-Print', the brainchild of Phillip Dossé, whose chief interests were motorcycle racing and other sports. In less than a year Dossé was to launch a magazine called *Music and Musicians* which, with *Dance and Dancers*, and later *Plays and Players*, *Films and Filming* and *Books and Bookmen*, became known as Hansom Books, a group that continued to exist somewhat precariously until 1980.

By the end of November I knew what my contributions to the first issue of *Opera* were to be: a second assessment of *The Olympians*, which I would by then have heard twice more; nine pages of Opera News (home and abroad); reviews of *Die Zauberflöte*, *Lohengrin*, and *Rosenkavalier* at Covent Garden; and, finally, a review of a book called *Stars of the Opera* which George sent me, along with a letter which said: 'I would suggest you might take an encouraging though pained view of it, rather than damn it as fully as the text would suggest to you. After all, they may want to bring out other books!' I took a rather more jaundiced view, and the review was consequently held over until the third number. We decided that each issue, at least in those early days, should include a profile of a singer, conductor, or producer, and that the first should be of a British singer, the natural choice being Joan Cross. It was in the second issue that we decided to call these profiles 'People', a series that has continued in the pages of *Opera* and which, by June 1982, had reached number 130.

As the first issue of *Opera* had a rather British look about it, we decided that the second should have an Italian flavour, and the third a German one. Puccini's *Tosca* was celebrating its fiftieth anniversary in 1950 and so we planned three features centred around that event; we also aimed to cover the opening of the 1949–50 season in the major Italian opera houses. George had already planned to go to Italy (and elsewhere in Europe) in early January to hear performances; he suggested that I might go over before him and cover performances in Milan, Rome and Naples; and so I arranged, as economically as possible, my first trip abroad since before the war.

I left London, somewhat apprehensively, on Boxing Day, to travel by train and boat to Milan.

My Milan correspondent, Roberto Bauer, had booked accommodation for me at a hotel with the operatic name of 'I Promessi Sposi'; he had also arranged tickets for the first night of *Boris Godunov* at La Scala on 27 December. Christoff, who had sung his first Boris in Russian at Covent Garden less than a month previously, now sang it in Italian in Milan. My first visit to La Scala, and the excitement and the sense of occasion made up for some slight disappointment in the actual performance. I was also very tired and became more so as the evening went on – the opera began at 8.30 and was not over until the early hours.

On the following night there was a *Bohème*, conducted by Victor De Sabata, who raced through the score at breakneck speed. I should have left early the next morning for Venice, to hear *Parsifal*; but not knowing anyone in that city and, at that time, having only a few words of Italian, I decided to go straight to Rome where I had arranged to stay in a small pensione owned by the parents of the wife of an Anglo-Italian friend, Teofile De Beneducci; he was a record collector and keen opera-goer, who with his Italian wife, Nanda, had recently moved to Rome where he was to become *Opera*'s first Italian correspondent.

Arriving in Rome two days earlier than I had planned enabled me to hear Giordano's *Fedora* with the splendid mezzo-soprano, Gianna Pederzini, in the title rôle, and the tenor Galliano Masini who, when he was not sobbing his way through the rôle of Loris, turned his back on the audience and blew his nose. On 31 December I went on to Naples; there I met the San Carlo's press officer, programme editor and general factotum; the Marchese Lucio Parisi, with whom I have kept in contact ever since. He took me to a rehearsal of

Leoncavallo's *Zazà* that was in progress, with the emotional Mafalda Favero singing Zazà. The conductor was the excitable Franco Ghione who shouted what were apparently rude epithets at the Neapolitan orchestral players throughout the rehearsal, and then, at two o'clock, when a gentleman, who was presumably the union representative, gave the signal for the players to down instruments, hurled his baton at the first desks and stormed out. I saw the point of the orchestra wanting to finish on time, for at 5.00 p.m. a late matinée (or early evening performance) of *Wozzeck* conducted by Karl Böhm was due to start; and that was the main reason for my visit to Naples. I also learned that had I come to Naples a few days earlier I would have been in time to hear the last performance of Verdi's *Nabucco*, conducted by Vittorio Gui with Gino Bechi in the title rôle, and a young and virtually unknown Greek-American soprano called Maria Callas as Abigaille, a rôle she never sang again in the theatre. I wish I had known!

That performance of Berg's *Wozzeck* was not the first given in Italy, for during the German occupation of Rome in 1942, Tullio Serafin had very courageously included it in a season of contemporary opera in the autumn of that year. In Naples, as in Rome, Tito Gobbi sang the title-rôle and the Belgian soprano Suzanne Danco was Marie. The opera was sensibly given in Italian, but that was not enough to attract a large audience; I do not think there were more than 500 people in the theatre but they were rightly enthusiastic. My own reactions were reflected in my review, when I wrote that:

> 'In more than fifteen years of opera-going, I have never spent such an absorbing evening in an opera house, nor have I ever emerged feeling so completely shattered emotionally and physically ... I left Naples convinced that of the many duties the Covent Garden Opera Trust has to fulfil to the opera public, an early production of *Wozzeck* is one of the most urgent.'

In fact, *Wozzeck* entered the Covent Garden repertory in March 1953.

Back in Rome on New Year's Day I heard a rumbustious performance of *Manon Lescaut*, and three days later *Il barbiere di Siviglia* in which, for the only time in my life, I was able to experience in the theatre the consummate *bel canto* art of Tito Schipa who was singing Almaviva. Gobbi, who had delighted me so much as Wozzeck, forsook the paths of good taste more than once as Figaro. I actually wrote those words in my review, and several years later when I met Gobbi and his wife for the first time, they had not forgotten what I had said! Rosina was sung by Giuseppina Arnaldi, whom I learned later had influence in certain government quarters. She was very pretty but 'her coloratura technique and shrill voice wrought havoc with the Queen of Night's second aria which she unwisely chose for the lesson scene'. I ended my review with the comment that 'the production, like the rest I witnessed in Rome, was negative in quality'. I was told later that my report had been ill-received by Rome Opera's administration, especially as they had gone to the trouble of placing a chair for me at the back of the stalls – the house was sold out – so that I could hear Schipa sing. They had also given me a large selection of war-time programmes for my collection. I was gradually beginning to learn that the reactions of opera houses to adverse criticism is the subject for specialist psychological attention.

I have no recollection of helping George and Dickie to lay out or make up the first issue of *Opera* during the next two weeks, but I suppose I must have been there. As publication date grew closer I became more excited but a trifle apprehensive. A launching party was planned in the splendid 'Red Room' at Dickie's Bloomfield Terrace house to which all the operatic establishment (and much of the musical world) had been invited. The date was 9 February, the day was a Thursday. Advance copies of *Opera* arrived a few days before and I proudly showed off my new offspring to my colleagues and headmaster (my sympathetic headmistress had by then moved on elsewhere), who was clearly impressed that one of his teachers could have been involved in something so utterly unrelated to the normal activities of a London primary school! Phyllis bought a new dress for the party; I splashed out and hired a car to take us from Norwood to Chelsea; and my mother-in-law came and baby-sat for us – by then we had a second addition to our family, our daughter Helen who had been born the previous summer.

The launching of the magazine and the party were widely re-ported in the popular press – hardly surprising, for it is not every day that the nephew of the King of England brings out a magazine devoted to opera! It was interesting to watch the contingents from the two London opera houses snatch up their free copies of the magazine and immediately turn to read the reviews of the recent performances in which they had participated. There was a certain amount of muttering about George's review of Covent Garden's controversial *Salome*, and even more about what I had written on *Lohengrin*. Does one invite someone to a party to launch a magazine in which a contributor had written about their performance that she 'gave a bewildering exhibition of shrieking, voice-pushing and over-acting'? In retrospect, I think not. After the party, George invited us to accompany him, the Steins, Benjamin Britten, Peter Pears, Joan Cross and a few other of his friends to a splendid dinner in a private room at Leoni's 'Quo Vadis' restaurant in Soho.

Two days later I was amazed to read in one paper that 10,000 copies of the first issue had been printed; in another that the number was 7,500 (I think that was nearer the mark). I was also surprised to learn that 'The assistant editor, Mr Harold Rosenthal, an LCC school teacher, had met Lord Harewood during the war when both were in the forces.' Never, in my wildest moments, could I have seen myself in a guards regiment! Far more encouraging was the review in one of the literary weeklies which praised the first issue and expressed the hope that the magazine would soon be able to appear every month.

Opera's first editorial (it was not actually called that but was headed 'Introduction', and in subsequent issues 'Comment') stated the aims of the magazine:

'To cover in prospect and retrospect any form of serious operatic activity amateur or professional, that is in our opinion of interest to the intelligent opera-goer. The views of those who practise opera and of those who only criticise it will appear side by side, and detailed articles on individual operas and composers will supplement news of British and foreign productions of operas ancient and modern. Letters or articles from readers will be welcome, and we shall try in every number to describe one or another of the great operatic figures of the day, be it a singer, conductor or producer . . .

'Our conviction, however, remains that the narrowing of the repertory spells eventual death for opera, and that the public in England is worse informed on the development and trends of opera than on any single other branch of art ... we hope that the names at least of the most important non-repertory pieces will be known to our readers before long; and that what at present amounts to a veritable horror of the unknown will eventually to some extent be superseded by no more than a mistrust for a doubtful quantity.'

Although these words were written by George, they also expressed my own thoughts; and more than thirty years later, those aims still hold good. Certainly today (1982) the British opera public is perhaps even better informed on the development and the trends of opera than its counterpart in other countries; and certainly not only the readers of *Opera* but a large portion of opera audiences – unfortunately, not all opera-goers are readers of the magazine – are aware of the names of what in 1950 were regarded as the most important non-repertory pieces, as well as those of many other works composed since. How far the magazine has been instrumental in affecting that change of climate I will leave for others to judge, but I certainly believe that *Opera* has helped in bringing about this change.

A glance at the contents of the first four issues of the magazine gives some indication as to how we pursued those aims. There were articles on Britten by Erwin Stein; on Vaughan Williams's *Hugh the Drover* by Sir Steuart Wilson; on Tchaikovsky's neglected operas by Desmond Shawe-Taylor; on Puccini by Cecil Gray; on Wagner by Neville Cardus; and on Milhaud's *Bolivar* by Tony Mayer. The 'People' series continued with profiles of Karl Rankl, Kirsten Flagstad (by Bernard Miles), and Carl Ebert. We published Richard Strauss's important 'Artistic Testament' which had been set out in a letter from Strauss to Karl Böhm, and had been written at the end of World War Two, when Böhm was still director of the Vienna State Opera.

To continue our 'crusade' and at the same time to cover current operatic events in greater detail than hitherto had been possible presented us with problems of space which George immediately said could be solved by publishing *Opera* monthly. This was a courageous decision to make, for after the elation of seeing most of the first issue sold, we came down to earth with a bump, and found that we were selling less than 5,000 copies a month. In any case, a bi-monthly publication which only shows the name of one month on its cover rather than two (e.g. June and not June-July) runs the risk of remaining unsold on the bookstalls during the second month. George was obviously prepared to invest, or rather lose, quite a large sum of money in order to establish the magazine firmly, until our circulation rose to over 6,000 (it is now well over 16,000) and, more importantly, until we had more readers who were prepared to become subscribers rather than buy their copies at a newsagent. Had George not been prepared to risk a large sum the magazine would not have survived those early years, and I would not be writing this book.

As well as George having to take that decision, there was one that I had to take. If *Opera* was to become a monthly magazine I would have to spend more time on it in my capacity as assistant editor; already I was finding that George was asking me, generally in long letters filled with 'directives', to chase contributors, collect photos, see the blockmaker, answer readers' letters, in fact to become something of a general factotum. I found this difficult enough while still doing a full-time teaching job, but to contemplate doing twice as much work over week-ends, during school holidays and in the evenings, was an impossibility; I told George this and he suggested that I gave up teaching. His decision to turn *Opera* into a monthly, and his suggestion that I should become involved in it more fully were put to me in a letter that I received from him at the end of June. He wrote:

'I am anxious that (a) you should become assistant editor in a rather fuller capacity than at present; and (b) that we should become a monthly as soon as possible, preferably in September (or August which is the same thing) ... You probably do not realize what I lost on the first two numbers, nor what I have paid out so far in hard cash ... If we work hard it should be possible to increase our sales from the rather low figure of 6,000 – assuming it does not get any lower – and take the risk of extra printing only when we have a good chance of selling the extra copies we print.

'What it boils down to is this. The work for an assistant editor is only part time – say three-quarters or so. There is no doubt that whoever takes on the job increases his or her chances of getting outside work, partly through the publicity connected with the magazine, and partly through the type of work.'

There then followed proposals about what I should be paid and I was offered £12 a week (£624 a year) which was slightly more than I was receiving as a schoolmaster, and powerful arguments why I would, in the long run, be better off. George then continued:

'I am sorry to have to make an offer that looks as though it were an attempt at bargaining, which it definitely is not. If you cannot accept it, you will have to let me know. On the other hand, I shall be very pleased if you do decide to accept, as I think we work together without much difficulty, and I believe you are one of the few people I know who is already well qualified to do this particular job!'

I never asked George who the others were!

He suggested that I should have a few days in which to think things over and then meet, as he wanted to get the position settled as soon as possible. Of course, I wanted to accept straight away; for here was the opportunity to do something I had always wanted; but there was, of course, the uncertainty. What if, after a year, *Opera* did not establish itself firmly and George decided to close it down? As a teacher I was in a 'safe' job with good prospects, so it was a difficult decision to make. Phyllis had no doubts at all – or if she did she very successfully kept them to herself; she urged me to accept, and was sure, perhaps more sure than I was, that I would make a success of it. With her backing, and knowing I would have her support I was able to tell George that the answer was 'yes'.

My colleagues at school arranged an end-of-term party for me to which Phyllis was invited and to which she brought four-year-old Simon and one-year-old Helen. My headmaster, on behalf of the staff, presented me with a copy of Scholes's *The Mirror of Music* (two volumes) and in an embarrassing speech extolled not only my achievements in the scholastic profession but also what he called my 'extra-mural activities', saying that I need have no worries about taking my place in the world of music as I had already proved that 'I could hold my own in front of the Countess' – (*sic*) meaning Marion Harewood; a remark that has remained a family joke to this day!

The announcement that *Opera* was to become a monthly magazine appeared in the August issue, which also carried the exciting news that La Scala Milan was to visit Covent Garden for a short season opening on 12 September. We also announced details of the competition, organized by La Scala to commemorate the fiftieth anniversary of Verdi's death, to find a new full-length opera to be produced in Milan during the 1951-2 season: 'Full details can be obtained from this publication': those few words indicated that even at that early stage of the magazine's life, we were beginning to be recognized as an international rather than a domestic publication.

Both George and I had known about La Scala's visit for some time, so we had planned a special issue to coincide with the London season, as well as a number of special features for early in 1951, when the opera world would be commemorating the fiftieth anniversary of Verdi's death. But by September we had run into difficulties, for we experienced for the first time a printers' strike; this resulted in the non-appearance of the October *Opera* and the late publication of our November and December issues, the latter being reduced in size from fifty-six to forty-four pages. This was hardly an encouraging beginning to our new monthly image, and it certainly was worrying for me personally that within less than three months of my decision to abandon teaching the future was looking distinctly unsettled.

However, George was reassuring and full of praise for the work I had done on the August and September issues. Because he had been away from London at the Salzburg and Edinburgh festivals, I had had to do the 'make-up' on my own. The printers had sent me a complicated chart and a set of instructions which included words like 'forms' and 'bleeding of blocks' which at that time meant absolutely nothing to me; so I paid a visit to our local public library to see whether I could find some technical books on printing! I found one which was quite incomprehensible; but after a telephone call to Dickie, I must have done the correct things, for the issue appeared without any apparent disasters.

The August, September and November issues of *Opera* included reports from the summer festivals which had proliferated since the end of the war. These were steadily to increase in number during the next decade – so much so that the amount of space needed to cover them in our pages began to crowd out the articles and other regular features; eventually, in 1960, we decided to publish an extra issue of the magazine devoted entirely to the summer festivals.

Although most of the editorial work was done at Friary Court and to a lesser extent at my own home, the official address of *Opera*, shown on our title page, was Mersey House, 132–4 Fleet Street, where Phillip Dossé held sway. This led to a great deal of confusion, so we decided that *Opera* should have its own editorial office as well as a base from which our advertising representative could operate. The photographer Roger Wood, whose marvellous action pictures of performances, especially at Covent Garden, were a regular feature in our early years, and whose studios were just off Westbourne Grove and within a stone's throw of the house in Bayswater into which George and Marion had moved, offered us 'house room'. It was not a very satisfactory arrangement, but it sufficed until May 1951 when we moved back to Fleet Street, this time to rooms in Ludgate House which we shared with *Ballet* and our joint advertising manager. Although that remained the official address of *Opera* for almost a year, we found it more convenient to make George's house in Orme Square our editorial base, and in February 1952 that address appeared on the title page of the magazine as did also the name of our new distributors and publishers, the Rolls House Publishing Company, which occupied a Dickensian office building just off Chancery Lane. They were to look after *Opera*'s interests and guide its fortunes on the bookstalls, generally very successfully, for the next sixteen years.

7

Performances in the Early Fifties

_____

Three weeks after *Opera*'s launching party a remarkable singer made
her Covent Garden debut as Mimi – the Spanish soprano Victoria
de los Angeles. Many had already heard her voice in a BBC studio
performance of Falla's *La vida breve* in 1948 when she sang the part
of Salud and elicited the highest praise from no less a person than
Ernest Newman. Then, the following year, she had delighted a
packed Wigmore Hall in her London recital debut when her ren-
dering of Handel's 'Oh had I Jubal's lyre' showed us that she was a
singer of rare talent. Her Mimi was sung in Italian, the rest of the
cast sang in English. Polyglot performances were quite usual at
Covent Garden in those days; Christoff had sung his first Boris in
Russian there in 1949 with the rest of the cast singing in English,
and a year later, Ludwig Weber came and sang the same rôle in
German! There had also been mixed-language performances of *Die
Meistersinger*, *Il trovatore* and several other works in order to accom-
modate guest artists who were unwilling to learn their rôles in English.
To be fair, quite a number of foreign singers prepared to struggle
with the difficulties of our language in order to satisfy both David
Webster and their own artistic consciences. Hotter, for example,
learned both the *Walküre* Wotan and Hans Sachs, neither of them
exactly short parts, in English, as did Flagstad the *Walküre* Brünnhilde;
and Schwarzkopf, Welitsch, Hilde Zadek, Rudolf Schock, Silveri
and Rothmüller were among the others who attempted what must
have seemed to them the impossible, sometimes with comic results,
but often with a great deal of success.

Polyglot performances sometimes reached the height of absurdity
and completely destroyed any kind of dramatic atmosphere that
might have existed. I recollect a performance of *Aida* in which the
Radames sang in German, the Aida in Italian and the rest of the cast

in English; and a *Tosca*, in which the soprano sang throughout in Italian, while the Scarpia (Rothmüller) sang in Italian in his scenes with Tosca and in English for the rest of the opera. He was unable to resist the temptation of throwing in the occasional word of English during his exchanges with the soprano when he thought the audience might need a little help in understanding the plot! His wicked sense of humour got the better of him when he instructed Spoletta in Italian to arrange the 'mock' execution of Cavaradossi ... 'Simulata! Come avvenne del Palmieri! Hai ben compreso?' and then, turning to the audience and winking, mouthed, quite loudly, the word 'simulated'!

By far the most important event at Covent Garden in 1950, and one with long-term effects for the future, was the engagement of Erich Kleiber to conduct for a three-month period. The manner in which that engagement took place did little credit to Covent Garden, for it was made without consultation with the music director, Karl Rankl. The same thing happened the following season with the engagement of Clemens Krauss, whose musical activities during the Hitler period were still, at that time, being regarded with suspicion, and of Beecham, who had been so outspoken in his criticism of the Rankl regime. These events led to Rankl announcing his resignation in May 1951.

I still remember the excitement in the house on the night of Kleiber's first appearance, and the prolonged cheers that welcomed him seemed to Desmond Shawe-Taylor, writing in the *New Statesman* 'uncommonly like the cheers of a beleaguered garrison at the sight of the rescuing force'. Kleiber, who had conducted at Covent Garden for Beecham in 1938, was director of the Berlin State Opera from 1923 to 1934, one of its most brilliant periods. A firm believer in what today we would call human rights he resigned in 1934 at the time of the controversy over Hindemith's *Mathis der Maler*, which the Nazis had banned, and did not return to Germany again until 1950. He spent most of the late 1930s and early 1940s in Buenos Aires, where his son, Carlos, who was also to become a distinguished conductor, was born. His reputation both as a musician and as being 'difficult' had preceded him. His performances surpassed all expectations and he endeared himself to orchestra, chorus and singers, and was instrumental in procuring engagements abroad for a number of the more promising of Covent Garden's British artists in whom he had great faith. It was true he could be difficult, and he was reputed to have said that if there was no trouble he would certainly make some. Many times he threatened to 'return to Buenos Aires', and when, in his second season, the question of a producer for *Wozzeck* was being discussed, he said he was firmly against the engagement of any of 'the clever young men'.

If there were difficulties for Webster at that time they were not of Kleiber's making, but arose from Rankl's understandable feeling that he was being edged out. I remember a particularly distressing incident when as Rankl walked into the pit to conduct a *Fidelio* performance, there were shouts from the gallery of 'Where's Kleiber?'; these were countered by applause from the stalls. Then, Webster had to break the news to his music director that the rumour that he (Rankl) had heard that *Wozzeck* would be conducted by Kleiber during his second season as a guest conductor was indeed true. Webster pointed out that *Wozzeck* was, after all, a 'Kleiber opera', the conductor having worked on it with Berg and conducted the first performance in Berlin in 1925. And if that was not enough, Webster had already informed Rankl by means of a letter that the title of music director was going to be dropped the following season. The atmosphere in the house was tense, to say the least, and Rankl would pass Kleiber in the corridor without so much as a nod. It needed all Webster's tact to prevent a public scandal.

Fortunately, there were some lighter sides. Webster, anticipating that Kleiber was going to prove difficult, and in an endeavour to keep him sweet, had engaged a South American soprano, Rayan Quitral, to sing Queen of Night in *Die Zauberflöte*, replacing the previously announced Wilma Lipp. Quitral had sung the rôle under Kleiber in Buenos Aires and was, by all accounts, a disaster. One can imagine Kleiber's dismay when he discovered that Miss Quitral was to be his Queen of Night in London. He immediately protested to Webster, who replied, 'But when we talked about the cast and possible Queens of Night you said, "You have never heard a Queen of Night like Quitral, who sang it for me in South America", so I thought we'd get her for you.' 'Yes,' replied Kleiber somewhat grimly, 'you never have heard a Queen of Night like that!'

George, reviewing the performance in the March 1951 *Opera* wrote: 'Quitral came from South America to sing the Queen of Night. Since she did not take her appearance here seriously enough to learn this very brief rôle in English, I can think of no reason, least of all her singing, why I should surpass her in this respect.'

During his first guest engagement with the resident company Kleiber also conducted a new production of Tchaikovsky's *The Queen of Spades*, a revival of *Carmen*, and what was termed a 're-studied' *Rigoletto* which was Covent Garden's sole contribution to the Verdi year. On 27 January, the fiftieth anniversary to the day of Verdi's death, it was *Rigoletto* that was performed, though originally another opera had been scheduled, the administration being blissfully unaware of the date of Verdi's death until I reminded them. Despite Kleiber being in the pit, it was a wretched evening; Walter Midgley who was to have sung the Duke of Mantua fell ill that afternoon, and Anthony Marlowe, an American tenor whose career had been mostly as a *comprimario* (i.e. in small rôles), was called in to save the performance, a task he did on more than one occasion, hardly with beneficial results.

As well as being the Verdi year, 1951 was the Festival of Britain year, and the latter part of the 1950-1 season was marked by several operatic events commemorating that occasion. These included the première of Vaughan Williams's *The Pilgrim's Progress*, a series of performances for Flagstad who had announced her intention of retiring from the stage, including her first London Leonore in *Fidelio* with Patzak as Florestan, Kundry in *Parsifal*, and her last Brünnhildes and Isoldes; and Beecham's long-awaited return to conduct *Die Meistersinger*.

Four of the five *Tristan* performances were conducted by Clemens Krauss, whose engagement had caused Rankl so much distress, but the last, which was Flagstad's final appearance at Covent Garden, was conducted by Rankl making his last appearance as music director. After twenty-one curtain calls, Flagstad spoke a few words to the audience: 'I want to take things more easily; please forgive me.' There was no word of thanks from Webster or anyone else for Rankl, whose work during the preceding five years had laid the foundation on which others were to build during the next decade, and make Covent Garden once again one of the leading opera houses in the world.

Flagstad, in fact, did sing two further performances of Isolde in Liverpool, where the whole opera company had gone for a three-weeks' season which included a new production of Balfe's *The*

Bohemian Girl. Beecham had inveigled the Liverpool Festival authorities, the Arts Council, and Covent Garden into mounting this old
war-horse as Liverpool's contribution to the Festival of Britain; it
came to Covent Garden for nineteen performances in mid-August,
when it was performed nightly, which necessitated two casts.

Everyone in the Opera House was apprehensive about 'Tommy's'
return after twelve years and was determined to show him that
things were not as bad musically as he had obviously hoped they
might be. He himself was on his best behaviour during the first
Meistersinger rehearsals★ and was full of praise for the orchestra and
chorus; later, he had some trenchant things to say about the cast,
even though he had been consulted about the singers. By the time
of the first full stage and orchestral rehearsals, everyone had been
lulled into a false sense of security. Beecham arrived late that morning, nearer 10.30 than 10.00, and announced, 'Gentlemen, we will
reseat the orchestra this morning'; at which a general post took
place, and after much noise and shuffling around, Tommy looked
over his half-glasses and turning to the double-bass player, Eugene
Cruft, asked 'Are you quite comfortable Mr Cruft?' to which Cruft
replied, 'No, Sir Thomas, I cannot get my instrument into a comfortable position.' 'Oh, what's the matter then?' asked Beecham.
'It's this rostrum,' replied Cruft, pointing to a little platform which,
of course, had not been moved in the general post. 'Rostrum?'
queried Tommy. 'Yes, Sir Thomas,' chimed in Thomas Matthews,
the leader of the orchestra, 'it was put in last autumn when the Scala
was here.' There followed a moment's pause while Tommy stroked
his little goatee, and then he roared, 'LA SCALA! God in Heaven!
Since when has Great Britain and Covent Garden in particular been
a dependency of the Italian Empire? Remove it!!' 'I can't,' said
Cruft, 'it's screwed down.' 'Well unscrew it,' stormed Beecham. By
now the chorus, who had crowded on stage for the beginning of the
opening scene, were laughing aloud. 'It's all very well for you to
laugh, ladies and gentlemen,' said Tommy, 'but mark my words,
your turn will come.' And it did, with a vengeance.

Act II of *Die Meistersinger* opens with the enchanting but musically
difficult scene for the apprentices and David; the chorus could not
get it right that morning, nor could Murray Dickie who was singing

★ Since the beginning of the 1951 season, I had been Covent Garden's official archivist
and so from time to time I was able to slip into the auditorium and listen to rehearsals.

David. Beecham's patience began to run out. 'What do you think you're singing?' he shouted, and one foolish chorister timidly murmured '*Meistersinger*, Sir Thomas'. 'Really,' he replied, 'I thought it was "Kiss me Up the Alley". Where's Mr Feasey?' (Norman Feasey was head of music staff and had worked with Beecham in the pre-war seasons.) Norman appeared, 'Yes, Sir Thomas?' 'Take Mr Dickie away, and don't bring him back until he knows his part.'

The La Scala season to which Thomas Matthews had referred and which had sparked off the whole episode was the famous two-week season at Covent Garden the previous September, when after a series of concerts at the Edinburgh Festival by the Scala Orchestra and Chorus, the complete opera company from Milan came to London for performances of *Otello*, *Falstaff*, and *L'elisir d'amore*. The two Verdi operas were conducted by Victor De Sabata, the only occasion on which he conducted opera in England; *Elisir* was conducted by Franco Capuana, the fiery little Neapolitan who was remembered from the San Carlo season at Covent Garden in 1946.

George smuggled me into the general rehearsal of *Otello* when De Sabata spent minutes on end just rehearsing the shattering chord with which the opera opens. Quite naturally George wanted to review the three operas himself, and as tickets were at a premium and the press office was not inclined to be over-generous with its meagre allocation, I had to be content with a seat in the press box, close to the stage on the balcony tier level, for *Elisir*; to stand at the back of the stalls circle for one *Otello*; and to be squeezed in at the side of the stalls for another and for *Falstaff*. That was the *Falstaff* which suffered because Webster had set his face against Stabile singing at Covent Garden and in which Gino Bechi gave a very muted performance of the title-rôle as he had a few evenings earlier as Iago.

None the less the *Otello* with Ramon Vinay as the Moor and Renata Tebaldi as Desdemona was a vintage one. *Elisir* introduced Tagliavini, Tajo, and Gobbi to London opera-goers, and brought back Margherita Carosio as a delicious Adina: *Falstaff* was not so strongly cast, for Maria Caniglia's (Alice) voice was by then showing signs of wear; Alda Noni was miscast as Nannetta and Valletti was a small-scale Fenton; only Fedora Barbieri as a racy, fruity Mistress Quickly was really worthy of a La Scala cast. But again, we had De Sabata and his marvellous orchestra.

Audiences and a few critics were enthusiastic; but the press, on the whole, was distinctly cool – there was something more than just sour grapes about it. George and I were amazed; so in addition to publishing George's own long review of the season in *Opera* which although pointing out the weaknesses of some of the performances also recognized the overwhelming strength of La Scala's ensemble, we decided to invite five independent writers to contribute their reactions to the season. A galleryite (Derek H. Johnson), a Viennese musicologist (Erwin Stein), a British conductor (Constant Lambert), a young *répétiteur* (Edward Renton), and an old opera-goer and amateur critic (Arthur Notcutt). It was Constant Lambert who hit the nail on the head when he wrote:

> 'May I express my surprise that the English critics of all people failed to appreciate the company's "team spirit" (a quality for which our island race is supposed to be renowned).
>
> 'To judge by the eminently justifiable letters of complaint in the press, more than one member of the public seems to have been both surprised and shocked by the carping and niggling of the London critics when faced with the full-bloodedness and all round excellence of La Scala. After some of the most memorable and breath-taking experiences of my musical life it was indeed shock-ing to find the critics next day were damning it with faint pseudo-academic praise, but it was not surprising to me. ... I realise only too well that the average English critic is a don *manqué*, hopelessly parochial when not exaggeratedly teutonophile, over whose desk must surely hang the motto (presumably in Gothic lettering) "Above all no enthusiasm".'

More than thirty years later that attitude still exists to some extent. I cannot end these comments on La Scala's London visit without quoting the headline that appeared above one of Ernest Newman's reviews in the *Sunday Times*: 'Oh to be in Milan, now La Scala's Here!'

After the stimulus of La Scala's London visit there was a feeling of anti-climax which not even the excitement of Kleiber's arrival at Covent Garden could wholly dispel. After Christmas, however, the atmosphere changed; Sadler's Wells celebrated the Verdi Year with its new production of *Don Carlos* in mid-January and gave the first stage performance in England of a Janáček opera, *Katya Kabanova*, conducted by the then virtually unknown young Charles Mackerras. In February Laurence Olivier turned impresario and brought the New York production of Menotti's political opera, *The Consul*, to the Cambridge Theatre. Because of Olivier, the theatre in which it was being staged and the general 'show-biz' atmosphere that surrounded the enterprise, it was reviewed by drama critics and gossip writers as well as by the musical press; and so we were regaled with such headlines as 'Vivien Leigh Weeps for Joy at Opera Gamble' (*Express*) and 'The Emotional English startled the Americans' (*Standard*). This was one of the first major new productions in London that I rather than George reviewed in *Opera*. 'Is it a work of art? Is it really opera? Will it live?' were three questions I posed at the beginning of my review. In that it was something of a nine-days wonder and is rarely, if ever, performed today, I feel my questions were well founded.

At the end of April, Vaughan Williams's *The Pilgrim's Progress* had its first night at Covent Garden and perhaps those same three questions should also have been asked about that work. George and I had the novel idea of inviting Cecil Smith, an American critic, to review the piece for us. Cecil was one of the leading American music critics of the day; he came from Chicago where he had occupied the chair of music at the university from 1943 to 1946; and from 1948 until 1952 he was editor of *Musical America*. A great Anglophile and even greater opera maniac he could hardly wait to come to Europe after the war. In 1951 he visited London for the first time as guest music critic on the *Daily Express*, changing places with my colleague, Arthur Jacobs. We met in a small pub not far from Covent Garden in April 1951; we both missed our next appointments because we discovered immediately our mutual love – opera. He was a man after my own heart, with a fund of anecdotes and recollections of operatic performances, stretching back to the 1920s and the great days of Mary Garden in Chicago. He endeared himself to everyone with whom he came in contact, performers no less than fellow critics.

George and Marion suggested I brought him to lunch at Orme Square and I remember when asked whether he had any preference for the white or dark meat of the chicken, he replied, 'I don't really mind, there is no colour bar as far as this American is concerned!' He returned to London in 1952, married an English widow, Madeleine, who became a close friend of us all. I invited Cecil to join *Opera*'s editorial board in 1954 and he enlivened our editorial meetings with his wonderful sense of humour. Alas, his stay with us was too short as he died of cancer in May 1956, just fifty years old. Anglophile though he was *The Pilgrim's Progress* was too much for him. He suggested that its ultimate hope might be a cathedral performance at the Three Choirs Festival.

> 'The dramatic form [he wrote] if such it may be called, is precisely that of a church pageant ... The score flows quietly, evenly and on the whole uneventfully, like a noble and stately river. The occasional rocks, narrows, and cataracts that interrupt its course are quickly passed and are not especially frightening.'

His remarks about Neville Coghill's production had a Newman-like touch to them:

> 'Vanity Fair looked, I am told (I have never actually seen one) like a scene from the Dick Whittington pantomime ... Mr Coghill taught Arnold Matters, the Pilgrim, the gestures of a village vicar, or perhaps a provincial Elijah, but provided him with little else ... The other individual members of the cast were no better briefed, and the delineation of lust and frivolity in the Vanity Fair scene were enough to send one to the nearest convent in the hope of a gayer time. As Madame Wanton, Audrey Bowman did, it is true, display one entire stockinged leg.'

Another English opera that surfaced for an even shorter period was George Lloyd's *John Socman*,* commissioned by the Arts Council and produced by the Carl Rosa Company at the Bristol Hippodrome on 15 May as its contribution to the Festival of Britain. The operatic establishment travelled down *en masse* by train; I shared a table in the dining car with Steuart Wilson, his wife, and Eric Walter White. The journey was more rewarding and far more amusing than the opera, which was set to a banal libretto by the composer's father and told of love and intrigue at the time of the battle of Agincourt. The opera was peopled with Gleemaidens, Lollards, Low Friars and the like. 'The music,' I wrote, 'was hardly original – it began with a Wolf-Ferrari like overture and then progressed through several passages that were reminiscent of Giordano, the

* Recently revived by the BBC in a studio performance in Manchester.

lesser-known Italian *verismo* composers, and of the early Richard Strauss, to a Falstaffian finale.'

Four other operas were commissioned by the Arts Council for the Festival of Britain year: Alan Bush's *Wat Tyler*, Arthur Benjamin's *A Tale of Two Cities*, Berthold Goldschmidt's *Beatrice Cenci*, and Karl Rankl's *Deidre of the Sorrows*. None of these has ever been staged by a major opera company in Great Britain, although the first three were either broadcast, or given by enterprising small groups; Rankl's opera, however, has never been heard. Far more successful was Peter Tranchell's *The Mayor of Casterbridge*, based on Thomas Hardy's novel of the same name, which was commissioned by the Cambridge Festival and staged there for a whole week at the end of July and the beginning of August; it has been once revived. Had these composers been living in Germany, several houses in that country would have mounted one or more of these commissioned works, but not so here.

Another example of our crazy operatic life in that summer of 1951 was the mounting of no less than three different productions of Purcell's *Dido and Aeneas* in London; one by the English Opera Group in Britten's new version of the score and produced by Joan Cross at the Lyric Theatre Hammersmith; one in Edward J. Dent's version and produced by Geoffrey Dunn at Sadler's Wells; and a third in a version by Geraint Jones and produced by Bernard Miles in his little Mermaid Theatre, which he had erected in the garden of his house in St John's Wood, and to which he had lured Kirsten Flagstad to sing Dido, a performance which William Mann described in *Opera* as the 'exquisite diadem to set atop the crown of her career' (i.e. her Brünnhilde in *Götterdämmerung*). And it was not only Flagstad that Mr Miles lured to St John's Wood, but also Maggie Teyte, Edith Coates, the young Thomas Hemsley, and Murray Dickie. 'Three productions of *Dido* may seem excessive,' wrote Bill Mann, 'but since it should surely be as prominent in London's operatic experience as say *Bohème*, which could be heard at least in five different theatres in 1949, one need not complain of unnecessary trebling.'

Glyndebourne got back into its stride that summer with twenty-five performances of four Mozart operas including the first professional production in England of *Idomeneo* with Sena Jurinac enchanting everyone as Ilia just as she had the year before as Fiordiligi. This was Fritz Busch's last season; he was already a sick man, and some of his scheduled performances were taken over by Glyndebourne's new young chorus master and assistant conductor, and a protégé of Busch, John Pritchard. Glyndebourne was also responsible for the two operas given at the Edinburgh Festival that summer, *Don Giovanni* and *La forza del destino*.

The Glyndebourne casting that year was somewhat uneven, to say the least, and not for the last time George and I had some very pointed remarks to make about some of the singers, and these did not go down at all well with John Christie - nor in one case with the singer in question. She was a young American soprano called Dorothy MacNeil who had come from the New York City Opera to sing Cherubino and Donna Elvira. I quite liked her Cherubino, and the fact that her voice was rather on the small side did not matter in the Glyndebourne auditorium; but when it came to the more dramatic rôle of Donna Elvira in the larger King's Theatre in Edinburgh the result was far from happy. I commented: 'Her Donna Elvira was a sad mistake; she had no feeling for the music, and little for the words she was singing. "Mi tradì" was an ordeal for all concerned.'

Shortly after, at the IMA Club in South Audley Street which had become a favourite meeting place for musicians, I was lunching with a friend and unwisely read out what I had written about that *Don Giovanni* in what was obviously a clear and presumably a loud voice. The tables in the dining-room at the IMA were mostly in separate alcoves, so one could not see one's immediate neighbours; as we left the dining-room, a lady's hand stretched out and tapped me on the arm, and as I turned to see who it was, an American voice said 'So you didn't like my Donna Elvira very much did you?' I learned from that day always to make quite sure that in a restaurant or anywhere else that might be frequented by artists, to take a careful look and see who was present before commenting on recent performances.

The 1951-2 Covent Garden season did not open until the third week of October when John Barbirolli returned to the opera house for the first time since 1937. He conducted the revivals of *Turandot* and *Aida* and brought an authentic touch of the Mediterranean warmth to Bow Street. 'Here at last was what Italian opera at Covent Garden has needed for the last four years and for what we have been campaigning for the last two!' I wrote, 'Italian music excitingly played and sung, carefully prepared and rehearsed; may we have lots more like it.' I got to know Sir John quite well during the next few years – he always called me by my surname in his gruff, throaty voice; and later I persuaded him to take part in some radio interviews for the BBC.

The highlight of the autumn season, however, was the first performance of Britten's *Billy Budd* on 1 December. Josef Krips had originally been engaged to conduct – a seemingly odd choice, though he had directed *The Rape of Lucretia* with considerable success both at Salzburg and with the English Opera Group. Krips cried off on the pretext that he found the reading of photostat copies of the score too much of a strain on the eyes, and so Britten himself conducted. The January issue of *Opera* devoted no less than thirteen pages to *Billy Budd*, a work that only came into its own in the 1960s though most critics and musicians warmed to it much sooner.

There were two issues of *Opera* in 1951 of which George was justly proud; that of February, which commemorated the fiftieth anniversary of Verdi's death, and that of May which was devoted to Britten. The Verdi number in particular has remained for me a model of its kind, containing as it did contributions from four leading British composers of the day: Vaughan Williams, Bliss, Britten and Berkeley, as well as essays by Francis Toye and Cecil Gray. George wrote an inspiring editorial on his favourite composer and I contributed one of those historical documentations which I have always enjoyed compiling on Verdi's visits to London.

Vaughan Williams's contribution to the Symposium is a classic and deserves to be reprinted in full; but for obvious reasons it cannot be included here. However, I cannot resist from quoting a few extracts from V.W.'s tongue-in-cheek (?) synopsis of *Rigoletto*, which he used to illustrate how 'song can carry on a plot in a way which words alone cannot do':

'In case readers are not familiar with the opera, I will rehearse the story of the last act (from memory, I fear, for I have lost my copy of the score). A wicked Duke has seduced (or is about to seduce, I forget which) the daughter of his Jester, who planning revenge with several "R's" persuades his friend, the keeper of a disreputable inn, to invite the Duke to his house, offering as a bait his, the innkeeper's, own daughter, who is quite ready to become seducee No. 2. The Duke is to be murdered and his body in a sack is to be thrown out of the window for the Jester to play with ...

'On the night appointed the Duke arrives and sits at a table in the inn garden, drinking wine and making love to the innkeeper's daughter, and singing to her the famous *La donna è mobile*, an obvious and banal tune, which is impossible to forget. ...'

The Britten number of *Opera* was far more serious, including assessments of his chamber operas by some illustrious German and French conductors and producers, and the tenth of our 'People' series, a profile of Peter Pears by Hans Keller, whose very individual style and approach to music has made him one of the most controversial and provocative writers in the field. Keller's language, even after all these years, still has me foxed. It certainly was never to the liking of my friend the bass singer, David Franklin, who often contributed to *Opera* during the 1950s. In his first article on 'Style in Singing' which appeared in November 1951, Franklin could not resist a swipe at 'the critic of the Highbrow Review' (who although unnamed, could be none other than Keller) 'snatching a few moments from his labours on the subtleties of the Inhibited Sub-Mediant to write glowingly about singing with a "freedom of rhythm, by rhythm, for rhythm"'. Franklin capped this in a subsequent article which he called 'Let the Critics Sing' when he wrote:

'One critic impressed us with his learning and subtlety who, examining the dreary harmony of one particular piece, was good enough to explain that it derived from the repeated frustrations of the composer's sex-life, which had led him to the extensive use of the "inhibited second". This penetrating analysis fascinated me, and I made a note of it. I didn't quite know where to file it, but in the end discreetly fitted in "Second, inhibited" next to "Fourth, diminished".'

The January and February 1952 issues of *Opera* which took us up to our second birthday included introductions to two operas that were George's particular favourites – Berg's *Wozzeck* which Kleiber was to conduct at Covent Garden at the end of January, and Massenet's *Werther*, which, at Sadler's Wells, was to have its first stage performance in London by a professional company since 1910.

Erwin Stein wrote about *Wozzeck* and Hugo Garten about Büchner, the author of the play of the same name; and in the same issue (January) we reprinted an article by Berg himself on 'The Musical Form in *Wozzeck*' which had originally appeared in the *Neue Musik-Zeitung* in 1928. In those first two years George and I set our sights very high and unfortunately too many learned articles did not help increase the magazine's circulation.

The Opera Diary in the February issue included my own review of a performance of *Die Meistersinger* at Covent Garden on 14 December. This had been a very special occasion; not only was it the 150th performance of the opera at Covent Garden, but also the 250th performance to be conducted there by Sir Thomas Beecham. After an evening lasting nearly five-and-a-half hours, David Webster presented Beecham with a laurel wreath. Beecham responded in a typically witty speech in which he deprecated being called an 'institution'. This event would not have been possible had not the administration been supplied with the necessary information by the archivist of the Royal Opera House, a position that had only been in existence for a year, and which I had suggested to David Webster. The archivist was none other than myself.

8

The Archives

When in 1944 I told Professor Dent of my plans to write a history of opera at Covent Garden, he generously put at my disposal his considerable library and in many conversations gave me the benefit of his vast knowledge and experience. We discussed the Opera House's lack of proper archives more than once, and it was largely due to his sympathy and understanding that late in 1950 I decided to approach David Webster and suggest that the post of archivist be created. I have no doubt that both Dent, who was a member of the Covent Garden board, and George supported my proposal, for within a few days of my having written to Webster, I was summoned to his office to discuss my proposals with him. 'Don't be intimidated by him, [said George] you will have to walk the length of his office to his desk, where he will be sitting Mussolini-like – and don't be put off if he gets up, whistles, jingles the coins and keys in his pocket, and looks out of the window.' I don't recollect him doing any of those things, but only agreeing to the idea, and giving me a free hand to build up the theatre's archives and to use them for the history I intended to write. 'You can begin on January 1st,' said D.W., 'I think we'll be able to find you a corner. Of course, we can't pay you very much, it won't be a full-time job in any case.' And so, from 1 January 1951, I was on Covent Garden's pay-roll at the princely sum of five pounds a week!

A preliminary reconnaissance behind the scenes at the Opera House revealed very little in the way of records of the theatre's past activities; this was because successive managements had presumably removed the various files of correspondence, contracts and other memorabilia they had accumulated when they moved out to make way for their successors. There was, however, a fairly complete set of nightly programmes of the opera seasons from just before the

turn of the century until 1939; these were housed in various cupboards, in cardboard boxes or tied up in dusty bundles in a couple
of rooms high up on the OP (opposite prompt) side of the stage,
where the Sadler's Wells Ballet had its administrative offices. In fact,
the small room I was first given was within hailing distance of
Ninette de Valois's office.

Michael Wood took me round the theatre and introduced me to
the various heads of departments and secretaries. There were two
important members of staff who had worked at Covent Garden
before the war, Sydney Cheney, the chief engineer, who remembered being carried onto the stage by Emmy Destinn as the child
'Trouble' in *Madama Butterfly*, and had a watch personally inscribed
by that famous soprano to prove it; and Frank Ballard, the chief
machinist, who had been at the Opera House since the days of
Caruso and Melba. When I got to know Mr Ballard and he discovered that I could talk knowledgeably about the pre-war seasons,
he proved to be an unexpected source of information, and he led me
to several hitherto unopened cupboards and cubby-holes where he
had hidden a vast amount of invaluable material which he had
guarded jealously.

Several months were to elapse however before I 'got on the right
side' of Mr Ballard, and thus gained access to his treasure trove. So
I spent the first few months sorting through the programmes and
checking performance details against the records I myself had compiled in the late 1930s and early 1940s at the Guildhall Museum and
the Enthoven Collection at the Victoria and Albert Museum. However, this was not adding anything new to the archives and so I
wrote a letter that appeared in *The Times*, *Daily Telegraph*, and the
weekly literary publications, in which I appealed for programmes,
play-bills, prints and indeed any material about Covent Garden
from the time of the opening of the first theatre in 1732 until 1939;
the response was promising. One morning a young Oxford undergraduate was shown up to my little room bringing with him some
libretti complete with casts from the 1850s and 1860s – his name was
Andrew Porter. A much older gentleman called Alec Balfour, a
relative of the famous politician of that name, whose opera-going
had begun in the 1890s, also introduced himself to me and gave the
Opera House many libretti and programmes; and Sydney Loeb,
son-in-law of the famous conductor Hans Richter, offered 'on

permanent loan' many of his superb photographs of Wagnerian personalities and programmes, which after his death passed into the theatre's possession. More Wagneriana came from a Harley Street specialist, Dr Cyriax, who had been a close member of the Bayreuth circle even earlier than Loeb, and had been a founder-member of London's first Wagner Society before the turn of the century. Then there were the dealers who had read my letter and were anxious to sell their treasures to the Opera House; that was more difficult, as there was little or no money for what I am sure some members of the board considered an unnecessary extravagance. However, I was able to persuade David Webster to sanction some modest purchases, one from a private collector in south London comprising bound volumes of programmes which included those of the period of Weber's musical directorship in the 1820s; another, a collection that was being auctioned at Sotheby's and included signed letters and photographs from Verdi, Wagner, Rossini and others which had once belonged to the theatre.

It was these successes and also my regular conversations with Mr Ballard that resulted in his inviting me one morning into his room in the corridor that runs between the stage door and the pass-door into the auditorium – the room had once been Melba's dressing room. He said he had something for me; and disappearing like Britten's Little Sweep half way up a chimney in the old fire place that still existed in his room, pulled down roll after roll of those green-and-white front-of-house posters that I and so many others knew from the pre-war days. These went back to the early 1900s and included the first performances in England of *Madama Butterfly*, *Turandot*, the famous Caruso–Melba evenings and other similar treasures.

Then, a few days later, obviously on Mr Ballard's suggestion which had been relayed to Michael Wood, Joe at the stage door said to me 'Oh, Mr Rosenthal, they've opened up the old music library for you.' 'Where's that?' I asked. 'Up the stairs two flights and behind those iron doors.' 'Those iron doors' had, I gather, not been officially opened since before the war and I thought from the name 'old music library' it must contain old orchestral and vocal scores; so up I rushed and saw shelf after shelf of old box files, countless cardboard boxes full of correspondence and contracts, and piles of photographs. Then, to my horror, my gaze fell on one of the several odd-job men I had seen around, seated on an upturned packing case, cap on head and in dirty overalls, tearing up papers and putting them into a large sack. 'What on earth are you doing?' I asked. 'I've been told to make this room tidy for the archives,' he replied. I snatched the piece of paper he had in his hand, and it was a letter from Richard Strauss to Beecham. 'Stop it,' I said, 'you're bloody well destroying the archives.' 'I've already done three sacks this morning,' he mumbled. What was lost I never learned, but at last here was what I had hoped to find at Covent Garden.

Gradually I was able to make some kind of order out of the chaos that existed and received some voluntary help from a Cambridge undergraduate during his vacation; he was an old Etonian and guards officer called Nigel Leigh-Pemberton, better known to opera-goers today as the tenor Nigel Douglas. Periodically David Webster would wander up the half flight of stairs from his office to see what I was up to. He rarely passed comment, always calling me 'Rosenthal', and after looking at the papers on the desk I had managed to get installed, vanished as quickly and quietly as he had arrived. Three years later, when George came to work in the Opera House as D. W.'s assistant, this room was turned into a proper office for him and the archives were then moved from the theatre to the top floor of a building which the Opera House had taken over at the corner of Wellington Street and Bow Street. In the move, quite a few things were 'lost'; and as there was no proper accommodation in Wellington Street, much archive material was not under lock and key, and several treasures were filched and pages torn out of the large inter-war series of press-cutting books. This at least led to some steel cupboards being ordered for the more valuable material, which included Rosa Ponselle's *Traviata* costume and Flagstad's Isolde dress that both artists had graciously donated to the theatre. Many pre-war singers, still living at the time, responded to letters I wrote and sent signed photographs or other small mementos. So by the time I resigned my position in 1956 I was able to leave behind a small but representative collection for my successors to build on.

I felt I had to resign at that time because my Covent Garden history *Two Centuries of Opera at Covent Garden* was well under way and was due to be published in 1958, the year of the present theatre's centenary. Because I wanted the post-war period of the book to be critical as well as factual and felt it could not reasonably be the former if I was still in the theatre's employ – that five pounds a week had risen slightly by then! – I invited D.W. to lunch at the IMA Club in South Audley Street to tell him of my decision. He arrived in marvellous good humour, chuckling at a 'card' he had seen in a newsagent's window on his walk from Covent Garden via Soho to Mayfair: 'Gentleman's Private Affairs Attended to: Phone Miss X' at whatever the number was. D.W. agreed that my situation was difficult and that he had been thinking about it for some time. There had certainly been problems arising from my being both archivist and assistant editor (and from 1953, editor) of *Opera*, and writing reviews of performances that had taken place in the theatre.

When George had joined the board at Covent Garden in September 1951 he had stopped reviewing performances there, though he still wrote about Sadler's Wells, Glyndebourne and overseas performances. I had suggested that it might be better to leave reviewing Covent Garden performances to my colleagues, but neither George nor David saw any reason for that; but Steuart Wilson, who was D.W.'s deputy certainly did, and the more so since George was brought in in a move that he saw as a threat to his own position. On one occasion he complained in print that the low morale that existed among the singers at the Opera House was largely due to the fact that adverse criticism of their performances often appeared in the magazine *Opera* which was edited by the archivist of the theatre and which bore the name of the controller of opera planning (George) on its title page as founder.

Before that, I had, perhaps rightly, been accused of breaking the Opera House protocol by writing a letter 'in my capacity as archivist' to the *Daily Telegraph* without first showing it to D.W., refuting a statement made by Sir Thomas Beecham in an article in that paper. Beecham had stated that on only one occasion when he was in charge at Covent Garden 'were we obliged to change an evening's opera'; I politely pointed out at least four instances when this had happened between 1934 and 1938. There were also other occasions when I obviously had upset the administration and board in print both in and out of *Opera*. So D.W. was, I am sure, relieved when I made the suggestion that my term as official archivist of the theatre should come to an end, for he disliked making the initial move. From then onwards I ceased to be 'Rosenthal' and became Harold.

I still advised on the archives, and I was always able to walk into the theatre through the stage door and make my way around with perfect freedom. I continued to provide historical material for the programmes, and helped George compile the *Centenary Souvenir Book* for the 1958 season. I was invited to serve on the committee that planned the large exhibition at the Victoria and Albert Museum in 1971 to mark the twenty-fifth anniversary of Opera and Ballet at post-war Covent Garden, contributing several articles to the sumptuous catalogue. In fact, despite two serious clashes with D.W., and many more with Garrett Drogheda during his chairmanship, I was still treated as part of the Covent Garden 'family'. I was especially gratified when I was invited to join the Council of the Friends of Covent Garden at its inception, and I eventually suggested that the Friends assumed full responsibility for the archives. In recent years, with so many changes in personnel and attitudes within the theatre, I have not been quite so certain where I stand.

9

The last Eighteen Months of George's Editorship

Three days before *Opera*'s second birthday, which was on 9 February 1952, King George VI died. As I was waiting for a bus in Fleet Street opposite the *Daily Express* offices, I noticed flag after flag being lowered to half-mast, and people began talking to each other, just as they had during the war: 'The King's dead'; 'No, it's not true.' But by the time I had reached Queensway, the early editions of the evening papers announcing the news were on sale. I was at Orme Square shortly after midday and found George in a black tie. However, it was work as usual, though as far as he and Marion were concerned they could not attend the last *Wozzeck* performance under Kleiber nor the first of the revival of *Le nozze di Figaro*, also under Kleiber, at Covent Garden.

The Opera House remained closed on 6 February and again on 15 February, the day of the King's funeral. The royal monogram on the red curtains, 'G VI R', was quickly removed, and the new 'E II R' appeared on 29 June, the night of Elisabeth Schwarzkopf's return to Covent Garden as Mimi. The revival of Vaughan Williams's *The Pilgrim's Progress* three days before the funeral seemed particularly appropriate. So did the colour of the cover of the March *Opera* which, because of a fault that developed during the printing of the issue, turned out a dull grey – quite unlike what we had planned. Some of our readers thought we had deliberately chosen this neutral colour because of the King's death. Others, rather less generously, suggested that the colour dull-grey was in perfect accord with the main feature of the issue, which was, in effect, a symposium on the subject of Music Criticism in Great Britain. It included contributions from Britten, Kenneth Clark, Winton Dean, Erwin Stein, and the

French critic and musicologist Fred Goldbeck. It was prefaced with one of George's best editorials, indeed one of the finest pieces he has written during the last thirty years. A few sentences from that extended 'Comment' are as valid today as they were in 1952:

'Criticism is not an end in itself, though it may be a means towards one. It seems likely that it has little effect on the artist (except to discourage him) or, in the ultimate reckoning, on the way the rest of us accept what he creates.

'Plain speaking has a habit of doing more good than harm – and if the number of people who clamoured to be allowed to contribute to this number is any indication, at any rate one thing has been established: criticism is under a misapprehension if it considers itself immune from criticism.'

The symposium aroused much discussion, and several critics, in the national as well as in the weekly and monthly learned journals, devoted space to it. It was Britten's contribution in particular, 'Variations on a Critical Theme', that was most widely quoted. Some people were particularly irked by Britten's remarks about 'those critics who wrote sourly because they were themselves "failed artists" who have had to turn to criticism to live' and again by his closing sentences:

'Please let us have humility. We are not writing or performing for the critic let him remember. Often his presence is a financial nuisance because his seat might have been sold to the public. And it is the public we are there for; they are open-minded and, if we can deliver the goods and have the goods to deliver, friendly and sympathetic as well.'

I believe that Britten was being rather naïve in suggesting that the public is open-minded. The opera public has nearly always resisted novelty and change, and still seems to display an inbuilt resistance, if not actual hostility, to anything that is new. I continue to despair of opera audiences whose behaviour is more in accord with the views expressed by Kingsley Amis rather than Britten. Amis has written that 'Public taste may not be the best taste, but it is the best available, certainly better than the critic's taste or expert's taste or bureaucrat's taste.' If that is truly the case, then we all would have given up years ago.

Two months later Britten actually reviewed a Covent Garden performance in our pages; it was *Le nozze di Figaro* conducted by Kleiber whom Britten considered a 'conductor of genius and energy'. I wish Britten could have been persuaded to write for us more often just as I wish he could have been persuaded to conduct opera more often.

The general interest aroused by the symposium was reflected in our correspondence columns during the rest of 1952. One letter from a Yorkshire reader gave us particular pleasure: 'We were staying in Salzburg and paid a visit to the Festspielhaus. The old Austrian who showed us around made our visit doubly enjoyable by his details. We were very impressed and very grateful to him for his services; and we remarked that Austria had much to be proud of: Mozart and many other composers. His reply amazed us: "Aber Madame, England has Benjamin Britten." '

The March issue was the last one in which Dickie Buckle's name appeared on the title page as art editor. We had been divorced from *Ballet* as far as distribution and subscriptions were concerned since the beginning of the year; and *Ballet* itself ceased publication in October. Dickie's direct influence on the visual look of the magazine had, in any case, been minimal after the first year; I don't think he ever really believed that pictures of opera singers should be larger than postage stamps. None the less a glance at 'Index to Artists' in the annual index to *Opera* during the period of Dickie's influence reveals an imposing list of names including Beardsley, Benois, Cosman, De Chirico, Messel, Neher, Piper, Utrillo, Keith Vaughan and Derek Hill.

The April issue was devoted to opera on radio and television; the two main articles coming from Andrew Porter (his first appearance in our pages) and Lincoln Kirstein. That issue also included a full-page photograph of *Fidelio* at La Scala, Milan, which had enjoyed a great success with Karajan conducting and with Martha Mödl as Leonore. Mödl was one of the great singing-actresses of the 1950s and 1960s and a favourite artist of both George and myself. I cannot remember who actually chose the photograph, but it was not to Mme Mödl's liking. She wrote a very long letter telling George that she found it unflattering. This was not the last time that a singer objected not so much to written criticism as to the photograph chosen to accompany a review. I certainly saw Lauri-Volpi's point of view a few years later when he protested in the strongest possible terms about a photograph of him in the title-rôle of Donizetti's *Poliuto* at the Terme di Caracalla in Rome, which clearly showed that he was no longer a romantic young hero (he was well into his sixties at the time) and, as if to add insult to injury, his tights looked as if they were on the point of coming down!

During the summer George and I agreed that I should make my first visit abroad since the magazine had been launched. I was to cover the Bayreuth and Munich festivals and the magazine would help finance the trip. Although I travelled to Munich alone, I was going to be joined there by Louis Yudkin, Covent Garden's gifted and lovable stage director who, like myself, was making his first visit to post-war Germany. I also knew that my colleague Bill Mann would be in Munich and Bayreuth at the same time, and so too would John Pritchard, whom I had met for the first time at Glyndebourne earlier that summer.

It was with a certain misgiving that I embarked on this, my first visit to Germany. After all, the war had only been over a few years, and the Nazi treatment of the Jews was something that few of us could forget, let alone forgive. As the famous Rhinegold Express (Hook-of-Holland to Munich) neared the end of its journey and we passed through a station called Dachau, my spirits fell; I would have liked to have pulled the communication chain, got off the train and returned to England as quickly as possible. Munich still bore its battle scars; elderly waiters and hotel porters were at times embarrassed by Jewish visitors, and I often felt distinctly uncomfortable when I was asked how I managed to escape from Germany, as people obviously connected the name Rosenthal with that of the famous china manufacturers whose business had been confiscated.

Opera in Munich was performed at the Prinzregenten Theatre; the old National Theatre, the scene of the first performances of *Die Meistersinger*, *Tristan und Isolde*, *Das Rheingold*, *Die Walküre*, and the later Strauss operas still lay in ruins. The members of the administration and indeed all the younger artists I met did all they could to put me at my ease – so did some of the older singers who for obvious reasons did not want to talk about the experiences of the Nazi period. The first opera I heard in Munich was *Der Rosenkavalier* conducted by Kleiber 'als Gast', with Maria Reining, Elisabeth Berger and Kurt Böhme in the leading rôles. On the Grümmer, Erna following evening I heard *Orpheus in the Underworld* at the Theater am Gärtnerplatz; and during the course of the performance wondered just what it was like a few years earlier when young people were hearing for the first time music by Offenbach, to say nothing of Mendelssohn and Mahler, whose works had been banned by the Nazis from 1932 until the end of the war.

Bayreuth is no holiday; the whole day is spent preparing for the evening's performance; the rabid Wagnerian makes his pilgrimage to Haus Wahnfried and stands in reverent silence at the Master's grave. The shops all sell scores, libretti and books on Wagner; the townsfolk, or a large number of them, gather outside the Festspielhaus and gape at the visitors. Even in 1952 the German miracle was in evidence, and the ladies were richly if not elegantly dressed; the men were well-groomed, many in smart dinner jackets and some in white ties and tails, and wearing their iron crosses and other war-time decorations without any sign of shame. Wine and champagne, or as the Germans call it 'Sekt', was much in evidence. *Tristan* on 23 July, the *Ring* on 24, 25, 27, 29 July; *Meistersinger* on 30 July and *Parsifal* on 1 August.

Meistersinger in Germany in 1952 was still something of a ritual for most of the audience and there was much dabbing of eyes during Sachs's panegyric on Holy German Art. I had the feeling that the demonstration at the end of the opera was more than just enthusiasm for the actual performance. *Parsifal* was something else. It was the second year of Wieland Wagner's 'new' approach to his grandfather's operas and the experience was so overwhelming both musically and spiritually that it made ample amends for the poor *Ring* (poor musically, that was) and the disappointing *Meistersinger*. There was a feeling that all had dedicated themselves to the undertaking and as we walked down the hill from the Festspielhaus it was as if the whole audience was unwilling to break the magic spell that had encompassed it by indulging in the usual post-performance conversation. I am not a religious person at all – in fact an agnostic; none the less I can well imagine if that is how I felt after that Bayreuth *Parsifal*, then the effect it must have had on those who belong to the Christian faith must have been almost unbearable. I am sure that much of the evening's magic came from the conductor, Hans Knappertsbusch.

Bayreuth had its lighter moments, thank goodness. There were

the enjoyable evenings at the Eule – the famous inn where genera-
tions of festival visitors and artists have foregathered after performances and eaten and drunk well into the early hours. On one occasion
Louis Yudkin and I were joined by Reginald Goodall who wor-
shipped at Knappertsbusch's feet, John Pritchard, and an amazing
character from Manchester called Harry Moon, who worked during
the year as a waiter, bar-tender, ship's steward, in fact whatever job
he could find in order to save up for his summer opera-going. He
contributed an article to *Opera* in 1953 called 'The Hitch-hiking
Opera-Goer'.

During one of the intervals of the *Tristan* performance Louis
Yudkin and I made our way into the Festival Restaurant for coffee
and cakes; there were two spare seats at our table and two American
ladies, hearing English being spoken, asked if they could join us.
They were 'doing' Bayreuth and then going on 'to do Salzburg'.
One asked the other, 'Say dear, who's conducting tonight?' (It was
Karajan.) 'Don't rightly know; show me your programme.' The
programme was handed over and perused. Its lay-out, plus a lack of
German obviously confused them; then one of them, lifting lorg-
nettes to her eyes and scanning the page triumphantly announced:
'It's Herr Mittwoch.' The day was Wednesday, and Mittwoch was
the word that caught their eye at the top of the page – obviously the
name of someone important!

Back in Munich we heard *Ariadne auf Naxos* on 2 August and
another *Meistersinger* on 3 August. *Ariadne* had the divine Sena
Jurinac as the Composer but the only thing I remember about
Meistersinger was that it was conducted in an express manner by
Joseph Keilberth who, without cuts, succeeded in getting us out of
the theatre nearly half-an-hour before schedule.

The fact that I was in Munich was of course known to the theatre's
press office and somehow was passed on to a young reader of *Opera*
whose name was Ruth Uebel. She was studying at Munich University and left a message for me at my hotel. I contacted her and she
introduced me to one of Munich's favourite restaurants, Schwarz-
walder. Over lunch she asked if she could send her reports to the
magazine, and I agreed. Then she told me she wanted to come to
England to perfect her English and asked whether I could introduce
her to a family with whom she could stay; this I arranged and in due
course she became a regular visitor to London. She invited our

children, Simon and Helen, when they were old enough, to go and stay with her family in Nuremberg, and has remained a very close friend of ours ever since. After a period working for Philips Records in Holland she went to live in New York where she became a successful artists' manager. For a time she looked after Leinsdorf and Mackerras, and now concentrates on a few gifted young pianists and singers. Her apartment between Lexington and Park Avenue is always at our disposal when we visit New York.

All in all it was a rewarding first visit to Germany; my great sorrow was that Louis Yudkin, whom I had got to know really well, was tragically killed in an air-crash in Rhodesia the following spring where he had gone to discuss the technical side of Covent Garden Opera Company's visit there in Coronation year.

Our 1952 autumn issues included reviews of what I had seen and heard in Bayreuth and Munich; George reported on Aix, and Edinburgh, and Bill Mann, Andrew Porter and Donald Mitchell on Salzburg. We had some distinguished contributors in Edward Dent ('A Background to *Un ballo in maschera*'), Martin Cooper (on *Samson et Dalila*), Ronald Duncan (on *Porgy and Bess*), and Edward Sackville-West (on *Mathis der Maler*). Most of those articles were commissioned by George, but always after discussing his ideas with me. Although I did not know it that autumn, George had been invited by David Webster to go and work at Covent Garden; but before he broke the news to me the following March and invited me to succeed him as editor, two events took place in London, each memorable and important in their way. The first was Callas's Covent Garden debut as Norma; the second a two-week season of Italian opera by a scratch company at the old Stoll Theatre that was so awful that it is impossible to forget.

I will return to Callas later, but suffice it to say that our November issue had her photograph on the cover (as did also our January issue – I believe the only occasion in *Opera*'s thirty years' history that the same singer has appeared on our cover after only an interval of two months) as well as a profile article, jointly written by George and myself. The same issue also had my first editorial comment. I wonder now when George asked me to write that first 'Comment' whether he was 'trying me out'. It was, in a way, an extension of some of the points raised in our Critic's issue and was prompted by the Italian season at the Stoll. I commented:

'What must the truly conscientious artist think when he receives the same kind of ovation for a good as for a bad performance, especially when he knows that he has just given one below his own accepted standard? What of the commercial impresario, what will his attitude be towards an indiscriminating public? We have just had a season of Italian opera in London; it has played to full and enthusiastic houses, musically and artistically it has been as bad as any opera season could be, yet it has obviously been a success from the box office point of view. From the inane remarks one could hear passed by members of the audiences, one might have thought that these were the best opera performances of the century.'

One of the first things that Callas did when I met her within a few days of her arrival in London was to congratulate me on what I had written.

In January 1953 we published the first of an outstanding series of articles on 'Mahler and the Vienna Opera' by Erwin Stein with some of the finest photographs of old singers ever to have appeared in *Opera*. In March, William Mann, at that time still one of *The Times*'s 'anonymous' critics, wrote a letter, which we gladly published, on the lack of understudies at Covent Garden; another pinprick that upset Steuart Wilson!

When George told me that he was going to Covent Garden and that he wanted me to take over the editorship I was flattered and apprehensive. Flattered, because he obviously was pleased with my work and had not approached someone like Winton Dean or Donald Mitchell; apprehensive because of the great responsibility that was going to become mine within a few months.

My first important task before taking over the magazine was to find an assistant editor; someone with whom I was in sympathy and with whom I could work. William Mann was a possibility, but he was committed to *The Times*; Cecil Smith was likewise under contract to the *Daily Express* and, in any case, he might well have decided to return to America when his three-year contract had expired. Much as I admired the knowledge and writing of Donald Mitchell and Winton Dean, neither was the kind of person who would want to commit themselves to the routine of editing other people's copy or to that monthly chore, the 'make-up' of the magazine. I discussed these problems with George, but quite rightly he said the final choice must be mine. And so I decided to invite Andrew Porter to become my assistant.

Andrew, as I mentioned earlier, had first introduced himself to me when he visited me at Covent Garden in my early days as archivist. Since leaving Oxford he had done some freelance writing for *The Times*, *New Statesman* and one or two other publications, and in 1952 joined the *Financial Times*. He had begun to contribute to *Opera* in 1952, reviewing performances in Florence, Milan, and Salzburg, as well as writing regularly about BBC operatic broadcasts; he even travelled out to Palmers Green in north London to see an amateur performance of *La Gioconda*. He reviewed his first Covent Garden performance, a *La Bohème* conducted by Barbirolli in the January 1953 *Opera*. He began his notice thus: 'The 243rd performance of *La Bohème* at Covent Garden was not a very good one although the conductor, Sir John Barbirolli, was not of the same opinion.' He followed this up with reviews for us of *Tristan und Isolde* – 'I have never liked Svanholm so well as during this performance without him', and *The Magic Flute*, 'we must note on the debit side a gurgling Sarastro'. His were just the kind of reviews that appealed to me – perceptive, enthusiastically written, and displaying an impish sense of humour. What really decided me however, was his article on 'Opera in Paris' which appeared in our April issue, for which he brought back to London some extremely good photographs, something that many contributors forget to do.

I had read Andrew's article for the April issue in early March, and having made my decision, which George thought a very good one, invited Andrew to come and have lunch with me in the restaurant of the Nag's Head, the famous pub opposite the stage door of Covent Garden. I told Andrew that George was going to work at the Opera House which meant his giving up the editorship of the magazine and that I was taking over, and that I would like him to be my assistant. There were a few moments of astonished silence, and then Andrew's face lit up with an enormous smile, and he replied 'I can't think of anything I'd like more.' He foresaw no difficulties *vis-à-vis* the *Financial Times* – nor were there any; and during the next two weeks we had several meetings to plan the issues for the rest of the year.

10

Fringe Benefits

———

As George had predicted when he invited me to become *Opera*'s assistant editor, there were many 'fringe benefits'. These included broadcasts, lectures, invitations to contribute articles on a freelance basis to various publications, and making useful personal contacts with people connected with the arts in general and the operatic scene in particular.

The invitation to do my first broadcast for the BBC came from that remarkable couple Anna Instone and Julian Herbage, who for years ran the weekly 'Music Magazine' programme on Sunday mornings. Anna was also head of the BBC Record Library and, as such, was responsible for the many programmes that relied on records for their content. Anna and Julian were always on the look-out for new 'young talent' and it was entirely due to their encouragement and remarkable ability to recognize potential that not only I, but many of my colleagues including Bill Mann, Andrew Porter, Alan Blyth and Rodney Milnes, became regular broadcasters.

When Anna invited me to take part in my first 'Music Magazine' programme I was both excited and nervous. My first meeting with Anna and Julian put me completely at ease; at least, I thought it was my first meeting with both of them, until Anna asked me whether I was related to the Mr Rosenthal who had been the headmaster of the Jewish School in Norwood. When I told her that he was my father, she reminded me that we had met in the mid-1930s, when she used to visit Norwood to help run the 'Girl Guide' troop that had been established there!

The first 'Music Magazine' broadcast in the autumn of 1950 led to my being invited to take part in a 'Record Review' on the Third Programme, which was introduced by Alec Robertson. My colleague, William Mann, who was also taking part in his first BBC 'Record Review', joined me in the Maida Vale Studios where we rehearsed in the late afternoon for the live broadcast a few hours later. Minutes before we were due on the air, one of the turntables fused and Alec Robertson, the studio manager and the engineers rushed us down the corridor to another studio, where we arrived just before the red light signalled that we were 'on the air'. In the panic, the records, which were old-fashioned 78s, and which one of the studio managers had snatched from the racks where they had been stacked in the correct order for playing during the broadcast, got mixed up; so when I told the unseen listening public that they were about to hear an extract from Massenet's *Werther* sung by Giacinto Prandelli, what in fact emerged from the speakers was the Act I trio from Mozart's *Così fan tutte*! Being virtually new to the game, I did not panic as apparently did Alec Robertson and everyone else in the control room and after a few seconds during which the red and green lights flashed alternately in the studio I calmly said, 'They must have put on the wrong record.' When we did get things right and the correct record was played, Alec rushed into the studio and congratulated me on remaining so calm. I doubt whether I would have been able to carry off a similar situation a few years later, for the more often I broadcast the more I suffered from the equivalent of stage fright.

I do not know whether it was because of that 'Record Review' or the 'Music Magazine' broadcast that I was asked whether I had any ideas to put forward for a series in the operatic record programmes that were a regular feature on the Home Service at lunch time on Sundays. These had proved extremely popular and were introduced by such well-known broadcasters as Philip Hope-Wallace and Stephen Williams, under the general title of 'Opera for All'. The idea was to build a series of programmes round a general theme that would be the excuse for playing recordings of famous singers past and present. My first series centred on first names that occur in more than one opera: 'Leonora and Alfonso', 'Lucy and Rudolph', 'John and Mary', etc; my second was called 'I sent a letter to. . . .' and gave me the opportunity of playing recordings of operatic scenes in which one character sends or receives a letter from another. Then there was a series which I called 'As others see us', which dealt with operas based on British history or, more often than not, the Italian or French composer's ideas of British history. It was all great fun, and in my series on first names, I included in the programme centred round the name of Elvira a recording of a then virtually unknown Greek soprano called Maria Callas singing 'Qui la voce' from Bellini's *I Puritani*. This anticipated her Covent Garden debut by just more than a year, and was the first time her voice was heard on the air in this country. The third and fourth programmes in that series were broadcast from Edinburgh where I had gone for the Festival; and the somewhat primitive conditions of the BBC Studios there meant that broadcaster, studio manager, producer, and turntable player were all in the same studio; so it was impossible to relax and chat while the recordings were being played.

One of the producers of those Sunday programmes, Diana Gordon, was a stickler on pronunciation. I had chosen to include a record by the bass Nicola Rossi-Lemeni and a discussion arose as to whether his name was to be pronounced Rossi-Lemēni, accent or stress on the second syllable, or Rossi-Lemĕni, with a short 'e'. Diana suggested that we should settle the argument by phoning the BBC pronunciation unit; she told them that in a programme due to begin in ten minutes, we had an Italian bass whose name was – and then she spelt out Rossi-Lemeni: 'What was the correct pronunciation?' she asked. We waited. The studio phone rang within a few minutes and a voice said 'We can't trace the base [bass] in question – can you help us further, is it a naval or an air base?'!

Those lunchtime broadcasts, 'Music Magazines', and 'Record Reviews' continued regularly, and my voice became well known to regular listeners to the BBC music programmes. That, in its turn, led to my being invited to give lectures on operatic subjects to music clubs, record clubs, university opera groups, and women's luncheon clubs. These latter groups, which were (and indeed still are) such a feature in the midlands and the north, generally asked to hear 'The Story of Covent Garden'. On one occasion, I think it was at Bury St Edmunds, I was somewhat put out when the chairman leaned over to me during lunch and said 'We are so much looking forward to your talk, Mr Rosenthal, so many of our members are enthusiastic vegetable gardeners.'!

My freelance writing activities also continued apace; I did a stint on both *The Yorkshire Post* and *The Scotsman*, deputizing for John Amis on the latter; I still contributed articles to *The Gramophone*,

Musical America and *Opera News*, though I found having to write about the same operatic performances for three different publications too demanding, and so decided to resign as the London correspondent of the two American publications.

Perhaps the most rewarding fringe benefits were the opportunities that arose both through the magazine and my work as archivist at Covent Garden of meeting singers, conductors and others 'in the business'. Some of these personal contacts were purely professional and others social, but quite a few of those contacts developed into real and lasting friendships.

Learning the Hard Way

According to a gossip columnist on one of the popular papers, George used 'with Lady Harewood at his side, to edit the magazine *Opera* from his Bayswater home. Now [July 1953] he leaves her to read proofs for the new editor Harold Rosenthal, while [at Covent Garden] he mulls over production costs, storage problems and salaries.' I certainly cannot recollect Marion ever reading proofs for me – but she did put up with my almost daily visits to Orme Square, which remained the editorial office of the magazine until the end of 1953. The idea of *Opera* renting an office from Rolls House in Breams Buildings was discussed, but it was not economically possible at that time, nor did it really appeal to me. The solution seemed to set aside a room in the large house in Muswell Hill which we had bought – or rather taken out a mortgage on – in September, and to which we planned to move from south London at the end of the year.

The July *Opera*, the first under my editorship, included an article in our 'People' series devoted to Elisabeth Schwarzkopf. It had been commissioned in April by George who had written to Walter Legge, Schwarzkopf's husband, asking him to suggest the most suitable person to write the piece. Walter Legge's reply to George began:

> 'When Pachmann [the famous pianist] was asked, "Who is the greatest pianist?" he replied "Godowsky is the second best." If I am considered liable to prejudice in writing about Schwarzkopf, then I suggest Confalonieri or Guido Pannain, both first class writers. It would be interesting to have an Italian on the subject.'

George and I decided that Walter should write the profile.

The copy duly arrived and I edited it before sending it to the printer. The article contained one or two very outspoken remarks about Covent Garden, which George agreed were 'rather near the knuckle', and so I deleted them; it also included a sentence which talked of Schwarzkopf's knowledge of English and ability to sing in that language, which was the policy at Covent Garden at that time. 'In the three years in which she sang there frequently' wrote Walter, 'in only one performance did she sing a part in the original language – Gilda, which she took over at twenty-four hours' notice.' This was, as I discovered to my cost, a 'deliberate mistake' put in the article by Walter, which neither George, Andrew, nor myself spotted. So, in mid-July I was somewhat taken aback when I received a broadside from Walter about the cuts I had made and about a mistake I had left uncorrected. He wrote:

> 'I put in the sentence a mis-statement about Gilda at 24 hours notice quite deliberately because I knew that as archivist you would spot the mistake immediately. I wanted to see if it was editorial policy of 'Opera' to alter contributions to the lines of what I assume to be its policy. Your action in finding time to cut certain vital parts of my article but not to correct simple mistakes confirmed what I feared.'

This was the beginning of a long state of undeclared war between us, which was *not* of my making. I could not have been happier when twenty years later, in 1971, Walter began to correspond with me and we established a close personal relationship, spending many enjoyable hours together whenever he visited London.

Andrew and I had decided to devote the first sixteen pages of the August issue to a symposium on *Gloriana*, Britten's Coronation opera that had enjoyed a *succès de scandale* rather than even a *succès d'éstime* at Covent Garden on 8 June. The contributors to the symposium were Tony Mayer, who headed his piece 'L'Affaire *Gloriana*' and wrote about the audience and its philistine reactions; William Mann, who analysed the vocal score; Andrew himself, who wrote about the libretto; and Cecil Smith, who reviewed the actual performance. I myself did not contribute, nor did I make any mention of the event in my editorial 'Comment'. Whether that was out of cowardice or because I was, in my position as Covent Garden archivist, still refraining from writing reviews of performances there, I cannot quite remember. Whichever it was, the absence of a comment on the part of the editor on the significance in our operatic history of so important an event, not least because Britten had been commissioned to write an opera for the Coronation, upset quite a lot of people, especially those in the Britten circle, which of course included George himself. This resulted in my receiving two long letters from George. In the first he criticized my choice of Cecil Smith to write the actual critique of *Gloriana* rather than one of *Opera's* regular contributors who understood and had studied Britten's music; and in the second, he made the valid point that my not mentioning *Gloriana* in my 'Comment' 'cast doubts on whether *Opera* thought it a good thing or not', and that I had missed the opportunity of pointing out 'without heat and firmly, what the Gala stood for, how it summed up the efforts made for English opera since 1945; how through it the arts generally and opera particularly were officially recognized as they had never been before in England.' George also said that he thought Ben Britten was justifiably hurt; and as if to rub more salt in the wound, he suggested that 'not to have given *Gloriana* the cover of the August *Opera*' – it was given in fact to Glyndebourne's *Alceste* – 'constituted an implied adverse criticism'.

After Walter Legge and George came John Christie, who wrote to me early in September what he called a candid letter. 'I am appalled by your September issue. Your editorial is just mere amateur stuff.' That editorial was a plea for more subsidy, which might lead to the eventual establishment of regional companies; and also a welcome to the return, under Arts Council support, of the Carl Rosa Opera Company which might well have become the training ground for young British singers. 'I don't know what the purpose of your magazine is', continued Christie, 'I thought it merely a disconnected account of opera in different parts of the world and without any fixed standard of comparison. . . . but now "Comment" is giving the magazine a purpose – and a purpose conceived, as far as I can see it, on an amateur basis.'

I replied to John setting out as clearly as I was able the aims of *Opera* as I saw them, and told him that if the magazine was nothing more than a disconnected account of opera in different parts of the world, then George and I would have given it up long ago! John replied in a much more understanding and conciliatory vein:

'Sorry for not replying to your letter of October 2nd. I think you have a difficult task to accomplish. You give an account of opera all over the world, but on what basis and on what standard? It can not but slowly be organized and achieved on a uniform basis. Individuals vary enormously and so do their views and their knowledge and perception. The essential difficulty is that those who write and criticize have not been brought up in the opera house and do not know how high standards are achieved. Most opera houses are – in my opinion – badly run, and are full of vested interests. Opera itself offers such difficulties: – they are nationally different, yet are handled by the same men with artists and audiences of other nationalities. What are we aiming at? The first step should be an investigation of other people's work and of the system in which their results are obtained. The critics have not done this. They write as from the front of the house. In general they are not practical. I am only concerned with the practical men, though of course I can enjoy the writing of some of the leading critics. Young men can be clever, but one wants more than that.'

In addition to those snipings during my first six months as editor, I had several problems of a practical nature with which to contend. Early in 1953 the Skyline Press which had printed *Opera* moved their premises from Islington to Waterloo; then, in April, we moved to a printer in Birmingham; and in August we changed yet again to another printer, Merritt and Hatcher in north London. Our advertising manager moved his offices from the Wool Exchange in the City to an office near Baker Street; and finally, on New Year's Day 1954, the editorial office of *Opera* was transferred from Orme Square to our new house in Muswell Hill, which has remained the editorial office of the magazine ever since.

The next two years were comparatively peaceful ones and were spent consolidating the magazine's position and strengthening its editorial team. I was still not reviewing Covent Garden performances and obviously Andrew, with his increasing commitments on the *Financial Times*, could not undertake to cover them all; and as we were regularly using Cecil Smith and Bill Mann, and from January 1954 Philip Hope-Wallace, we decided to invite them to become 'associate editors' from July that year; they were joined in January 1955 by Desmond Shawe-Taylor. This newly-constituted editorial board used to meet regularly to discuss policy and to make useful suggestions about articles, possible contributors and the like. The team remained constant until the sudden death of Cecil Smith in May 1956. Then, in the summer of that year, Andrew, who had taken over the editorship of the *Musical Times*, resigned as my assistant, though remaining on the board. He was replaced by my good friend John Warrack.

Philip Hope-Wallace's first contribution to our pages was a review of *Aida* at Covent Garden in January 1954 before he had actually joined the board. It demonstrated immediately what a perceptive critic he was; his dry wit and vivid word-pictures continued to enliven our pages both in reviews and articles, especially on French opera which was his love, for many years. I cannot resist quoting from that first *Aida* review:

> 'There has been some refurbishing of the old production; new dances which meant well, and some arty but not too long prolonged groupings of the Egyptian maidens atop the tomb where Johnston and Gré Brouwenstijn struggled for breath. Otherwise much the same, except that the priests after the Judgement scene, shambling on like fairies with wands in *Iolanthe*, do not seem to get the cue to shamble off again; the "going-away" music is clearly indicated.... Though big, she [Brouwenstijn] looks well, even athletic, like one of those great lady athletes her country produces. She looked as if she could outrun most of the Egyptian army if it really came to "fuggiamo"!'

Desmond Shawe-Taylor, on the other hand, was the more elegant and fastidious writer; he has always made more alterations to his proofs than any other contributor to our pages! Little price to pay, however, when one rereads his outstanding series 'A Gallery of Great Singers' which began in January 1955 with an article on Jean and Eduard De Reszke, and continued with pieces on, among others, Melba, Calvé, Destinn, Maurel, and Battistini. Most of these articles were illustrated by superb photographs from the collection of Lady de Grey (subsequently the Marchioness of Ripon) who had played a very influential rôle at Covent Garden between 1888 and 1914 and whose photograph albums had passed into the possession of her daughter, Lady Juliet Duff, a friend of Desmond.

Another series of which I was justifiably proud appeared in *Opera* during 1954 and was devoted to 'The Scala under Toscanini'.

It was written specially for us by Claudio Sartori, a leading Italian critic. This series was a logical follow-on to the articles on the Vienna Opera under Mahler that Erwin Stein had contributed during George's editorship. Erwin continued to write for us, contributing a stimulating new series which he called 'Success in Opera' and participating in the symposium on Covent Garden's new *Ring* production in the summer of 1954.

In September 1954 the Vienna State Opera paid its second postwar visit to London; on that occasion, however, it did not perform at Covent Garden nor indeed in any other theatre, but on what can only be termed a makeshift stage at the Royal Festival Hall. When I reviewed the season in the November issue I commented that visits by foreign opera companies to England always seem to have an extraordinary effect on the critics and public, who either find all that the visitors do superlatively good, or so bad as not to be worth seeing or hearing. I reminded readers that when the Scala, Milan, came to Covent Garden in 1950 my predecessor as editor had complained about the scurvy way in which they had been treated by the majority of the critics, who having been brought up to regard everything in music that was 'Teutonic' as being good and everything 'Latin' as bad, had condemned nearly everything they had witnessed, and only found good words to say about the orchestra. The exact reverse happened regarding the Vienna visit; only Ernest Newman put things in the right perspective. One of our leading young composers appeared on a television programme in which he said that until one had seen opera performances such as the Viennese were giving in London, one had never really seen opera! 'No Scala? No Munich? No Glyndebourne?' I asked.

I also had the temerity to point out that the casts of the three Mozart operas that the Viennese performed in London were not typical of what opera audiences in Vienna normally got. They were, I said, 'Festival' casts; and for people to say, as many did, that Covent Garden should learn how to put on opera from them was just being ridiculous. I pointed out that during the 1953–4 season *Figaro* had been given in Vienna fifteen times, but that not on any one occasion was the cast that of the first night at the Royal Festival Hall (Della Casa, Jurinac, Seefried, Anday, Schoeffler, Kunz, Czerwenka, Dickie). In fact, only once in the preceding two years had the three sopranos sung together in *Figaro* in Vienna. Seefried, who appeared six times during the Vienna fortnight in London had made only fourteen appearances in Vienna between September 1953 and the end of June 1954. As for the cast of the London *Don Giovanni* (Grümmer, Jurinac, Streich, Simoneau, George London, Kunz, Berry, Weber) it had never appeared in Vienna, though its various members had sung in that opera at one time or another. Only the famous *Così fan tutte* (Seefried, Hermann, Loose, Simoneau, Kunz, Schoeffler) was a typical Vienna cast and one that the State Opera kept intact as far as possible to take around Europe. I also criticized the makeshift scenery, the acoustics, and the lack of a real opera-house atmosphere on the South Bank.

For my pains *Opera* was bombarded with letters from outraged readers who seemed to think that it was sacrilege to have written one word of criticism about the season. I was accused of jealousy, of prejudice, and of being the mouthpiece of Covent Garden! 'How can you, as the editor of *Opera*, who is also on the staff of Covent Garden, expect your magazine to be taken seriously by intelligent opera-goers? The magazine promised well when it began, but it now appears to be the official house organ of Covent Garden Opera House', wrote one of our regular readers. 'Perhaps one is not expected to take "H. D. R." seriously' wrote another, who then went on to say that my remarks were likely to make readers consider cancelling their subscriptions to the magazine. Readers from abroad, including Vienna, joined in the correspondence which continued for three months. I did get some support for my views, including a charming letter from a Baron Rupert Hirsche of Vienna, who wrote:

'Forgive me to practise my English, but as a good citizen from Vienna I must reply to the Sir from Italy who believes the good singers sings always in Vienna. Since August I think the Seefried has sung 2 t. at the Opera. Schoeffler is in America since 8 weeks, the Jurinac in Italy since 6 weeks. Lisa della Casa nothing after London. The Höngen is ill; the Güden is ill; and the Welitsch will not sing again till January. Of the great ones only Kunz and Weber make the performances each night both big and small. For we do not always get the best, your *Opera* is quite right to make the criticism.'

The following year the Festival Hall played host to another opera company from abroad, the Stuttgart Opera or the Württembergische

Staatsoper, to give it its official title. Stuttgart was the one city in Germany in which Wieland Wagner regularly produced outside Bayreuth and the repertory of the company's short London season included his controversial production of *Fidelio* which was praised to the skies by Ernest Newman and booed by a large proportion of the audience, including Victor Gollancz, who stumped out of the auditorium shouting 'scandalous!' The Festival Hall had promoted the Stuttgart visit as a 'Gala Season' and had charged gala prices accordingly. My adverse comments and critical reviews hardly drew a murmur from our readers. Stuttgart was not Vienna!

One of the occupational hazards of editing a magazine is to have to abandon an article at the last minute either because the author objects to some of the alterations or cuts made to it by the editor or because the lawyers are worried about the risk of a libel action – fortunately there have been only two occasions during the whole of *Opera*'s life when that has happened. Frustration can also occur when a feature planned to coincide with an important operatic event fails to arrive because the author has not kept to his deadline or, as has happened more than once, it arrives and is printed, and then there is a last minute change in the cast or even the repertory at the opera house, which renders the article quite irrelevant. This happened in our October 1955 issue. We had commissioned an article on the baritone Tito Gobbi, which was to appear at the time of his first appearance at Covent Garden as Iago in the new production of *Otello* that was scheduled to open Kubelik's régime at the Opera House. Not only did the article appear but so also did a photograph of Gobbi as Iago on the cover. But there was no Gobbi that month at Covent Garden as Iago or in any other rôle.

Like *Otello* itself, Kubelik's régime opened with a storm that blew up during the final week of rehearsals. Kubelik, who was conducting his first *Otello*, had quite rightly insisted on a long rehearsal period for this new production. Gobbi, who had sung Iago more than a hundred times, had been given permission to arrive later than either Vinay, the Otello, or Brouwenstijn, the Desdemona. When he failed to materialize by 5.30 p.m. on 11 October (the other principals had been in London since 3 October and the first night was announced for 17 October) Kubelik decided to cancel Gobbi's contract and replace him by Otakar Kraus. Although there was naturally general disappointment at not being able to hear Gobbi in one of his greatest

1. *Above* With my parents and sister at Cliftonville, 1928.

2. *Left* As Maurice Mullins in Emlyn Williams' *A Murder has been Arranged* during my army days, May 1942.

3. *Above* The launching party for *Opera* at Richard Buckle's house in Bloomfield Terrace, February 1950. George and Marion Harewood are in the centre of the picture.

4. *Below* At the famous Eule restaurant in Bayreuth after a performance in 1952. On my right the late Louis Yudkin, and next to him, Reginald Goodall.

5. *Above* With Eva Turner, Dudley Scholte, Eamonn Andrews, Walter Midgeley and Anne Ridyard outside the BBC's television theatre at Shepherd's Bush, before Eva Turner's 'This is Your Life', September 1959.

6. *Below* Making a presentation to Maria Callas at a private party in London, 1957.

7. *Above* Thanking the guests at *Opera*'s Tenth Birthday Party in the Crush Bar at Covent Garden, February 1960.

8. *Below* With Anna Instone and Julian Herbage at the party to launch the first *Opera Annual*, October 1954.

With Joan Sutherland, William Beresford, Phyllis and Richard Bonynge in Sutherland's successful debut at the Opéra as Lucia, April 1960.

With Phyllis at the 1969 Verdi Conference in Parma – obviously during one of oring contributions!

11. *Above* At the first-night party at the Deutsche Oper, Berlin, on the occasion of Covent Garden's visit there in April 1970. From left to right: the American soprano, Evelyn Lear, Josephine Veasey, David Ward and Joseph Rouleau.

12. *Below* At the famous Al Colombo restaurant in Venice with the conductor Peter Maag and the bass Noel Mangin, April 1971.

13. *Bottom* Off-duty in Chicago in October 1974 with colleague Charles Osborne (centre) and host Lee Freeman.

14. *Above* On stage at the
London Coliseum after the
evening organized by the
Friends of the English
National Opera to celebrate
the fiftieth anniversary of
Sadler's Wells Opera,
January 1981. From left to
right: George Harewood,
Anne Howard, Dennis
Dowling, Ava June, Geoffrey
Chard, Alberto Remedios,
Mark Elder, Douglas Craig,
Lord Goodman and
Harold Blackburn.

15. *Right* With Placido
Domingo at a party in
London, February 1980.

16. *Above* Blowing out the candles on my twenty-fifth anniversary cake, assisted by the American soprano, Roberta Knie, at Colin Davis's party for me at Covent Garden, June 1978.

17. *Right* With Phyllis at Colin Davis's party to celebrate my twenty-five years as Editor of *Opera*, June 1978.

rôles, the public and critics mostly supported the new music director on this matter of discipline. Many Covent Garden regulars feared that Gobbi would never sing again at Covent Garden but he was back the following summer for *Rigoletto*, and was a regular visitor to London during the next twenty years. His Iago was eventually heard in June 1962 during Solti's first season as music director, when he came to replace the previously announced Geraint Evans in the rôle. It was in the December 1955 *Opera* that I wrote my first review of a Covent Garden performance for nearly five years, Kubelik's opening *Otello*.

12

Spreading my Wings

———

In the June 1950 issue of *Opera* George had reviewed the reprint of the opera-goer's 'bible', *Kobbé's Complete Opera Book*. He had concluded his review by suggesting that perhaps the next reprint,

> 'Should be a collaboration between Kobbé, whose views are still fresh and vigorous more than thirty years after his death, and someone sufficiently enthusiastic and self-effacing to re-arrange all the material and re-write such of it as was not from Kobbé's pen.'

In due course, this resulted in George being invited by Roger Lubbock, one of the directors of Putnams who published Kobbé, to undertake the task himself and to bring it up to date.

George decided that the cast lists which prefaced each entry in Kobbé and which were American-orientated, should be entirely rewritten so as to include details of important European performances that had been given during the inter-war years and in the 1940s and 1950s. Knowing that I had been compiling such records, George asked me if I would assume responsibility for that aspect of Kobbé and I gladly accepted. The revised Kobbé was due for publication late in 1954; that meant that my lists had to be ready early that year. This brought me into personal contact with Roger Lubbock and he asked me about my projected book on Covent Garden, George evidently having told him that I was assembling material for a history of the Opera House. He asked me whether I had a publisher, and when I told him I had not, he immediately offered me a contract. We decided that May 1958, the centenary of the present Covent Garden Opera House, would be the ideal time for publication; and this meant delivery of the manuscript by the end of the summer of 1957, thus giving me three years to complete the book.

I anticipated that editing *Opera* and writing my Covent Garden book would occupy most of my time; while the odd lecture and broadcast that could be fitted in would help to augment my income. But I never found it easy to say 'No' to other writing assignments that were offered to me – there were also sleeve-notes for gramophone records and occasional articles for other magazines. Then, in the summer of 1953, I met the young publisher, John Calder, an operamaniac if ever there was one; he told me he wanted to publish a yearly operatic book or annual on the lines of the *Ballet Annual* which Arnold Haskell had edited with such success for several years; and he said he wanted me to edit it; and *faute de mieux*, I accepted.

The first *Annual* was described as 'an experiment'; it was generously received by my critical colleagues and warmly welcomed by the public. I was able to persuade several of *Opera*'s regular contributors to write for it. Professor Dent, whom Winton Dean in his review of the *Annual* called 'the senior contributor and also the spriteliest and most literate, characteristically deflated the pretensions of conductors, critics, Strauss-worshippers and foreign singers'. The *Annual* also carried a series of appendices; one a cumulative operatic obituary 1940–53, and another a listing of operatic premières that had taken place during the same period. From this latter compilation was born the idea of a supplement of Loewenberg's *Annals of Opera*, which materialized some twenty-five years later.

The success of the first *Annual* encouraged John Calder and me to plan a second one. As 1956 was to be the Mozart Bicentennial Year, I thought the second *Opera Annual* should be almost entirely devoted to that composer and accordingly I invited several distinguished Mozarteans to contribute to it, including Dent, the conductors Karl Böhm, John Pritchard and Vittorio Gui, and a number of Mozart singers both active and retired; these included Irmgard Seefried, Maria Ivogün, Jarmila Novotna and John Brownlee. There were two refusals to my invitation to contribute; one from Sir Thomas Beecham who wrote:

'Frankly I do not like writing or speaking about so called classical composers; whenever I do I find myself involved in controversy, something which I genuinely dislike.

'My own feelings about the interpretation of such men as Bach,

Handel, Haydn, Mozart and Beethoven differ materially from that which prevails widely in this country, and the Press rarely loses an opportunity of emphasising it, generally to my disadvantage.'

The other refusal came from Elisabeth Schwarzkopf. I assume that those alterations to Walter Legge's Profile of his wife still rankled – and continued to do so until well into the 1960s.

The success of the *Annuals* prompted John Calder to invite me to write a short book about present-day sopranos, which I foolishly agreed to do, for publication in 1956. I chose twenty-five sopranos, including Callas, Tebaldi, Joan Cross, Flagstad, Jurinac, Milanov, Schwarzkopf (!), Varnay and Welitsch. The book was written in a hurry and I was not particularly proud of it; but once again my colleagues were generous, perhaps over-generous, in their reviews. The book was well illustrated and there was a short discography appended to each entry.

When I was gathering together the photographs for the illustrations I wrote to most of the singers asking them to send me a selection of pictures. My letter to Callas elicited this reply:

> 'Every now and then we write to each other, or rather every now and then you remember me.
>
> 'I'm sending a few of my latest pictures – hoping you will like them.
>
> 'I'm fine and I suppose and hope the same for you and your family.
>
> 'It's such a long time we don't see each other. Have you all missed me? Have other singers stolen me your admiration and love!
>
> 'Best regard to you and family.
>   'Love,
>   'Maria'

Of course, I missed Maria, and certainly no other singers had stolen my admiration and love! She had not appeared in London since the summer of 1953 and I had not been to Italy to hear any of her La Scala performances. I think she was happy with what I had written about her in *Sopranos of Today*, where I summed up her art as follows:

'Of course she has her detractors; what great artist has not? "The voice is ugly", "She has three voices", are criticisms that one often hears, and indeed even her greatest admirers would admit that there is some truth in these statements. But to answer her critics I would say that the innate beauty of her voice is such that it can move listeners to tears in certain passages, and her ability enables her to recreate an operatic character in such a way that the listener feels he is hearing it for the very first time. She is one of the truly greatest of present-day operatic artists, and, I would venture to say, one of the finest singing-actresses in operatic history.'

That was written in 1956, which was before London had heard her Violetta, Medea, and Tosca; before her La Scala Anna Bolena and Imogene in *Il pirata*; and before she had benefited from working with Giulini and Visconti.

During the five years from 1953, the year I took over the editorship of the magazine, until 1958, the year my Covent Garden history was published, I was spreading my wings in another important way. I was beginning to travel abroad regularly – not as frequently as George had been able to when he was editor – but often enough to become known as the editor of *Opera*. That was important, for I have always found personal contact with press officers, administrators, artists and foreign colleagues of great value. Not only did those contacts enable people to put a face to a name they knew from the signature at the end of a letter or a review, but they were (and are) immeasurably useful in helping those engaged in performance on one hand and in criticism on the other to understand each other's point of view. And so my visits to Munich and Salzburg in 1954, to the Holland Festival in 1955, to Bayreuth and Munich again in 1956, and to Aix-en-Provence in 1957 were rewarding from every point of view. Phyllis was able to accompany me on the 1956 and 1957 trips and that was an added pleasure, for I was able to introduce her to colleagues and friends, and she was able to see the warmth with which I was welcomed and I am sure she sensed the growing respect there was in operatic circles for the magazine.

There were performances I heard during each of those trips that have remained in my memory – and not always because they were outstandingly good. I recall a performance of Wagner's rarely-performed *Rienzi* that I heard in an open-air performance in Augsburg on my way to Munich in 1954. *Rienzi*, all five acts of it, would, if played uncut, last almost as many hours; but even cut as it was on that occasion, it was an experience not to be missed. *Rienzi* is an opera in the Meyerbeer mould – grand and heroic with huge choruses and processions, battles and banquets, and a grand finale showing the Capitol in flames. In Augsburg it was performed at the Roten Tor amidst the ruins of the Roman fortifications at the edge of the city, and the wall at the back of the *al fresco* stage allowed real, enormous spectacular flames for the climax. That, with the very un-Wagnerian noises supplied by goods trains being shunted in the nearby railway sidings and the occasional aeroplane overhead, made more of an impression than the singing and conducting.

In Munich I heard my first *Frau ohne Schatten*, Strauss's fairy-tale opera with its mixture of symbolism and mysticism on the one hand and spectacular claptrap of earthquakes and magic transformations on the other. It was only redeemed for me by some glorious singing from the soprano, Leonie Rysanek, and by Kempe's magnificent conducting. More memorable was Hans Hotter's performance as Cardinal Borromeo in Pfitzner's long-winded *Palestrina* the first act alone lasts only ten minutes short of two hours. I wrote at the time that I was glad to have had the opportunity of seeing the work in the theatre, but would not mind if I never saw it again.

My visit to the Holland Festival the following summer was the first of many I made during the next ten or so years when Peter Diamand was its artistic director. I fell in love with Amsterdam, and visiting critics were always royally treated. There was no nonsense as there is in some quarters today about not being invited to after-performance parties, where it is thought that if artists see critics at a party they will not enjoy themselves! The 'clou' of that 1955 festival was the visit of the Scala company under Giulini to perform Rossini's *L'Italiana in Algeri* with Giulietta Simionato as a most winning Isabella. The production was by the then relatively unknown Franco Zeffirelli, whom I noted as 'a gifted young designer and producer'.

Bayreuth and Munich in 1956 set the pattern for many future visits abroad: first the business side of the festival, then a holiday somewhere in Europe. That 1956 visit to Germany was centred around our friend Ruth Uebel who invited us all to stay with her family in Nuremberg, and to leave the children with her, while we went to Munich and Bayreuth. It worked wonderfully well. This was the year of Wieland Wagner's revolutionary production of *Die Meistersinger – Die Meistersinger ohne Nürnberg* as the German press labelled it. Wieland attempted to universalize this most German of operas, playing down the 'Holy German Art' side of the work, but also sacrificing the magic of Midsummer Night in old Nuremberg on the altar of symbolism. But as with all Wieland's productions there were many wonderful moments, and the setting of the first act, St Katherine's Church, which we saw face-on instead of obliquely, with the chorus singing straight out at the audience remains the finest first act of *Die Meistersinger* in my experience. The festival meadow in the last act became a cross between the Royal Choral Society assembled in the Albert Hall and a bull ring; yet when I returned to Bayreuth a few years later and saw this production again, Wieland, as was his custom, had made several modifications and I was converted. There were two great individual performances in that 1956 *Die Meistersinger*, Karl Schmitt-Walter as Beckmesser and Fischer-Dieskau as Kothner. Schmidt-Walter played Beckmesser absolutely straight, and he was made up to look neither ridiculous nor ugly; a pedant, soured by his lack of success in the past, yet with a sly sense of humour. Fischer-Dieskau played Kothner as a young and pompous committee man who obviously knew by heart all the constitution of the Mastersingers' Guild and certainly had a young and pushing wife behind him! There were wonderful performances too that summer from Astrid Varnay as Senta and Kundry, and Ludwig Weber as Daland.

Aix the following summer was something quite different. Not only were there the scenic, gastronomic and climatic delights and attractions, which indeed often surpassed the musical ones, but there was a complete absence of the rush and fuss, and smart foreign tourists; all of which helped to give the Aix Festival an almost domestic atmosphere – a pleasant contrast to the highly organized, commercialized and generally crowded and noisy Munich, Bayreuth, Salzburg and even Edinburgh Festivals.

And the operas? First *Così fan tutte* with Aix's two Teresas – Stich-Randall as Fiordiligi and Berganza as Dorabella. Berganza had been discovered at the Toulouse Singers' Competition the previous autumn by Aix's artistic director, Gabriel Dusurget; it was he who had really discovered Graziella Sciutti and had brought such fine tenors as Léopold Sèmoneau and Luigi Alva to Aix. Sciutti was the Susanna in *Figaro* and Rolando Panerai the Figaro and Guglielmo. The two Mozart operas were performed in the courtyard of the Archbishop's Palace on Cassandre's specially constructed stage. In those days it was the best open-air theatre in the world; the seats were comfortable and although the stars twinkled overhead one was hardly conscious that one was listening to opera in the open air, except when a very slight breeze ruffled the leaves of the plane tree which emerged, as if part of the scenery, from a corner of the balcony. As years went by the tree lost more and more of its branches until it eventually had to be cut down. In the early 1970s, the balcony was taken down for safety reasons, and the whole auditorium was reseated on an ascending tier system, with horrible metal chairs that are small and uncomfortable.

Despite several subsequent visits to the Aix Festival, the magic of our first encounter with that most individual of Provençal cities has never quite been recaptured; mostly because of the festival's growing popularity which has brought about a corresponding increase in tourism, and so an endless stream of cars and mopeds now screech up and down the Cours Mirabeau, except on Sundays when the police put up barriers and the street becomes a pedestrian precinct.

13
Crises during the Fifties

——

Opera has always been faced by crises either financial or artistic, and more often than not one has engendered the other. Since opera became subsidized in Great Britain, companies have always pleaded shortage of money, and with such regularity that the almost annual cries of 'wolf', if not actually unheard, have not generally been believed. During the first decade of post-war operatic activity the main crises were artistic rather than financial and it was not until the late 1950s that Covent Garden and Sadler's Wells were both faced with major crises in which money, policy and personalities all featured.

Steuart Wilson was never really happy at Covent Garden; his contract as deputy general administrator was due to expire in the summer of 1955; but since George's appointment as an administrative assistant in Coronation year, he had been feeling more and more frustrated. In addition he had a bee in his bonnet about what he saw as the influence wielded by what he called the 'homosexual clique' in the musical world in general and in ballet and opera in particular. In the spring of 1955, Steuart made a direct approach to the Covent Garden board, but the then chairman, Lord Waverley, refused to allow him to appear before the board in order to criticize the administration. Garrett Drogheda who, as Lord Moore, was secretary of the board described in his own autobiography *Double Harness* how he was deputed to tell Steuart of their decision. The result was that at the end of April that year Steuart left the Opera House, though remaining on salary until September; but even before his appointment had officially ceased he gave an interview to the Sunday newspaper, *The People*, in which he said he was going to spearhead a campaign against homosexuality in British music; the interview included such innuendos as that there was an 'agreement among homosexuals which results in their keeping jobs for the boys'. The threatened campaign never got off the ground, but Steuart kept the pot simmering, and almost a year later he launched a second attack, first privately by sending another memorandum to the Covent Garden board, then publicly in a letter to the *Daily Telegraph* demanding a full inquiry into the way Covent Garden was being run – for this he had the backing of an editorial in the paper.

The moment chosen for this attack was a good one or bad one according to how one viewed the situation; for early in June 1956 the Opera House published its first report in the form of *A Review 1946-1956*, the aim of which was to tell the public what Covent Garden had achieved, and to ask for more money. The opera public might have been impressed, the press on the whole was not, and there was open criticism in leaders in the *Daily Telegraph* and *Evening Standard*. Martin Cooper, the highly respected critic of the *Daily Telegraph*, followed up his paper's editorial with an article which suggested that Covent Garden was too large for most British singers who, according to Cooper, had small voices, and that there should be a restoration of the old pre-war international opera seasons. Several letters appeared in the correspondence columns of the *Daily Telegraph*, mostly supporting Martin Cooper. I wrote a letter pointing out that it was not the size of the singer's voice that mattered, but the way it was projected. Singers like Patti, De Luca and Martinelli had not possessed especially large voices; and in our own day Sena Jurinac, Irmgard Seefried, Erich Kunz, Lisa Della Casa and several others certainly did not have larger voices than most British singers who were then appearing at Covent Garden. More letters followed; there were questions in Parliament, and then, inevitably, Beecham gave voice in an article in the *Daily Telegraph*. He claimed that English voices were 'of comparatively moderate volume' and that the attempt to make Covent Garden the home of a national opera company had been a 'ghastly failure'. There were more questions in the House, more outbursts from Beecham, including a particularly vicious attack on Kubelik, to which the latter replied in a letter to *The Times* in which he defended British singers, attacked stars and snobbism, and concluded thus:

'Critics should not condescendingly dismiss their artists with two or three lines of good or bad criticism, but ought to help them build a British opera which would compete with the best houses in Europe, even with those houses which were fortunate enough to have much longer background work already done in the past. This will never be possible by asking for *stagione* style – a few singers gathered together with almost no rehearsal for *ad hoc* performances. The finest ensemble must consist of high-class singers, confident in their own ability as soloists. I believe that to achieve this should be my work at Covent Garden, and I will do my utmost to find ways in which to work on this policy. I declared this when I signed my contract with the authorities at Covent Garden, and this line I will hold during my stay there.'

Beecham attacked again, reminding us that twice Covent Garden had engaged a foreigner as music director in the post-war period: 'In defiance of all common sense they have engaged as musical director a foreigner, and let him loose upon the unhappy creatures who had been led to expect beneficial results from this monumental piece of stupidity!'

I sprang to the defence of Covent Garden again, and in a letter to *The Times* reminded Beecham that when his Covent Garden company had collapsed in 1920, he had published a pamphlet in which he said: 'For half a century we have talked English opera, we have dreamt English opera, we have wrangled about English opera, but we have done nothing'; I continued 'Post-war Covent Garden has neither talked, dreamt nor wrangled. It has acted; and taken more than a first step to ensure the permanence of a British national opera.'

Beecham had been only too successful in sowing seeds of doubt in the mind of Kubelik, who even before my letter appeared, had offered his resignation, which was refused. Lord Waverley's letter, published in *The Times* on 29 June, expressed the confidence of the entire board in Kubelik; that day also happened to be Kubelik's forty-second birthday, and he held a press conference saying how deeply he had been affected by what Beecham had written. That should have been the end of the affair; but John Christie thought that he must have his say, and Beecham could not refrain from sending yet another letter to *The Times*. But it was Steuart Wilson who again felt that he had to have the last word in a letter to the *Daily Telegraph* on 9 July. Once again he demanded an official enquiry into the powers wielded by David Webster and the qualifications of the board where:

'Amateurs and "patrons" of the arts outnumber by six to two those with real musical knowledge and experience; into the system of engaging artists by which the Opera House insists on a singer abandoning the concert platform without guaranteeing his regular appearances at Covent Garden, where he may remain weeks or even months unemployed ... [And finally into the] unfortunate effect on the singers, as described by Mr Rafael Kubelik, of adverse criticism – but not so much in the public press as within the Opera House itself and particularly in the magazine *Opera* which bears the name of the Assistant Administrator on its title-page.'

No reply was made to the Wilson letter either by the board, David Webster, by George, whose name continued to appear on the title-page of *Opera* as its founder, or by myself, as editor of the magazine that was allegedly publishing adverse criticism of Covent Garden. In fact at that time we were pleading in the pages of *Opera* for more subsidy and as a result of this we received many letters from readers accusing us of being afraid to criticize Covent Garden!

No sooner had Covent Garden got over that crisis, than they were faced with one of quite a different kind. In July there were to be three performances of *Tosca* sung in Italian. The cast included Zinka Milanov as Tosca, Ferruccio Tagliavini as Cavaradossi, Scipio Colombo as Scarpia, and in the short but important character rôle of the Sacristan, one of the leading Italian comic basses of the day, Melchiorre Luise. Equity, the British actors' union, which was always consulted by the Ministry of Labour before issuing work permits to foreign singers, opposed Signor Luise's engagement on the grounds that the rôle could have been filled by a British singer. None the less, the work permit was granted, but Equity refused to issue Luise with a membership card and threatened to call all their members at Covent Garden out on strike if Luise sang the second and third performances. He did not, and Howell Glynne, who had been rehearsing in Bournemouth with the Sadler's Wells Opera for their forthcoming new production of *Martha*, was summoned back to London to sing the Sacristan.

In my editorial in *Opera* the following month I deplored Equity's action and pointed out that the opera sub-committee was made up of two soloists and four choristers from Covent Garden; four soloists and five choristers from Sadler's Wells; eight other well-known operatic soloists; and eight comparatively unknown names. There were obviously several axes to grind. 'What guarantee is there', I asked, 'that this committee might not say, "We have a British artist who can sing Tosca as well as Mme Milanov, or why import Signor Gobbi for Rigoletto when we have British artists for the role?"' And answers came there none. However, some time later I was asked by Equity whether I would mind, from time to time, giving my opinion on certain foreign singers whose names might not be well-known to the opera sub-committee, for whom Covent Garden might be applying for permits. So for several years on an unofficial basis I provided them with factual information and copies of reviews of several foreign artists. Today, no labour permits are required for singers who are resident in an EEC country; but Australian, Canadian or other Commonwealth singers cannot now sing here without a permit.

In 1957 it was the turn of Sadler's Wells to be confronted with a serious crisis. At the end of May the Sadler's Wells Trust issued an official statement saying that it was no secret that Sadler's Wells had been in financial difficulties for some time, and that despite large audiences and increased Arts Council support, the income was not enough to meet rising costs. It continued: 'In consequence, Directors have decided, with the utmost regret, that following the highly successful première of *The Moon and Sixpence* last week, no further new productions can be undertaken this year.'

The Moon and Sixpence had been composed by John Gardner who had been on the music staff at Covent Garden, its libretto, an adaptation of the Somerset Maugham novel, was by Patrick Terry, the manager of the Covent Garden Opera Company; and it was directed by a young producer whose name was Peter Hall. 'Brilliant, and there is no other word for it, was the production of Peter Hall,' I wrote; 'he succeeded in making his singers act in the most convincing manner and never attempting to be "clever" for the sake of being clever, and always was the servant of the music.' Prophetic in a way – for today Peter Hall's operatic productions are praised for precisely those virtues.

In order to try to cut costs Sadler's Wells was only able to offer its chorus a thirty shillings a week pay rise for the 1957–8 season. The chorus refused it and went on strike and the programme for the opening weeks of the season had to be entirely rearranged so that only operas that had no choruses were performed: *The Moon and Sixpence*, *Così fan tutte* (which can just be done without a chorus), *The Consul* and *The School for Fathers*. I am sure that it was at that time that the seeds of the labour problems with which Sadler's Wells and later the English National Opera have been plagued in recent years were sown.

In the 1950s such problems did not trouble the Carl Rosa Company, but they, like every operatic organization, were faced with financial difficulties. As early as 1952 they had been forced to cancel their autumn tour because of the lack of funds. A year later the Arts Council granted them a subsidy of £20,000 to enable them to resume activities. A Trust was set up to administer the grant which by the 1956–7 season had been increased to £51,000 but that was not enough, and each year there was a deficit. None the less by the spring of 1957 the company's repertory was an enterprising one including Puccini's rarely-performed *Manon Lescaut* and, the even less familiar Berlioz's *Benvenuto Cellini*, which except for a production in Glasgow in 1936 had not been heard in Great Britain for more than a century. I travelled specially to Brighton to hear it on 5 April, a few days before the company opened its London season at Sadler's Wells with the same work. Although I was glad to add yet another opera to my list and to have the opportunity of hearing Berlioz's music in the theatre, I was, like most of my colleagues, unimpressed by the standard of the performance, though we all tried to be kind to the company, praising their enterprise and enthusiasm.

The reviews of that London season in *Opera* and elsewhere were hardly flattering. I recall a horrendous *Don Giovanni*, which my colleague William Mann described as being 'atrociously played', and a *Tannhäuser*, during which one did not know whether to laugh or cry. Despite the adverse critical reactions the company's autumn tour went ahead as planned, during it Mrs H. B. Phillips, the company's artistic director, announced her retirement. Her husband, H. B. Phillips, had been the Carl Rosa's guiding spirit from 1924 until his death in 1950 when his widow succeeded him. She was a very formidable lady who had very definite ideas, not only of how the company should be run but also how opera should be put on;

and she had a firm ally in her music director, Arthur Hammond. When she announced her retirement she made it quite clear that she would retain her seat on the company's board and 'continue to give all the help and advice of her long experience'. Professor Humphrey Procter-Gregg, who at that time occupied the chair of music at Manchester University, agreed to become the company's artistic director for a limited period. He had a long experience of working in opera as stage manager and designer for the Beecham companies and during the war years he had worked with the BBC and had translated several operas.

Long before the change of artistic director, the Carl Rosa board was far from happy about the way the company was being run and several members of the Trust resigned, including Edric Cundell (the director of the Guildhall School of Music), James Smith (a member of both the Covent Garden and Sadler's Wells boards), and Norman Tucker. This, together with Sadler's Wells' own financial problems, contributed to a much more serious crisis in the spring of 1958 when the Arts Council produced another of its half-baked plans – a merger between Sadler's Wells and the Carl Rosa! The primary aim of the scheme as outlined by the Council was to save money, for by that time the Carl Rosa was in debt to something in the region of £17,000 and Sadler's Wells to £45–50,000. The announcement was followed by the immediate resignation of Norman Tucker, the director of Sadler's Wells, together with that of his music director, Alexander Gibson, and the general manager Stephen Arlen. There were protest meetings, statements by singers, and leaders in the press – not only in the 'heavies' but in the popular papers too. I joined with my colleagues Andrew Porter, Arthur Jacobs and Donald Mitchell, and gladly added our names to those of Joan Cross, Lawrance Collingwood and several other distinguished pre-war Sadler's Wells artists in a letter of protest that appeared in the *Daily Telegraph*. *The Times* published a leader headed 'A Bad Day for Opera', and Ernest Newman in the *Sunday Times* contributed to the debate in an article headed 'Thoughts on the Present Discontents'. The music section of the Critics' Circle, of which at that time I was the secretary, passed a motion deploring the 'Intention of disbanding the present Sadler's Wells'; 'Such a step', we stated, 'would result in an immeasurable loss to the cultural and operatic life of the nation as a whole.' We strongly urged that an independent inquiry should be held into the administration of opera in Great Britain, and that indeed was set in motion not long after. In less than a fortnight, the Arts Council bowed to public pressure and the proposed merger of the two companies was dropped.

In the April (1958) *Opera* we devoted fifteen pages to what we termed 'The Opera Crisis'. That was the month during which the Carl Rosa opened its first London season under Procter-Gregg's direction at Sadler's Wells. It was true that he had tried to strengthen the company's musical side by engaging Bryan Balkwill and Edward Renton as conductors and inviting Sir Adrian Boult to conduct *Don Giovanni*, the first time he had conducted an opera in the theatre for nearly twenty years. Several new young singers were engaged, but the net results were hardly encouraging. Once again the season had a bad press. 'Professor Procter-Gregg's "new look" Carl Rosa was something less than that on the opening night', I commented. 'The performance was marked by an astonishing degree of unevenness from which the sets were not exempt' wrote John Warrack about *Faust*; and the same critic remarked on the chorus's 'panicky medi-ocrity'. It was not long after this that Procter-Gregg resigned, following what he bitterly called 'ten months of relentless animos-ity'. During those ten months Mrs Phillips, supported by a few members of the Trust who resented all attempts to improve stan-dards and demanded that every move by the artistic director be reported to them, continually interfered with the running of the company. This proved more than some members of the board could tolerate, and Sir Donald Wolfit, the singers Astra Desmond and Norman Allin, and Frederick Cox, director of the Northern College of Music in Manchester, all resigned. The Arts Council withdrew its subsidy and decided to set up a new company to function in con-junction with Sadler's Wells. Many of the Carl Rosa personnel, soloists, choristers, music staff and orchestral players, joined the new company which was to be known as 'Touring Opera 1958' – its director was Procter-Gregg!

True to its name 'Opera 1958' did not last beyond the end of the year, and then it was absorbed entirely into the Sadler's Wells organization. This enabled Norman Tucker and his colleagues to embark on a scheme that had been carefully worked out to give opera and operetta in London, coupled with a greater amount of provincial touring. That, in its turn, eventually resulted in Sadler's

Wells Opera moving to the London Coliseum where already, in the summer of 1958, it had given a successful series of performances of *The Merry Widow*. As for the Carl Rosa, it attempted a come-back in 1960 which proved disastrous and then, after having been in existence for more than eighty years, quietly but sadly disappeared from our operatic life.

During the operatic troubles of 1958 Covent Garden kept a discreet silence; 1958 was, after all, the present theatre's centenary year, and on the very day that the proposed Carl Rosa-Sadler's Wells merger was announced, Covent Garden made public its plans for its centenary season which was to include the now famous Giulini-Visconti *Don Carlos*; a revival of *La traviata* with Callas; a new production of *Tristan und Isolde*; and a gala attended by the Queen and Prince Philip. Three months before that splendid season got under way, Kubelik, who had never really recovered from the attacks made on him by Beecham, announced his resignation as music director.

14

Covent Garden's Centenary – Then into the Sixties

——

The year 1958 remains one of the most exciting of my life; not only because of its operatic events but also because my book *Two Centuries of Opera at Covent Garden* was published on 12 June, four days after the Opera House's Centenary Gala. The book, some 850 pages long, with copious appendices and lavishly illustrated, was, after all, the realization of my teenage dreams and to hold in my own hands the result of so many years' labours, was quite a moving experience. The rush to get it out on time was traumatic; during the previous summer I had got up very early on most mornings, working from 5.00 a.m. until breakfast in order to get the manuscript completed, it was already well over six months late and almost twice as long as originally envisaged. By the end of 1957 the galley proofs had been corrected; page proofs followed very soon afterwards and were completed by the end of February, and the first copies of the book were ready to be sent to reviewers by the end of May.

I suggested to Roger Lubbock that the launching party should be at Covent Garden itself, and he readily agreed, as happily did David Webster. And what a splendid party it was in the Crush Bar of the Opera House, with singers of the past like Maggie Teyte, who became Dame Maggie Teyte on the day of the party in the Birthday Honours List, Agnes Nicholls, the widow of Hamilton Harty who had sung at Covent Garden in the early years of the century, Parry Jones and Miriam Licette from the Beecham days as well as many of the younger generation of singers; and, to add lustre to the occasion, Maria Callas, to whom I presented a copy of the book: 'I hope it is not full of my tantrums' she remarked according to one paper, though another reported her as saying 'I suppose it's full of my tantrums!' You can take your choice.

The reviews of the book were really very good. I greatly appreciated the way Martin Cooper devoted his long Saturday article in the *Daily Telegraph*, two days later, to a review of the book, which he began thus: 'The centenary of the Royal Opera House has been celebrated in several ways, but none so worthy as Harold Rosenthal's monumental historical survey ...' While my colleague Andrew Porter in the *Financial Times* commented 'The most enduring moment of the centenary of the present Royal Opera House will prove to be Harold Rosenthal's chronicle.'

But all my colleagues were generous in their praise; and there were reviews in the European press and in several American papers and periodicals, and Philip Hope-Wallace contributed a review illustrated with gramophone records of several famous singers whose names featured in the book, to the BBC's Sunday morning 'Music Magazine'. I still have the transcript of that broadcast which ended in a typical Philip way:

> 'Oh, there has been big stuff in this big house; whatever else you learn from Mr Rosenthal's book (the odd details, about the forty geese hired for *Königskinder*; the tenor who swallowed his false beard, the tantrums, the rows, the uncertainties), it is incontestably a *great* tradition which is enshrined in the Royal Opera House whose two centuries Mr Rosenthal's huge, dogged compilation so loyally celebrates.'

On 18 July, there was a Foyles Luncheon at the Dorchester Hotel, presided over by David Webster, to mark the centenary of the Opera House. Among the speakers were Joan Hammond, George and myself. It was all very intoxicating; but if I had any illusions about making much money from the book, they were quickly dashed. My advance from the publishers had been £75 plus another £75 on delivery of manuscript. Royalties continued to trickle in during the next few years, but I doubt whether I earned more than £300 in all for my years of labour.

The book was not my only contribution to the Covent Garden centenary. With George and Michael Wood, the Opera House's press officer, I helped to plan and write the souvenir programme book; then there was the centenary exhibition at the Arts Council; and finally an hour's programme on the BBC.

One Sunday evening the previous autumn, anticipating the centenary, I had given a lecture in the Crush Bar. Instead of illustrating the talk with gramophone records, I had invited a few Covent Garden singers to provide the musical examples. To illustrate Melba's long reign, I had chosen the young Australian soprano, Joan Sutherland. Her husband, Richard Bonynge, suggested, in his turn, that Joan should sing the 'Fountain' aria from *Lucia di Lammermoor*, one of Melba's favourite operas. This was more than a year before Joan's great triumph as Lucia at the Opera House, and, I believe, before it had been definitely decided that she would sing the rôle. I agreed, and Joan stunned us all with a display of vocal pyrotechnics just as she was to do to a much larger audience in February 1959. I was happy and pleased that I was, in a way, responsible for letting her sing a snatch of *Lucia* in Covent Garden in advance. I felt that my Covent Garden lecture contained the seeds of a possible radio feature on the coming centenary, and so I suggested to Anna Instone that perhaps something rather more than a short item in a 'Music Magazine' programme would be more fitting to celebrate the event. She agreed and as a result I was asked to compile a sixty-minute programme on the Opera House to be illustrated by recordings and which would also include interviews with famous artists past and present who had featured in Covent Garden's history.

With the help of a BBC staff producer I set about building the programme. I wrote letters to singers and conductors; recorded interviews with some Covent Garden regulars whose opera-going days went back to the 1890s; these included Alec Balfour, who remembered Jean and Eduard De Reszke, and was present at Caruso's London debut in 1902 – he recollected having had to put his hands over his ears, so loud was the sound coming from the Italian tenor's throat, and Sydney Loeb, the son-in-law of the famous German conductor, Hans Richter, who recalled his father-in-law's Wagner performances at Covent Garden as well as those conducted by Nikisch and Beecham. The BBC, through their representatives in America, Germany and elsewhere, were able to record messages from Frida Leider, Lotte Lehmann, Bruno Walter, Eva Turner, who was then teaching in America, Rosa Ponselle, Martinelli, Flagstad, Set Svanholm, and Hans Hotter, to all of whom I had written about the programme. I myself visited and recorded conversations with Sir Adrian Boult, who had played the off-stage bells at the first Covent Garden performances of *Parsifal* in 1914 and who himself had been a pupil of Nikisch, whose conducting methods and approach to Wagner he contrasted with those of Richter; with Karsavina, who recalled dancing at King George v's Coronation Gala; with Agnes Nicholls, who had sung Zerlina in *Don Giovanni* in 1904 in a cast that included Destinn, Caruso and Scotti, and which was conducted by André Messager; with Miriam Licette and John Barbirolli, who had appeared at Covent Garden in the 1920s and 1930s; with Dame Ninette De Valois, who when she was a dancer had appeared in the opera ballets during the Beecham seasons in 1919 and 1920 and remembered standing high up in the flies above the stage to listen to Melba; and with several of those involved in more recent events.

The two outstanding operatic events at Covent Garden during that centenary summer were the production of Verdi's *Don Carlos* and the series of *La traviata* performances with Callas. *Don Carlos*, together with *The Trojans* produced the previous summer, have been generally acknowledged as the two greatest achievements of the Kubelik régime, and each represented, in its way, a path that could be followed by Covent Garden in the future. Berlioz's work was sung in English by a cast which, with one exception, was drawn from Covent Garden's resident company, and included Amy Shuard, Joan Carlyle, Jon Vickers, Jess Walters, Michael Langdon, and Joseph Rouleau – the guest artist was the American mezzosoprano, Blanche Thebom, who sang Dido. Kubelik was the conductor and John Gielgud the producer. *Don Carlos*, on the other hand, was sung in Italian, not incidentally in the original language of the opera which is French, something that few opera-goers either know or, if they do, care to acknowledge. The hand-picked cast of international singers (except for Covent Garden's own new discovery Jon Vickers) consisted of Gré Brouwenstijn, Fedora Barbieri, Tito Gobbi, Boris Christoff and Marco Stefanoni; Giulini was the conductor and Visconti the producer. Both operas were received with high critical acclaim.

The Trojans was a project that both David Webster and George had long wanted to realize, and Kubelik had conducted it as a young man in his days in Brno. *Don Carlos* was George's own special choice for the centenary, and his love of Verdi in general and his faith in *Carlos* in particular helped him persuade the board to accept it. It was *Carlos* rather than *The Trojans*, in other words international star opera rather than home-based ensemble opera, that was to set the pattern for the future, a pattern that Solti was to build on during the 1960s. George, looking back on the way opera had gone at Covent Garden some eight years after he had left the Opera House, admitted that what at the time had been planned for a special occasion set such a high standard, that the public and some of the critics expected that kind of production to be the norm for the future. And so it happened that opera in the original language (even if *Don Carlos* was not exactly that) with guest artists soon came to be accepted as the normal thing at Covent Garden. It was sad that the original post-war aims of the Covent Garden Trust as far as opera was concerned were thus abandoned.

The *Don Carlos* production was a revelation; I do not believe that even George or David Webster believed that it was going to be the success it was. As well as writing a long review of the two performances I attended officially as a critic, the first night and the centenary night itself, 15 May, I devoted my editorial in the June *Opera* to it. 'Not only is it one of the finest operatic productions ever seen or heard at Covent Garden', I wrote, 'but it serves to vindicate completely the art of Grand Opera.' I remember several years later at one of the many revivals of the production at Covent Garden, hearing a very young man, who could only have been in his early teens, if that, in 1958, trying to impress a group of bright young things who were standing round him in the Crush Bar, use those very words and large chunks of the rest of my review, as if they were his instant reactions to the evening's performance. I was both flattered and amused.

I still think that the staging of the Fontainebleau scene that was so often cut in previous productions elsewhere, but was restored by Giulini and Visconti, has not been surpassed on the operatic stage anywhere during the last twenty or so years – though perhaps it was equalled in Peter Hall's production of Britten's *A Midsummer Night's Dream* at the 1981 Glyndebourne Festival which evoked that same kind of magic. In the Visconti production as dusk fell and the lights came on in the windows of the palace at the end of an avenue of trees the whole atmosphere on stage matched the music that Verdi gave to Carlos and Elisabeth de Valois.

To sit in the stalls at Covent Garden on 15 May 1958 and to know that exactly one hundred years earlier on that very night the great opera house had begun its life with Meyerbeer's *Les Huguenots,* another French grand opera – for that is after all what *Don Carlos* really is – appealed to my sense of history; it also moved me, for, romantic that I am, I felt sure that there were many ghosts present on both sides of the footlights that night. It was during that series of *Don Carlos* performances that my friendship with Tito Gobbi and Boris Christoff and their wives (who incidentally are sisters) began; a friendship that ripened over the years and was soon extended to Phyllis. The Christoffs, with no children of their own and essentially lonely people, have always been generosity itself, especially when it came to Simon and Helen, whom they took under their wing when they came with us to Rome a few years later. No adverse criticism, spoken or written, about either of those two singers has made the slightest difference to our relationships; indeed, I have always found that I seem to set myself even more demanding standards when writing about artists with whom I have developed close personal ties.

Maria Callas, of course, I had known for five or more years and she always valued what I wrote about her; we talked about her performances and her vocal problems, about her approach to the music and to the character she was portraying. She sang five Violettas that summer in London, I saw four of them. One I was fortunate enough to witness from the side of the stage, and this taught me even more about that remarkable singer's art than the performances I heard from my usual seat in the stalls. I wrote about three of the performances in the longest review of an opera I ever contributed to the magazine. The way Callas found the right 'tone colour' for certain phrases marked her as someone unique in our day. Single words and phrases would take on a new meaning – the emphasis she put on the word 'due' in the phrase 'Di *due* figli?' when Alfredo's father, Giorgio Germont, tells her that Alfredo is not his only child; or 'E vero, è vero', uttered in a resigned tone when Germont pointed out that one day she would grow old and that Alfredo would tire of her, will, I know, never be equalled. Nor the way she started 'Dite alla giovine' when the phrase sounded as if it was suspended in mid-air.

Callas's last act was superb. One suffered with the dying Violetta as she dragged herself from bed to dressing table, from dressing table to chair; 'O come son mutata,' she gasped, as she looked at her wan reflection in the mirror. When her faithful maid, Annina, told her that Alfredo had arrived, she hurriedly tried to tidy her hair and look her best; then came the reunion of the two lovers, with Violetta's hands (and how Callas had made use of her beautiful long fingers throughout her performance), clasping at the longed-for happiness and hardly believing that Alfredo was really a flesh-and-blood figure. 'Ah! Gran Dio! Morir si giovane' (Oh God, I am too young to die) was sung with terrific intensity – and at the final performance Callas took the whole phrase in one breath. As the drama moved to its close and Violetta gently gave Alfredo her locket, it was impossible to keep back my tears. The death scene was almost horrific, the last 'E strano!' was uttered in an unearthly voice, and as Violetta rose from her chair to greet what she thought was a new life, a glaze came over her eyes, and she literally became a standing corpse.

If I have devoted too much space to describing one of the greatest operatic performances it has been my privilege to experience it is because I believe that Callas's Violetta deserves to be recorded in detail, for I am as sure today as I was in 1958 that we will not hear another like it. Those *Traviatas* spoiled many of us for all others; we did not want to hear another Violetta for a very long time, and when we did it was always Callas's inflections that sounded in our inner ear. And not a few fine sopranos since Callas have been very wary about singing Violetta in London as long as the memory of those performances remained so vivid. Recently in 1981, however, the British soprano Josephine Barstow who sings regularly with the English National Opera has shown herself to be a worthy successor to Callas in that rôle.

The Russian-English impresario, Sander Gorlinsky, who had played an important part in bringing La Scala to London in 1950, had always nurtured the hope that one day he could put on his own seasons; and indeed, in 1957, had brought an Italian company to the old Stoll Theatre which had introduced the young Renata Scotto and the then unknown Spanish tenor, Alfredo Kraus, to London. He had also included *Lucia di Lammermoor* in the repertory, thus anticipating Covent Garden's production of the work for Sutherland by two years. During the Stoll season he had inserted a questionnaire in the programme asking the public which operas they would like to hear in subsequent seasons. The result, in order of popularity was: *Andrea Chénier, La forza del destino, I Puritani, La Sonnam-*

bula, *La Gioconda*, and *La fanciulla del West*; of these *Chénier*, *Forza* and *Sonnambula* were included in the 1958 Drury Lane season. We had conducted a similar poll in *Opera* as far back as 1954; our list was headed by *Otello*, followed by *Lucia*, *Forza*, *Tannhäuser*, and *Andrea Chénier*; *I Puritani* came tenth, *Gioconda* thirteenth, *Sonnambula* twentieth, and *Fanciulla* twenty-fifth. By the time we held a similar poll in 1968, which was during Solti's seventh year as Covent Garden's music director, the first four operas of our 1954 list i.e. *Otello*, *Lucia*, *Forza* and *Tannhäuser* had been added to the Covent Garden repertory. Other works in the first twenty that reached Covent Garden include *Manon Lescaut*, *Falstaff*, *I Puritani*, *Don Giovanni*, *Don Carlos*, *Arabella*, *Les Troyens*, and *Sonnambula*! As far as our 1968 poll was concerned it was headed by *Nabucco* followed by *Guillaume Tell*, *Gioconda*, *Vespri Siciliani*, *Prince Igor*, *Faust*, *Huguenots*, *The Bassarids*, *Eugene Onegin*, *Lulu*, and *Andrea Chénier*, of which only *Nabucco*, *Faust*, *Onegin* and *Lulu* have, at the time of writing, been mounted at Covent Garden, though *Chénier* is promised for later in the 1980s. On the other hand many works that came low down on the list have been given at one or other or sometimes both the London houses, including *Poppea*, *Lucrezia Borgia*, *L'Africaine*, *L'elisir d'amore*, and *Maria Stuarda*. The public does not always get what it wants, and when it does, is not always prepared to support it.

In 1958 Gorlinsky organized a season of Italian opera at the Theatre Royal, Drury Lane which certainly had its lighter moments. The tenor in *Chénier* started in vocal difficulties and was replaced by another singer after a prolonged first interval; the spotlight played a game of 'find the tenor' in *Turandot* – never quite catching up with him as he moved from one side of the stage to the other in an effort to be trapped by the lighting man. In *Les Pêcheurs de perles*, which was sung in Italian as *I pescatori di perle*, the tenor Ferruccio Tagliavini greeted his friends in the chorus, who were lined up in straight lines, with handshakes all round, and lots of the chorus were wearing wrist-watches and their own socks! In *Il trovatore*, which was performed in the best (or worst) Italian provincial style, Mario Filippeschi was roundly booed by a large section of the audience after an unforgivable display of vulgar singing and top-note hogging in 'Di quella pira', of which his claque demanded an encore which was granted. In *William Tell*, in which the same tenor appeared and in which most of the soprano's music had to be omitted as Onelia

Fineschi lost her voice shortly before curtain time, it was the dancer, Alicia Markova, who scored the greatest success and won the evening's warmest applause for her exquisite and feather-weight dancing. The greatest bonus that season brought us was the return to London after nearly thirty years' absence of the Italian conductor Tullio Serafin, who was to coach Sutherland and conduct her Covent Garden Lucia the following year.

In truth, visiting Italian companies have not fared particularly well in this country since the war. I do not refer, of course, to the companies that came from the major houses like La Scala and San Carlo in Naples, but to the *ad hoc* troupes. Late in 1959 a company was assembled to give a short season at the Adelphi Theatre; it performed two operas *La Bohème* and *L'elisir d'amore*. There were some well-known names among the soloists including Tagliavini, the bass Italo Tajo, and the soprano Gabriella Tucci; but the real purpose of the season was to launch a young Anglo-Italian soprano, who had been studying in London with Dino Borgioli; her name was Rosalina Neri and she was better known as a popular singer on television. During the course of the evening she changed her costume at least four times as her singing went from bad to worse. The audience expressed its feelings in no uncertain manner and Miss Neri only sang that one performance of *L'elisir d'amore*.

A few weeks earlier, on 4 December to be exact, Covent Garden gave *Der Rosenkavalier* in German for the first time since 1938; the occasion was the London opera debut of Georg Solti and the star cast included Elisabeth Schwarzkopf as the Marschallin, Sena Jurinac as Octavian, and Kurt Böhme as Baron Ochs. Solti's engagement as Covent Garden's new music director from September 1961 was announced a few months later.

Although Solti had been invited by the Covent Garden board to become the Opera Company's music director during the time he was in London for *Der Rosenkavalier*, he was at first reluctant to do so, feeling that he had reached a stage in his career when his future lay more in the concert hall than the opera house. However, he discussed the offer with Bruno Walter whom he regarded as his 'musical father', and Walter, perhaps remembering his own happy days at Covent Garden in the 1920s, urged him to accept. That advice, plus the fact that Covent Garden was turning from the repertory system to the *stagione* system, tipped the scales and Solti accepted. Like many involved in opera, Solti felt and obviously still feels, that the day of repertory opera is over; I am not sure about that, and often ask myself whether it would not be possible to build up an ensemble such as existed in Vienna under Mahler, at La Scala under Toscanini, and in Munich under Clemens Krauss. When I write or speak on that subject I am always told that it is not feasable today; that singers would not stand for it; and that it would be impossible to find a conductor prepared to give up a lucrative international career in order to stay in one place for virtually a whole season. Such an approach seems to be working at the Metropolitan in New York under James Levine.

When Solti arrived in 1961 he said that his aim was simply to make Covent Garden the best opera house in the world. If that meant that the house was to become a frame for a series of magnificent festival-like productions with hand-picked casts, then he most certainly succeeded; but if, on the other hand, a great opera house is an institution that develops its own special style, forming and nurturing a permanent ensemble, and one in which a logical pattern of building up and expanding the repertory can be discerned, then he did not. None the less, given Solti's artistic *credo*, Covent Garden established itself as an international house to be reckoned with.

It was during Solti's second season as music director that the 'Friends of Covent Garden' was formed. This is an organization similar to the famous Metropolitan Opera Guild in New York; its main aim was and remains 'To raise additional monies to promote opera and ballet through the Royal Opera House in whatever way may seem most effective'. It subsidizes tickets for students, offers scholarships, arranges lectures, recitals and social events, and allows members to attend rehearsals at a nominal fee. Several times during the 1950s, especially when Covent Garden was faced with one of its numerous financial crises, I had urged, in *Opera*, the formation of such a body. In November 1958 I published an Editorial Comment which dealt with the enlargement of the Sadler's Wells Company and the operetta season at the Coliseum. Praising Norman Tucker's 'new-look' Sadler's Wells company, I commented that

'In the present circumstances, one cannot help feeling a pang of sorrow for Covent Garden which, as everyone must now know, is threatened with closure unless more money is forthcoming. By next year [i.e. 1959] Mr Webster's prophecy [i.e. that no one running an opera company in England could be certain to have a company to run by the following year] could be fulfilled only too truly as far as his own theatre is concerned.'

I then went on to urge, yet again, the formation of a supporters' club and the possible establishment of a subscription series. I sent David a proof of my editorial so that, if he so chose, he could reply to it in our pages. David was as unpredictable as ever, and I received a letter from him a few days later that began:

'Thank you for your letter enclosing the drivel you propose to publish. The only point that appeared to me to make sense is that we could run a Club in order to promote a magazine which could probably put a final closure to 'Opera' and that is something which appeals to me a lot!'

Early in July 1962 I received a letter from Garrett Drogheda, telling me that Covent Garden was 'about to launch a new venture which is to be called "The Friends of Covent Garden"' and inviting me to serve on its Council. In addition to the aims outlined above, The Friends was going to publish its own magazine to be called *About the House*. Despite that fact, and remembering David's statement that such a magazine might well put *Opera* out of business, I none the less agreed to serve on the Council. I still do, and *Opera* magazine is flourishing as never before!

The organizing secretary of The Friends, who not only runs its office, edits the magazine, arranges the lectures, helps to arrange the gala performances and big luncheons, visits New York to see how the American Friends of Covent Garden are progressing, and yet still manages to find time to attend performances and invite me to lunch at the Garrick Club from time to time, is the amazing Honourable Kensington Davison. He had a distinguished war-time record in the Royal Air Force but after the fire raid on Dresden was not afraid to express pacifist views and rather left-of-centre feelings.

Solti certainly needed the support of The Friends during his first few turbulent seasons; but there were some people at Covent Garden who viewed the organization with some suspicion and others who regarded it as a nuisance, nicknaming it the 'Fiends'. The first issue of *About the House* appeared in November 1962 and included an article by Sam Wanamaker, whose production of *La forza del destino* conducted by Solti, had had its first night at the end of September when it was very badly received by the critics and public, and there was a great deal of booing. Opposite the first page of Wanamaker's article Ken Davison had included extracts from six reviews of the performances, some in favour, some against. Unfortunately, in succeeding years, very little has appeared in *About the House* that actually criticizes anything to be seen or heard at Covent Garden; that seems to me to be a pity, for even if it is a 'House Magazine' it should, after twenty years, feel able to criticize or at least reproduce criticisms from the press on what the Opera House is doing. The Metropolitan Opera Guild's *Opera News* is not afraid to do that.

Wanamaker also contributed an article to the November issue of *Opera* in which he explained his approach to *Forza*. It was a reasoned and reasonable piece, and he concluded:

'If there are rules and regulations for opera productions that have escaped me I should be pleased to be informed. For the present the "rules" that I follow are simple. ... Listen to the music, study and understand the libretto, the characters, the situation, the background. Find the truth in each. Never violate the musical truth, never interfere with the musical statement, but enhance it. Help the singers to realize the words, thoughts and feelings of the characters. Help them to try to appear as human beings and not opera singers in costume. Remember that opera is theatre and drama, and not a dressed-up concert in scenery and coloured lights. Try to find a way to make opera exciting and alive for today, for a young audience. Above all, enjoy it and love it oneself.'

Clearly a man after my own heart!

Originally the Italian artist Renato Guttoso was to have designed the production, but it soon became an open secret that there had been violent disagreements about the scenery and costumes, and in the event it was Wanamaker himself, with the help of Michael Knight, who provided the settings, and Dinah Greet the costumes. Wanamaker chose to use projections of Goya paintings to illustrate the action. That was not at all to the liking of some of the cast, especially the famous Italian tenor, Carlo Bergonzi, who was returning to London for the first time since 1953. Even less to his liking was Wanamaker's article in *Opera*, especially his remarks about 'bad opera actors making "grand gestures" to express phoney and typical "larger-than-life" emotions'. He continued:

'As it happens such gestures and emotions *were* displayed by one of the cast, Mr Carlo Bergonzi as Alvaro – because he was unable to be present until the final week of rehearsal (others rehearsed for three or four weeks) and refused to attend further rehearsals in order to integrate his own performance with the style of the production. How bitter it was for me to find some critics praising, in the event, something which represents for me all that is worst in operatic convention of performance and stage deportment!'

No self-respecting tenor, especially an Italian tenor, was going to leave that unanswered; and so I was hardly surprised when in early December I received a letter from Bergonzi, who was at that time singing at the Metropolitan in New York, protesting about Wanamaker's article in general and what had been written about him in particular. I published his letter in the January 1963 issue of the magazine:

'Here in New York, being in possession of your November issue, I happened to read the somewhat indiscreet article [on *La forza del destino*] by the producer Sam Wanamaker. I shall be glad to have this ill-bred gentleman correctly informed of the reality of my situation.

'I arrived in London (to sing the role of Alvaro) a few days after the death of my poor father (this had been the first reason for my late arrival) very much shaken and depressed. Immediately the same afternoon, I sought to turn my attention away towards my work, and went to a stage rehearsal arranged by the producer. But at rehearsal the next day I felt physically very ill and went to Mr Solti to ask him to release me from my engagement in order that I might return to Italy to cure my depression. After Mr Solti had entreated me to stay on the ground that he had found no tenors to replace me, I stayed on, but excused myself for two days from rehearsal and stayed in bed to get well with the aid of restorative and anti-depressive injections.

'When the dress rehearsal arrived I got up and duly took part. Everything went well but I was very tired by the end. After this fatigue the producer had the courage to invite me to another stage rehearsal. I gently declined, saying I was very tired, and I went to rest in order to be on form for the first performance of *La forza del destino*, which was, for me, an important return to Covent Garden.

'If this innocuous gentleman is, therefore, very displeased with my success, I am similarly happy at his failure. His production was to my mind quite ruinous, his stupid movements not being in character with the score composed by our great Verdi. The scenic setting was similarly stupid because it was remote from realism; such "imagination" is not acceptable to the true opera-lover. The most intelligent critics and the distinguished London public understood this very well.'

Singers whose vanity was wounded, administrators who felt their policies were misunderstood or misrepresented, and a chairman of the Royal Opera House who thought I disapproved of virtually everything that went on there were recurring problems with which I was faced as the editor of *Opera* during the 1960s, the second decade of the life of the magazine.

15

The Magazine in the Sixties

———

On 29 January 1960 *Opera* celebrated its tenth birthday with a party in the Crush Bar of Covent Garden. It was attended by many artists, colleagues, and representatives from the arts world in general. Desmond Shawe-Taylor, on behalf of the editorial board, presented me with two beautifully-framed silk programmes of royal gala performances given at Covent Garden in 1897 and 1907, which still hang on one of the walls in my office.

The birthday issue of the magazine, published in early February, was enlarged to ninety-six pages and boasted our first colour cover which was a reproduction of a Victorian music cover, showing Jenny Lind in scenes from *La sonnambula* and *Robert le Diable*. George wrote a guest editorial in which he expressed 'pleasure but not surprise that *Opera* had reached its tenth birthday', and then went on to make a plea for 'constructive criticism'. The issue included reproductions of forty-five of our front covers, depicting the most important operatic events of the previous ten years, and we reprinted extracts from reviews, articles, and news items reflecting those events. There were messages from composers, conductors, singers, producers, administrators and a whole host of well-wishers from all over the world, including many with whom we had broken a lance during the preceding ten years – and that was something that greatly heartened me. I particularly relished the message from Moran Caplat, the general manager of Glyndebourne, who wrote:

'*Opera*, like *The Lancet*, is a professional publication probing the mysteries of a profession. Both are avidly read by professionals who mostly profess to disagree, and both are sometimes dangerous in the hands of amateurs. *Opera*, though the much younger of the two, has undoubtedly established itself and you, the Editor, are much to be congratulated on its clear individuality and independence. May you both continue to flourish.'

While the message from the soprano, Amy Shuard, was typical of the many received from performing artists:

'Because we trust the high standards it has maintained over the years we take its criticism seriously and value its praise, should it come. *Opera*, in fact, has been many things in the past ten years: friend, stern critic, guide, newspaper. May it go on being all of them.'

In mid-October, our first 'Festival' issue appeared; it contained eighty pages instead of the usual sixty-four or seventy-two, and was offered at the same price as a normal issue, half-a-crown. In addition to the reviews of seventeen different summer festivals we devoted several pages of editorial to the background and achievements of one special festival, Glyndebourne, thus initiating what was to become a special feature of subsequent festival numbers. By the mid-1960s we had increased the number of pages of the Festival issue to 112 and its price to 5s. Today (1981) with 128 pages it costs £1.20!

In 1961, John Warrack was appointed music critic of the new *Sunday Telegraph* and resigned as my assistant editor, though he continued to contribute to the magazine and remained a member of the editorial board. The choice of a successor was not an easy one and we had many discussions as to who would be most suitable for the job. Our final choice was Arthur Jacobs, who had contributed many stimulating and often provocative pieces to our pages in the past; he had been the music critic of the *Daily Express* from 1947 to 1952, and had produced a first-rate *Dictionary of Music* for Penguin. Unfortunately, Arthur's rather brusque manner and his unfortunate habit of rubbing people up the wrong way had prevented him during the 1950s and 1960s from achieving the kind of position for which his talents so obviously fitted him. Our regular editorial board meetings, never the easiest of gatherings to control, became even more fraught after Arthur joined the board. His lack of what one might call social graces led to clashes with his predecessor, the more conventional and establishment figure John Warrack, and with the conservative Desmond Shawe-Taylor. I have always hated quarrels and arguments, and generally managed by appearing to agree to the many proposals that he made, but acting only on those of which I approved, to keep Arthur happy for nearly ten years!

Arthur's assistant editorship – he incidentally insisted on having the title changed to 'deputy editor' in 1964 while I was away in America for nearly three months and he had to hold the fort – was marked by several changes in the format of the magazine. It was entirely at his suggestion that we introduced such features as 'We hear that ...', which was a kind of superior gossip column about artists' future activities, and a 'Coming Events' section, which we printed on a tinted paper and which was inserted in the centre of the magazine. Arthur also felt that we should include reviews of musicals, which he thought were a branch of music theatre and thus qualified for coverage in our pages – I humoured him over this for a time, and then quietly dropped the idea. He also felt that we neglected Eastern Europe as far as our news and foreign reports were concerned; again I went along with him, but the great difficulty was (and still is) to find Eastern European critics who do not send reviews that are either politically biased or parochial in the extreme.

As well as musicals and reports from East Europe, Arthur also wanted us to build two or three issues a year around a special theme: Criticism, Education, Contemporary Opera, and so on. This last topic was the main feature of our June 1964 issue, and for the first and last time we printed two of the main articles in both German and English. The front cover of the issue, which was printed in black and white, depicted a scene from Weill's *Mahagonny* showing protesters carrying banners with such devices as 'Better Dead than Red' and 'Workers of the World Unite'. Arthur, ever the optimist, suggested that we should print several hundred extra copies, which we did, but in the event sold less than our usual monthly total.

At least once a year he suggested (and still suggests at our editorial board meetings) that we could change the size of the magazine from its convenient $5\frac{1}{2}''$ by $8\frac{1}{4}''$ to something much larger; and every time this suggestion is discussed we all reject this proposal. The last time this suggestion was made (July 1981) I not only sounded out all the board but also our founder and first editor, as well as several friends who have long been readers of the magazine, and without exception they all replied 'keep it at its present handy size'. One of the board even went so far as to exclaim 'over my dead body!' So *Opera* has remained and, as long as I edit it will remain, the size of *Readers'*

Digest, so that it can easily be slipped into the pocket and, when bound, take its place on the bookshelf.

During the 1960s the price of the magazine was twice increased: to 3s in 1963 and to 3s 6d two years later. Our editorial board was enlarged and strengthened. Edmund Tracey, at that time the assistant music critic of the *Observer* joined us in 1965 but remained with us for only a year before being lured away from journalism to go to work with Norman Tucker and Stephen Arlen at Sadler's Wells, where it was largely due to his influence that Reginald Goodall began his second successful career as one of the outstanding Wagner conductors of our day.

Edmund was replaced by Alan Blyth, who had occasionally helped with the make-up of the Festival issue, and was given the imposing title of 'overseas news editor'. His help was invaluable and in July 1968 I made him joint associate editor with Arthur; this gave me an excuse for abolishing the title of Deputy Editor which had never really appealed to me, and which, I felt, firmly committed its holder to becoming editor should anything happen to me.

Looking back through the contents of the magazine during the 1960s I see that our contributors included such distinguished names as E. M. Forster, Arnold Haskell, Brigid Brophy, Victor Gollancz, Neville Cardus, Pierre Boulez, and Rolf Liebermann. It was Desmond Shawe-Taylor who had the brilliant idea of inviting people from outside the world of opera to write about their operatic memories, and it was Desmond who approached Forster whose charming contribution entitled 'My First Opera' appeared in our June 1963 issue. His first opera was *Tristan* at Covent Garden in 1904 in which he recalled that in the second act 'Ternina waved a scarf with magnificence, and came in at the end of the third with a song for which my ears had now been adequately trained'.

Haskell recalled being taken to hear Caruso, Melba, Destinn, Battistini and 'other giants of that period', when 'If one closed one's eyes, it was an advantage. One did not see the prison wall in *Faust* shaking in the back-stage draught or the apoplectic rather than the consumptive figure of Melba-Mimi made yet more mountainous by her muff. One went to hear, perhaps to be seen, but not to see.' Gollancz wrote about Wagner's *Ring*, and Boulez about 'blowing up all opera houses' to which Liebermann replied.

One of Arthur's suggestions which resulted in another interesting series was to ask various practitioners of the operatic art to write about their work; and so we had contributions from Zeffirelli, Peter Hall, and Dennis Arundell on various aspects of producing opera; John Pritchard and Charles Mackerras on conducting; Charles Bristow on lighting; Osbert Lancaster on designing; the soprano Helga Pilarczyk about the problems of singing in modern opera; and Henze about composing *The Elegy for Young Lovers*, for which Auden and Kallman had provided the text, and which had its first performance in the original English at Glyndebourne in July 1961, much to the consternation of many Glyndebourne regulars.

John Pritchard's article in July 1964 on rehearsing opera compared conditions at Glyndebourne with those existing at Covent Garden, to the detriment of the latter. This, following close on a feature entitled 'The Plight of the Lyric Theatre', a joint contribution by the ballet critic, Clive Barnes, and myself, was not to the liking of David Webster, and when at the end of August I sent him a draft of the 'People' article I had written about him, which for reasons I have still to discover, upset him, our personal relations deteriorated rapidly, but not as seriously as they were to two years later, when he read a proof copy of my *Covent Garden, A Short History*, which out of courtesy I had sent him in advance.

A 'crisis' of a different kind arose in the spring of 1968 when the April issue of *Opera* had to be considerably curtailed owing to the last-minute withdrawal of an article by its author – the only time in the magazine's thirty-one-year history that such an incident occurred. Alfred Alexander, an ear-nose-and-throat specialist, who regularly looked after the vocal cords of several famous singers and is often called in by Covent Garden when an artist suddenly goes down with a throat infection that puts a performance in jeopardy, had set himself up as an expert on Mascagni's *Cavalleria rusticana*, especially on the difficulties that had been experienced by Mascagni's librettists in their dealings with the Italian novelist Verga, on whose short story the opera was based. Dr Alexander had submitted an article which he called 'The Strange Story of *Cavalleria rusticana*' which included his own translation of the original Verga story; this made the article almost five times as long as we had planned and I wrote to tell him that we proposed to omit the translation and also make a number of small alterations to the article in order to make it of manageable proportions. Dr Alexander found himself 'unable to accept the "new form" of the article' and threatened us with legal action should we publish the shortened version. We decided to take the easy way out and did not pursue the matter.

In the April 1961 issue of *Opera* I donated a half-page advertisement to the National Campaign for the Abolition of Capital Punishment, a cause that I, like George, had long espoused, and whose moving spirit was the publisher, Victor Gollancz. I believe the advertisement lost us a few readers but it brought me into close contact with Gollancz whom I had only known casually until then. It was when we were at Bayreuth together, however, in 1965 that I got to know him really well. A few months earlier he had told me that he would like to publish an *Opera Bedside Book* to include some of the more striking articles that had appeared in *Opera* since its inception; he suggested that I should edit the book, choosing the extracts, grouping them together under specific headings, and write a short introduction, while he himself would write a foreword. Every contributor I approached gladly gave his or her permission for their pieces to be reprinted; and the result was a late autumn (or early Christmas) book.

The *Bedside Book* was well received and Victor Gollancz, with his long experience of promotion, cajoled 'quotes' from Solti, Gobbi, Eva Turner and even Garrett Drogheda who by that time had begun to call me 'Harold' and whose 'puff' read 'Serious competition to the Covent Garden box office I fear'. But what thrilled and moved me more than anything else were the final sentences in Victor Gollancz's own foreword: 'It fills me with admiration to think that the pieces to be found in this Volume are but a meagre selection of the riches that Harold Rosenthal and Lord Harewood, his predecessor, have assembled over the years in the pages of *Opera*. Both are editors of genius.' Maybe an exaggeration, but it's always nice for one's ego to read something like that in print.

16

Abroad in the Sixties:
Discovering the New World

—

Although I had made several trips abroad to hear opera during the 1950s, they were on a rather modest scale, but gradually during the 1960s they became both longer and more frequent. There were several reasons for this: the magazine was doing fairly well and so could afford to finance a few more foreign visits; then, in my capacity as editor, I was receiving far more invitations to attend not only festivals but also mid-season performances; and, perhaps most important of all, Phyllis was now free to accompany me far more often than in the past, and it is always more enjoyable to travel with someone than alone. By the mid-sixties Simon was at Cambridge and Helen in her teens and quite domesticated. On a number of occasions the children came with us to Munich, Salzburg, Paris and other delightful places; they took opera-going, being entertained by singers and going back-stage, if not as the normal way of life, at least as great fun.

In April 1960 Phyllis and I went to Paris to hear Joan Sutherland make her Paris Opéra debut as Lucia. Covent Garden's press officer, Bill Beresford, was also in attendance. I recall a lunch at one of the smarter Paris restaurants to which we were summoned by Bill, with Joan, her husband, Richard Bonynge, and Evan Senior, the Australian editor of the ill-fated *Music and Musicians* – come to think of it, Phyllis and I were the only non-Australians present – when Evan, refusing all the splendid dishes offered as *hors d'œuvres* asked for sardines, not fresh sardines but the tinned variety, and a whole tin was brought to the table, opened ceremoniously and then devoured by Evan!

As for the *Lucia* itself, it was a great success; Zeffirelli, who had

already produced the opera in London, Palermo, Genoa and elsewhere, gave the Opéra its first new *Lucia* for some fifty years; the
Paris Opéra chorus, however, some of whose members must have
been singing that long, decided to continue the tradition of singing
in French, although the rest of the cast sang in Italian. This was the
first of many performances I attended during the next twenty years
when a British singer – and for me Sutherland was always a Covent
Garden-trained British artist – scored an outstanding success on the
stage of a famous foreign opera house. I still get excited when this
happens, and not a little proud that *Opera* and its editor have helped
to make our singers accepted abroad.

At the end of the year I paid my first visit to Milan since 1950 and
heard Callas in *Poliuto* (twice), *Fidelio* with Birgit Nilsson and Jon
Vickers, waywardly conducted by Karajan (once), and *Don Carlos*
(twice) with not one but two great Bulgarian basses in the cast:
Christoff as Philip and Nicolai Ghiaurov as the Grand Inquisitor.
There was no love lost between the two men, and so the great
confrontation between Church and State was more convincing than
usual; otherwise the *Don Carlos* did little credit musically or artistically to La Scala's reputation.

According to my diary, I heard more opera in Italy in 1962 than
ever before – performances in Rome, Naples, Milan and Florence.
Then there was a week at the Holland Festival, a fleeting visit to
Salzburg and Munich on our way to Yugoslavia for a visit to the
Dubrovnik Festival combined with a family holiday; and performances in Paris and Strasbourg. 'You've had quite a Harewood-like
year' commented one of my colleagues! There were many things to
remember from that year: hearing Montserrat Caballé, for example,
in the small rôle of Naiade in *Ariadne auf Naxos* in Rome; travelling
from Rome to Naples to hear Donizetti's *Maria di Rohan* and finding
myself in the same compartment on the train as Rossi-Lemeni's
parents – his father was a retired colonel in the Italian army, his
mother a Greek – they were going to Naples to hear the same opera
as I was, for their daughter-in-law, the beautiful Rumanian soprano
Virginia Zeani, was singing the title-rôle. But the most memorable
Italian experience that year was hearing Magda Olivero, one of the
truly great Italian singing-actresses, whose career began in 1933, and
who, in 1980, was still making occasional appearances, really 'giving
a performance' as Minnie in *La fanciulla del West* at the San Carlo

in Naples, and raising the temperature on stage and in the audience by sheer emotional impact.

Opera-going in Naples is always fun; the audience so unashamedly enjoys itself, reacting with obvious pleasure to every bit of good singing, taking deep breaths and hissing anything bad, and welcoming a beautifully turned phrase or even note with an audible 'Ah, che bella voce' or some similar phrase. In the circumstances, one can forgive the wonderful unpunctuality of the Neapolitans – one six o'clock performance began at 6.35 and another at nearly seven o'clock.

What else is there to remember from the mid-1960s? A visit to Hamburg to hear the first stage performance of Stravinsky's *The Flood*, given in a double bill with Dallapiccola's *Il prigioniero*. This was followed by a reception for Stravinsky at the Vierjahrszeiten Hotel, where we all waited expectantly for a splendid buffet supper which never materialized! Then there was the opening of the rebuilt National Theatre in Munich in November 1963 when the festivities were blighted by the terrible news received between the opening *Frau ohne Schatten* (invited guests only) and the official first night, *Die Meistersinger*, of the assassination of President Kennedy. All the parties and receptions that had been arranged were cancelled, and the stage lighting failed at the beginning of the 'Prize Song' and was not restored until Sachs began his panegyric on 'Holy German Art'.

The opening ceremony at 10.30 a.m. on 21 November was attended by many famous old Munich singers including Maria Ivogün, Viorica Ursuleac, Delia Reinhardt, Julius Patzak, Ludwig Weber, and sitting in a special place of honour the eighty-nine-year-old Paul Kuhn, a famous Mime and David from before the First World War whom the Nazis had driven out of Germany in the 1930s. The morning ceremonies concluded with the playing of the German National Anthem and then, for the first time since it was banned by the Nazis, the Bavarian National Hymn, after which we all adjourned to drink the health of the new opera houses in champagne, and wander through the white and gold Ionic Halls greeting acquaintances and spotting musical and political celebrities. A few months later I was back in Munich for a Strauss Festival, this time with Phyllis; and was to return there several times during the next ten years, but rather less often after that.

Then I remember ten days in Stockholm in 1968 when I heard

Gedda as Hoffmann and Elisabeth Söderström in the title-rôle of *The Queen of Golconda*, an opera by Berwald that he had written for Jenny Lind but which she never sang; and, indeed, it had not been performed until Söderström sang it in 1968; and naturally there was a visit to the lovely Court Theatre at Drottningholm where I heard Gluck's *Orfeo* with Kerstin Meyer. There was a *Semiramide* at the Florence Festival that year with Joan Sutherland who was cheered, and with Monica Sinclair as Arsace who was booed, as was also Richard Bonynge who conducted – an event which is not mentioned in the latest biography of the Australian soprano.

En route to Florence we spent a couple of nights in Milan where we saw and heard what still remains the most stunning production of *Cavalleria rusticana* in my experience. Karajan, whose conducting I have generally found contrived and even heartless, made the hackneyed old score sound much better than it actually is, and Giorgio Strehler, one of the few really great stage directors, combined with the designer Luciano Damiani to give us an almost anti-religious and down-to-earth production, making the usually boring processions gripping and realistic. The acting of the principals, including Fiorenza Cossotto who sang Santuzza as if her very life depended on it, had one sitting on the edge of the seat. When La Scala magic works, the result is a unique kind of operatic experience, for La Scala at its best remains unbeatable.

On the way home from Florence we stopped off in Geneva, where we heard a performance of *Die Walküre* in the splendid Grand Théâtre which at that time was under the direction of Herbert Graf, whom I had got to know when he came to produce Handel's *Samson* and Wagner's *Parsifal* at Covent Garden in 1958. Graf had always encouraged young American and British singers, and in Geneva his theatre worked in close conjunction with the opera school at the local conservatory, using a number of the most advanced students in small rôles. We were invited by the chief producer of the theatre, Lotfi Mansouri, who was also on the staff at the school, to attend an end-of-term concert in which two young British singers, Anne Evans and Katherine Pring participated. They also sang two of the Valkyries in the *Walküre* performance; when they returned to England they joined the Sadler's Wells Opera, and made distinguished careers for themselves. I had particularly looked forward to hearing Anja Silja as Brünnhilde, but she was ill and was replaced by Liane

Synek, a dull German soprano who had replaced Silja at a *Fidelio* performance a few years earlier when the Frankfurt Opera came to London.

It was the discovery of a new operatic world across the Atlantic that provided a new dimension for me in the 1960s. I had long wanted to visit the States, ever since those days in the 1930s and 1940s when I religiously clipped out the operatic reports from *Musical America* and *The Musical Courier*. I mentioned this one day to Francis Mason, the cultural attaché of the American Embassy in London and a great opera fan, and he suggested that if I could organize a few lectures on university campuses and for some of the opera guilds which would help finance my trip, he would see what he could do to get me invited officially by the State Department. And so, without the help of an agent, I began to arrange a coast-to-coast trip, tying in lectures with the operas I wanted to hear in New York, Chicago and San Francisco. Francis, as good as his word, pulled strings in certain government departments, and on 18 September 1964, I received an official letter from the Ambassador, David Bruce, inviting me to participate in the 'Foreign Leader Program of the Department of State'. This, he told me was 'to give distinguished citizens of other countries who would not be well acquainted with the United States an opportunity to observe at first hand aspects of American life which may be of interest to them'. I was able to call on the Department to help organize a programme of activities and arrange introductions to people I particularly wanted to meet.

No one had warned me about the immense size of the United States, and in my ignorance I had arranged more lectures than I should have done – something like twenty between 18 October and 9 December with even more operas than that to attend over the same period. Looking again at my schedule, which I quickly learned to pronounce 'skedule', I just do not know how I managed to do it. From Washington I flew to San Francisco, hearing a performance of *Il trovatore* the evening I arrived there, and falling asleep; then within less than a week there followed five more operas and two lectures, including one at Berkeley. From San Francisco I flew to Chicago, where I participated in an operatic Round Table, I interviewed Irmgard Seefried for a BBC programme I was to do when I returned home, and went to Bloomington, where Dean Bain had turned the opera school of the music faculty into an operatic power house. From Chicago I returned to the West Coast, this time to Santa Barbara where I met Lotte Lehmann, and to Los Angeles where I gave two lectures, one of which was attended by Carl Ebert who invited me to visit him and his wife at his splendid home at Pacific Pallisades, two generous actions on the part of one of the great men of opera. Then, back to Chicago for another week of opera, three lectures and an early-evening dinner given by the English Speaking Union at which I was to be the guest of honour.

Nineteen sixty-four was the 400th anniversary of Shakespeare's birth, and the English Speaking Union had asked me to talk about 'Shakespeare and Opera', one of the subjects on my lecture list. Imagine my dismay when half way through dinner, the chairman, a formidable lady in a flowered hat, leaned over to me and said 'Say, Mr Rosenthal, would you mind speaking about something else – we understand you have been hearing opera all over the States and we would like to hear your reactions to the American opera scene.' Who was I to say 'No'?; and so making some hasty notes on the back of my menu card, and hardly knowing what I was eating during the last fifteen minutes of the meal, I did what the lady had asked. My 'speech' – the Americans often call lectures speeches – got a mixed reception, especially that part of it in which I was rash enough to suggest that until there was a subsidy for opera in the United States, opera could never really be established on a firm footing. I said that it seemed to me to be a waste of effort to set up large fund-raising organizations to ensure that opera seasons took place at all. As my 'speech' was just a few days after Harold Wilson's victory in the 1964 general election, I made no secret of my socialist sympathies, and that obviously was a mistake. When I had finished, one very angry gentleman came to me and in a very loud voice, accompanied by much banging on the table to emphasize his points, said 'It ill-becomes an English visitor to our shores to tell us how to spend our money, especially as you Europeans existed on American money after the war!' I had forgotten about Chicago's republican and isolationist traditions.

From Chicago I flew south to New Orleans, where I was greeted on my arrival at the airport by a delegation of avid readers of *Opera*, including John Gehl, who was then a young schoolmaster, but who later gave up teaching to set up a travel agency and organize opera tours to Europe, and who has become a firm friend. I saw one opera while in New Orleans, or rather three of the four acts of *Il trovatore*, for a combination of heat, humidity and some sea food eaten on the plane, forced me to flee the theatre after the third interval.

From New Orleans I went to New Mexico, then to Texas, but it was, of course, New York to which I was looking forward, especially my first visit to the Metropolitan Opera, the old Met that is, which was then in its last season. My host, or rather hostess, was Ruth Uebel. She arranged for me to meet Lorenzo Alvary, Hungarian bass who had settled in America in the late 1930s and who had a splendid apartment on West 57th Street; he had, late in life, married a wealthy Kentucky widow called Hallie, who was worth her weight in gold from every point of view! Lorenzo ran a weekly radio programme called 'Opera Topics', and from 1964 until the late 1970s he would record an interview with me either in New York or London, and once I think in Paris. I never got paid for radio interviews in the States; free publicity for myself and the magazine was considered reward enough. I could write pages about the Alvarys, their generosity, their hospitality and their marvellously contrasted characters. Over the years, I saw Lorenzo in a number of character rôles at the Metropolitan and in San Francisco; I have argued with him about politics – he is very right wing and still thinks he sees reds under every bed – about opera, which he maintains is too popular and too easily obtainable, firmly believing that it should be the preserve of the élite.

At the Met I heard eight operas in almost as many days, including a Saturday afternoon performance of *Lucia* with Sutherland and an evening *Meistersinger*, which was mercifully cut. In the March 1965 *Opera*, I wrote about my impressions of the Met in a five-page feature which I entitled 'Rudolf Bing's Metropolitan'. Bing, like David Webster, was touchy about critics, and later I heard from David himself, that Bing had told him that he was not exactly pleased with what I had written. I do not know whether he objected to being called a 'benevolent dictator' or to my saying how badly the orchestra played on most evenings, or about my criticism of the New York audiences who came late, left early, chattered during the opera, and seemed more interested in the Met as a social institution than a cultural one. Whatever it was, my subsequent meetings with Bing were always cool.

New York's attitude to opera was perfectly demonstrated to me at a Gala Performance I attended. It was to raise money for the Met's Welfare and Pension Fund, and was made up of Act I of *Der Rosenkavalier* (with Elisabeth Schwarzkopf, Lisa Della Casa and Otto Edelmann, conducted by Thomas Schippers), Act I of *La Bohème* (with Renata Tebaldi, Carlo Bergonzi, Cesare Siepi and Fernando Corena, conducted by George Schick) and Act I of *La traviata* (with Joan Sutherland and John Alexander, conducted by Schick). During the second interval, the chairman of the Met's board of directors, Lauder Greenway, made a speech in which all the usual thanks were expressed to all the usual people 'who had made the occasion possible'; then, we were invited to pay tribute 'to the person without whom opera in New York would be impossible'. I thought someone would bring Rudolf Bing onto the stage – not a bit of it; everyone stood up, turned about as if to royalty, and cheered Mrs August Belmont, the 'emeritus director' of the board, who, waving her hand and bowing returned the audience's tribute. To that kind of audience opera meant, and means, stars, top notes, glamour and a social occasion; I would much rather have subsidy and something more democratic and infinitely more artistic. Unfortunately, recent economic events have made audiences at Covent Garden, Salzburg and elsewhere in Europe behave far more like their American counterparts, even giving standing ovations to people who don't really merit them.

As Francis Mason had predicted, the fees from my many lectures helped finance my first American trip; they also allowed me to return to Europe in luxury, crossing the Atlantic on the *France* as a first class passenger; and even after that there was some money in hand which helped us buy our first car. The *France* had its own radio and TV studios, and as someone in authority had obviously discovered who I was, I was invited to give a ten-minute talk one evening before dinner on my operatic experiences in America.

17
Some More Performances Abroad

—

Although I did not return to New York until September 1967, I did have the opportunity of hearing the Metropolitan Opera perform in Paris in June 1966, when the company was invited by Jean-Louis Barrault to appear at the Odéon as part of his Théâtre des Nations season. Early in March that year I received a letter from Lorenzo Alvary in which he wrote:

'As you probably know, the Metropolitan Opera was invited to Paris and while my personal contribution, as Antonio in *Figaro*, is not the outstanding event of the visit, I would like to ask you, if you intend to come to Paris for the occasion, to accept my invitation to be there as my guest. It would give me great pleasure to meet you again. Independently from this, we definitely count on your visit to New York for the opening of the Metropolitan, where again my artistic contribution in the opening night's *Cleopatra* [that was Samuel Barber's specially commissioned opera, *Antony and Cleopatra*] and in the following *Frau ohne Schatten* will be modest; but your presence in New York certainly will put the occasion on its proper level. I mean by this the level will be determined and measured by you.'

Those Paris performances were hardly a credit to the Met's reputation. Perhaps because of the size of the theatre and the fact that Beaumarchais was a French writer, Bing chose *Il barbiere di Siviglia* and *Le nozze di Figaro* as the two operas to be given: 'Two of the Met's weakest and most vulgar productions', I wrote, and continued: 'Whoever decided to bring the two Beaumarchais pieces, so tastelessly done, to Paris of all places, was guilty of a colossal blunder.'

This was, in fact, admitted by Bing himself some time later in his autobiography *5000 Nights at the Opera*, when he wrote: 'I did not have the strength to resist the temptation of a Paris visit. The responsibility was entirely mine – Mr Bliss [Anthony Bliss] a leading member of the Board and more recently the Met's general manager advised against the visit and proved right.' However, Bing could not resist his usual dig at the critics, remarking that 'The press is approximately as hostile as the New York press so that is nothing new.'

The *Figaro* performance I attended was a gala for the American Library in Paris and was attended by the US Ambassador, who, like half the audience, was delayed by the terrible Friday night traffic jams, and so arrived after the curtain had risen. Before the performance, Barrault made a speech from the stage in which he virtually told the audience to behave itself and applaud.

My second transatlantic trip in 1967 was a result of a number of invitations from universities and operatic organizations where I had lectured in 1964, asking me to pay them return visits. In addition, the director of Canadian Opera in Toronto, Hermann Geiger-Torel, another of those wonderful refugees from Nazi Germany who contributed so much to cultural life on the other side of the Atlantic, suggested that I should come and see his company at work; and the Women's Committee of Canadian Opera invited me to participate in the company's Jubilee Symposium as 'Key' speaker. Then there was the possibility of going to Montreal for EXPO '67 where during the time I would be there, the Vienna State Opera and the English Opera Group were due to appear; and so I needed little persuasion to arrange my second American tour.

I left for Toronto on 11 September and was immediately plunged into a round of parties, receptions, lectures, conferences, and performances. Geiger-Torel and his staff were kindness itself; I was issued with a stage-door pass by the Canadian Opera management, and met several old friends and made some new ones. The Toronto company worked in close co-operation with the Opera School at the University of Toronto, which in its turn was part of the music faculty. The Dean was an old acquaintance from BBC 'Music Magazine' broadcasts, Boyd Neel; the Director of the Opera School was Peter Ebert, Carl's son, later to work with Scottish Opera; and among the voice teachers was Howell Glynne, the Welsh bass. Glynne had been a wonderful Kecal in *The Bartered Bride*, Mr Crusty in Wolf-Ferrari's *School for Fathers*, Lavatte in *The Olympians*, Fiesco in the first performance in England of *Simon Boccanegra*, and a fruity Baron Ochs. He and his wife entertained me on several occasions in Toronto; and on one memorable day they drove me to the Niagara Falls. During my stay in Canada I heard twelve operas in as many days (six in Toronto and six in Montreal), which was not something I would care to do again, especially as these included the premières of two Canadian operas, Raymond Pannell's *The Luck of Ginger Coffey* and Harry Somers's *Louis Riel*; the latter was an historical piece that told of the attempts between 1869 and 1885 of Louis Riel, leader of the Metis, a race that originated from the union of a French-Canadian man and an Indian woman, to secure rights for his people, and the struggle between them and the Dominion of Canada. Somers used quite a bit of folk music in his score and the opera was a considerable success and certainly deserves to be heard outside Canada.

I did not find Toronto a particularly attractive place; it seemed too much like another 'American' city; but Montreal, with its French atmosphere and background, and excellent restaurants, was quite another matter. The Vienna Opera's performance of *Elektra* that I heard with Birgit Nilsson, Leonie Rysanek and Regina Resnik in the three leading women's rôles, superbly conducted by Karl Böhm, remains the finest I have ever heard of that opera. After the performance Regina Resnik invited me to join her and some friends for supper and we arranged to meet again in New York on 30 September, my birthday.

The English Opera Group's EXPO season, which included Britten's *A Midsummer Night's Dream*, Church operas, and his arrangement of *The Beggar's Opera*, as well as a double bill comprising Handel's *Acis and Galatea* and William Walton's *The Bear* in its first performance outside England, had to compete with the Viennese for audiences; and if less glamorous was at least as artistically successful. The first night of the double bill ran into difficulties as a strike of public transport in Montreal meant that the audience had to find its way to the theatre by car and taxi. Curtain time was held until the audience had assembled, and Walton's one-act opera did not begin until nearly 11 o'clock. There were quite a number of empty seats, and many people left during the opera to find their way home as best they could.

On 28 September I went to the new Met for the first time, to hear *The Magic Flute*. The house was all glitter and glamour, and the acoustics were superb. Since I had last been in New York, the management had enforced the 'No admittance into the auditorium once the house lights are down' rule; but they were still unable to do anything about the early-leavers or the elderly gentlemen who fell asleep and snored, or the ladies who jangled bangles. The audience still applauded every stage picture as it was disclosed (good, bad or indifferent), the entrances of favourite singers, and the ends of arias, despite the request in the programme which asked them 'respectfully and urgently not to interrupt the music with applause'.

My birthday fell two days later and before the promised celebration with Regina Resnik, I suffered a matinée performance of *La Gioconda* Ponchielli's creaky old warhorse, which American audiences love, and which a vocal minority are always trying to urge Covent Garden to revive. Renata Tebaldi, having by then persuaded herself that she was a dramatic soprano, sang the title rôle in which she was hopelessly at sea; and the ballet, which includes the famous 'Dance of the Hours', was almost as funny as it had been in Walt Disney's *Fantasia*. Much more enjoyable was my birthday party with Regina, her family, and a few friends at one of New York's Chinese restaurants.

The New York City Opera always gives a Sunday afternoon performance, beginning at the early hour of 1.15 p.m. The State Theater, as well as being the home of the New York City Opera, also houses the famous New York City Ballet, and it is certainly more suited to the dance than opera from every point of view. As its prices are considerably cheaper than those at the Met it attracts a far less smart audience, and one which always seems genuinely to be enjoying itself and the music.

The performance that afternoon was Rimsky-Korsakov's *Golden Cockerel* with two of the company's undisputed stars and most popular artists, the soprano, Beverly Sills, and the bass-baritone, Norman Treigle, who died some eight years later. The production designed by Ming Cho Lee and directed by Tito Capobianco was lovely to see as well as to hear. Julius Rudel, the company's imaginative and gifted music director at that time, was the conductor. Three weeks later I went again to see and hear Sills and Treigle in Handel's *Julius Caesar* in a performing edition that understandably

upset Handelian experts on this side of the Atlantic when the recording of it was released in the early 1970s. Handel opera, however,
was virtually an unknown quantity as far as American opera audiences were concerned, and in the inter-war years just as Beecham
helped popularize Handel's oratorios in England with his controversial performing editions and Raymond Leppard brought Monteverdi and Cavalli operas before the public at Glyndebourne during
the 1960s, so Julius Rudel's edition of *Julius Caesar* served a useful
purpose. I often feel that my musicological colleagues have little
theatrical sense or feeling, and that for them cosy, homely productions with original instruments, and with *castrati*, if one could get
them, would be the ideal solution!

The City Opera's *Julius Caesar* was certainly the best operatic
performance of that second visit to America! 'Beverly Sills was the
Cleopatra of one's dreams,' I wrote in *Opera*, 'beautiful to look at,
seductive as to voice, and every inch a queen.' I put her picture,
together with that of Treigle on the cover of the January 1968 *Opera*,
and two months later received a letter from Beverly, who wrote: 'I
was never so excited as when I saw *Opera* in January, and never so
pleased to read what you wrote – I just had to write to you ... I
think *Opera* is greatly responsible for a flurry of offers from Europe
... Again – I'm so pleased, thank you.'

By 1969 she had made her debut at La Scala as Palmira in Rossini's
Siege of Corinth and the following year she was at Covent Garden
for *Lucia di Lammermoor*. I was present at both those occasions by
which time I had already made personal contact with her, her
husband and her handicapped little girl. Although she had a considerable success in Italy and returned there on several subsequent
occasions she failed to please the London critics and regular opera-
goers, though Andrew Porter recognized her considerable qualities,
and when he went to New York as critic of the *New Yorker* became
one of her most ardent supporters. Beverly is now director of the
New York City Opera, and is making a great success of her new
career.

In between those two City Opera performances, I had flown to
San Francisco where Phyllis, who was flying out from London to
join me for the rest of my trip, was due to arrive. One of the most
amazing functions we attended was the annual opera ball and 'Fol
de Rol' at the Civic Auditorium, a barn of a place that used to house

San Francisco's cultural activities before the Opera House was built. The purpose of the evening was to raise funds to support not only the opera company but to help the Opera Guild's educational programme. The keynote of the occasion was 'Return to Elegance' – elegance was and is an 'in word' in the States, where apartments, restaurants, audiences and clothes are all 'elegant'. The committee's appeal for elegance resulted in what Phyllis assured me were the most amazing hair styles and costumes she had ever seen on or off stage. The entertainment, however, was fun, with Grace Bumbry (the season's Lady Macbeth) singing 'Can't help lovin' that man'; Régine Crespin (the season's Marschallin) singing 'La Vie en rose', and Rossi-Lemeni (the father in *Louise*) giving a Chaliapin-like performance of 'The Song of the Flea'.

During our week in San Francisco we heard five operas and I gave several lectures including one at Berkeley, one at Stanford, and one to an enormous audience at the famous Mark Hopkins Hotel, for the Junior League of the Opera, which was reported at length in the *San Francisco Chronicle* and which obviously reached the Metropolitan press office and presumably Rudolf Bing's desk by the time we returned to New York the following week. The report began:

> 'One of England's most highly respected opera authorities paid high compliments to the San Francisco Opera last week, and at the same time was decidedly less enthusiastic about the Metropolitan Opera. ... The Met audiences, like those in Chicago, expect opera to be three stars dressed up in costume on a stage. Because the Met has no subsidy and depends on box office and its backers, this audience has to be pandered to.'

I must hasten to add that in recent years under the Bliss–James Levine–John Dexter administration standards at the Metropolitan have improved out of all recognition.

If the City Opera's *Julius Caesar* was the best performance I saw on that visit, the Metropolitan's *Falstaff* was certainly the worst. My diary and review in *Opera* of the performance on 5 October records:

> 'An unhappy evening at the Met and one of the worst performances I have ever heard in a major house. *Falstaff* was conducted by one Bruno Amaducci who succeeded in making long stretches of the score virtually unrecognizable. He chopped the work up into little passages, highlighted instruments that should never be

heard separately, and wrought havoc with the ensembles. How does a man like that come to be engaged at the Met? . . . I was so saddened by it all that I left the theatre at the end of the second act.'

Two weeks later I felt I should give Mr Amaducci a second chance, and so tearing ourselves away from a dinner party given by Blanche Thebom (Covent Garden's Dido of a few years earlier) we arrived at the Met for Acts II and III. There was little improvement, and the magic of the last act was just non-existent. Bing, in his autobiography published five years later, wrote about the *Falstaff*:

'The moment the dress rehearsal came on to the stage it was clear we had a problem. Members of the chorus, orchestra players, soloists complained. The fault was mine: I had hired Mr Amaducci without ever hearing him conduct, something I do not believe I have ever done before at the Metropolitan . . .

'The real villain of the piece was the press, because the New York critics had indeed, as Mr Amaducci claimed, given him mostly good reviews, one of the lesser critics claiming that one day he would be ranked among the Toscaninis and Bruno Walters. . . . Some well-known members of the New York musical press, whose negative opinions are for ever cited to demonstrate how inferior the Metropolitan is to all other opera houses all over the world were so ill informed that they hailed his arrival as a significant acquisition to the company.'

I wrote to Bing, referring him to my own review in *Opera*; but he never acknowledged that at least one critic, albeit an English one, had not been happy with Amaducci's conducting of *Falstaff*.

There was another event during that long American sojourn that I would like to chronicle, which is almost farcical in retrospect. I had been invited to visit Syracuse in New York State to take part, so I assumed, in a radio show and then meet some of the musical personalities of the local university. I did not think it particularly strange at the time that I was asked to take an early morning plane from Newark, New Jersey, airport where I was to pick up my ticket rather than New York's La Guardia. I was met at Syracuse by a young man who conducted me to his waiting car. I said I was looking forward to meeting his father, whom I assumed was the man in charge of my radio programme. 'What do you mean, my father,' my chauffeur responded, 'I'm in charge of the university radio station, and we'll just drop your bags at home and go straight to the studio.'

Arriving at the studio, I was reminded that in our correspondence I had been asked to say something about Tito Gobbi; and so I thought I was going to have a run-through with an interviewer. That was not to be; I was seated in a studio, given an enormous pile of Gobbi recordings, and told 'We'll be on the air in five minutes. So long as you can make sure that there are breaks for news and "messages" [i.e. commercials], it's all yours for the next two hours!'

The first 'message' was to advertise the airline that had provided me with my free ticket, and that explained why I had had to get up at the crack of dawn and get myself to New Jersey. Coffee and sandwiches arrived and I nibbled at them during the commercial and news breaks. I just managed to get through the next two hours, though I am sure my regular BBC producers would have had kittens at the programme that went out. Whether it was the emotional stress of the situation in which I found myself, the fillings of the rather awful sandwiches that I was given to eat, the prospect of the evening dinner party, or a combination of all three that made me feel sick and ill by the end of the afternoon, I do not know. But I do remember having to excuse myself in the middle of dinner that evening and not being able to face another proper meal for the next week; a week that included visits to Bloomington and Middleton for lectures and social engagements.

When I related my experiences to Lorenzo and Hallie, they were appalled. Lorenzo wrote to the Mayor (I believe) of Syracuse, and I received the equivalent of a fee and expenses, something which had never been mentioned while I was there. When I returned to London, I dined out on that story for several months!

18

My 'King Charles's Heads'

———

It was either at a Covent Garden press conference or in a letter arising from something I had written in *Opera* that Garrett Drogheda chided me about 'trotting out one of my King Charles's heads'; but until I looked up the origin of that phrase in *Brewer's Dictionary of Phrase and Fable*, I did not know that it derived from 'Mr Dick, a harmless half-wit in *David Copperfield*, who, whatever he wrote or said, always got round to the subject of King Charles's head, about which he was composing a memorial'! I trust that Garrett did not regard me as a harmless half-wit, though he, like others in the Covent Garden establishment, were most certainly irked from time to time by my particular hobby-horses, which seemed to them far from harmless.

My particular King Charles's heads were, and, indeed, still are, opera in English as opposed to the original language; the engagement of second-rate foreign singers and conductors when there were better British ones available; the evolvement of what I liked to call a house style of production; and the growing élitism of opera at Covent Garden. George Christie would probably add to that list criticism of Glyndebourne audiences and what, from time to time, I have regarded as the Glyndebourne cult; while George Harewood might add my obsessions with conductors' tempos, which, he tells me, I invariably find too fast or too slow.

I suppose it is true that all those subjects recur like a Wagnerian *leitmotiv* in my writings, broadcasts and lectures, and I suppose like my obsession with getting dates or facts one hundred per cent correct they have become something of a joke among my colleagues and certainly of the magazine's readers. As far as Covent Garden was concerned, I set out those criticisms in my *Opera at Covent Garden: A Short History*, published by Gollancz in the spring of 1967, and, as a result of what I had written, there was a further deterioration in my personal relationships with David Webster, Garrett Drogheda and one or two other people connected with Covent Garden.

In October 1966 I had asked Gollancz to send a proof copy of the book to David Webster, not only because I thought it the courteous thing to do, but also because it had been at David's suggestion that I embarked on a short popular history of the house – a kind of cheaper alternative to my larger *Two Centuries of Opera at Covent Garden* that had been published in 1958. Shortly after David had received the proof copy I sensed a certain coolness in his attitude towards me, a coolness that got progressively icier as the weeks passed by. Then, when I went to the first night of the revival of *Simon Boccanegra* on 11 November, I found that my programme note and synopsis of the opera from the previous season had been replaced by one, obviously hastily written, by Sheila Porter, Covent Garden's press officer, who was suitably embarrassed when I asked her why this had happened without my first being told. Tito Gobbi, who was in London to sing the title-rôle in the revival of the opera, and who had also produced it the previous season when he had expressed his approval of the content of the programme note in question, was as surprised as I was when he discovered the change.

This happened a few weeks after I had been virtually commanded to attend a meeting with Garrett Drogheda and John Tooley in Garrett's penthouse office at the *Financial Times*. John had obviously been asked by David to represent him and then report back on what happened as Garrett went through Part 3 of my book, the section I had called 'The Age of the Producer, 1945–?', as opposed to 'The Reign of the Singer, 1732–1903', and the 'Dictatorship of the Conductor, 1903–1939'. Objections were raised to various views I had expressed and Garrett suggested, even demanded, that certain changes should be made. The fact that I had reiterated yet again the original aims of post-war Covent Garden and had praised the Kubelik régime which had respected and furthered them, but had questioned the aims of the Solti period, certainly did not go down well, especially with Garrett who looked on Solti as 'his man'. As I wrote:

'When Solti came to Covent Garden in 1961 he said that his aim was simply to make Covent Garden the best opera house in the world. If that is taken to mean that the house was to become a frame for a series of magnificent festival-like performances, then he has most certainly succeeded. If, on the other hand, a great opera house is an institution in which an indigenous style of opera-giving is to be developed and nurtured, in which an ensemble is to be built up as in Vienna under Mahler, in Milan under Toscanini, and in Munich under Clemens Krauss, and in which there is a discernable and logical pattern in the building up and expansion of the repertory, then, after five Solti seasons, there is still a question mark over Covent Garden.'

I did make some changes in the text, not in my opinions but rather in the way they were expressed. What I refused to change, however, and this I am sure was what so upset David, were my views about the manner in which Karl Rankl had been treated after he left Covent Garden in 1951:

'No sooner had Rankl's resignation been announced than the Covent Garden Board spoke of his "valuable pioneer work in the formation of the training of the company, orchestra, chorus and principals alike, and in the organization of the workings of the Opera House after a long period of silence" ...

'Covent Garden's gratitude to Rankl never went as far as inviting him back to conduct as a guest. In fact he did not set foot in the opera house again for 14 years, when he attended the first night of Schoenberg's *Moses and Aaron* in 1965.'

I do not know whether David and Garrett expected that when the book eventually appeared in the spring of 1967 that that particular passage would have been toned down, if not removed, but it was not; and I am as convinced today as I was then of the truth of what I had written.

I reported all this to my good friend and colleague, the late Sydney Edwards of the *Evening Standard*, who immediately took it up in a feature entitled 'Inside Page'. He asked David Webster whether he had any views 'On the snubbing of Rosenthal'. 'It might not be untrue,' said David in a typical D. W. reply, 'but I don't see why!' Garrett commented in the same column that if Covent Garden tried to keep to its original policy of opera in English,

'the standard would not be what it is today. British singers infinitely prefer to do opera in foreign languages; it is part of their

stock in trade and gives them opportunities to sing abroad. ...
It would be a disaster if we went back to giving opera in English.
I can't conceive why we should be asked to do it.'

Have I waged a losing battle? Am I, I wonder, in 1981 as committed a campaigner for those ideals as I was in the 1960s? I doubt it.
Not because I am any less convinced of the rights of my case, but
because sadly, I am persuaded that it is a minority view for which I
can expect little support either from the opera public at large or
from most of my colleagues.

In June I was invited to attend a conference organized by UNESCO
in Sofia to discuss the problems that face young singers on the
threshold of their careers; this coincided with the third international
competition for young singers, the final sessions of which the delegates attended. There were 118 of us from twenty-four different
countries, and some fifty of us took an active part in the conference
either reading prepared papers or making speeches. The delegates
included Walter Felsenstein, Peter Ebert, Dean Bain, the French
soprano Janine Micheau, Lionel Salter from the BBC, and Boris
Kaikin the chief conductor of the Bolshoi Opera. Both Covent
Garden and Sadler's Wells had been invited to send delegates; and
the latter was represented by Tom Hammond, and Covent Garden
by Joan Ingpen, whom Solti had invited to Covent Garden as
'director of opera planning'. When I saw her at Heathrow Airport
while we were waiting to be called for the flight to Sofia, she
jokingly said, 'You'll have to be careful what you say now, Harold.
I'm coming to keep an eye on you!' Although the remark was made
in fun, I did have the uneasy feeling that the 'establishment' was still
worried in case I spoke out of turn about Covent Garden's policy
vis-à-vis young British singers.

Between 1967 and 1970, my personal relationship with David
improved somewhat; and as chairman of the music section of the
Critics' Circle I arranged a lunch to pay tribute to him on the
occasion of his retirement in the summer of 1970. This took place at
the Westbury Hotel, and as well as the critics and our guest of
honour I invited John Tooley, who was to succeed D. W., to be
with us. David wrote a letter saying how much he enjoyed the
occasion and thanked me for organizing it. John, in a hand-written
letter, was much warmer in what he said, and it was he who told me

how deeply touched D. W. had been by the idea. But I was sad and still am, that he and I never really established the kind of personal rapport that existed between him and some of my colleagues. I am equally sure that it was that souring of relationships during the late 1960s that prevented my going to work at Covent Garden when John Tooley took over in 1970. I had put out feelers as far back as 1960, when George left the Opera House and there was obviously the vacancy for the kind of job I had long wanted to do. I can recall a conversation with Garrett about it, when he asked me whether I thought I could work with Solti. In retrospect I know I could not have, as those deeply-held views that I have mentioned certainly would not have accorded with those of the new music director.

It was rather different, however, by the end of the 1960s when Solti's successor Colin Davis and Peter Hall, who was to have become Covent Garden's director of productions, made known their artistic *credo*, which was far more in accord with the views I had been expressing over the years. I lunched one day with Peter Hall and told him I would love to come to work with him and Colin, and I suggested that the post of *dramaturg*, the person who in a German opera house combines the duties of adapter of librettos, editor of the programmes, and helps advise on repertory and casting, should be created. That was at the end of February 1970, and Peter confirmed in a letter that he would talk about my proposal to both Colin Davis and John Tooley; and he was not the only person to have spoken on my behalf, at least to John, for George also did. After two months of silence I thought I would ask John whether he had given any thought to the possibility of creating a *dramaturg*'s post; and I took the opportunity while in Berlin, where I had been invited to attend some of the performances given at the Deutsche Oper by Covent Garden on their first large-scale foreign tour. John asked me to have lunch with him but he had little to say to raise my hopes. He knew I was disappointed, and wrote a kind, consoling letter to me early in May. I am sure that it was probably Colin Davis more than he who had proved less than enthusiastic – not so much about the post of a *dramaturg*, but about my working at Covent Garden at all. In fact, over the years Colin suggested that some of my more astringent reviews of performances at the Opera House were prompted by the fact that I harboured some kind of resentment because I had not been asked to work there. Nothing could be further from the truth – critics always think they can cast operas better than those whose job it is actually to do it!

George also suggested that despite all the annoyance that *Opera* gave the 'establishment' from time to time, it might well prefer to have the magazine run as it had been for so long, than to risk somebody else taking it over, which of course is what would have happened had I gone to work at Covent Garden, or indeed in any other opera house. That was not the first time that I had that view point put to me. Some years earlier I had applied for the position of music director of the Arts Council to succeed John Denison who was leaving to become general manager of the Royal Festival Hall. I remember at the interview Lord Goodman asking me 'What will happen to *Opera*, if you were to be appointed?' I began to wonder whether the saying that no one is indispensable in their job might not hold good as far as the editor of *Opera* was concerned! A thought strengthened by a sympathetic letter from George soon after I had told him of my disappointment about Covent Garden, in which he wrote:

'You must not allow the disappearance of the greater objective to blot out from your mind achievements you have made with the smaller. I think *Opera* has done so well over the last few years that you forget that its consistency and value are very considerably the result of your hard work and knowledge. Of course, it might have been done as well by somebody else, but the point is that it hasn't, and that just because you have been doing it for so many years, you should not get into a frame of mind that tells you it runs itself. I am quite certain that it doesn't, and that you have every reason to be proud of its position in the world of opera at the moment.'

I now realize how true that was; but in 1970 when I had been editing the magazine for sixteen years I felt I was in a rut, and in need of a change. If it was not to be Covent Garden then perhaps it could be somewhere else; and just over a year later another opportunity presented itself.

Rudolf Bing, the general manager of the Metropolitan, had announced at the end of 1970 that he would retire in June 1972; his successor was to be the Swedish producer and administrator of the Royal Opera, Stockholm, Göran Gentele; Bing's comment when the appointment was announced was 'The poor dear doesn't know what he's in for.' I had first met Gentele in Edinburgh in 1959, then at Covent Garden, where he staged the first opera of the Solti régime, *Iphigénie en Tauride* in 1961, and again on my visit to Stockholm in 1968 when we spent some time together. I had discovered that we had a lot in common in our approach to opera as an art form and especially about such controversial topics as the star system, the *stagione* and repertory systems, and the language question.

In the autumn of 1971 Gentele went to New York for Bing's last season so he could see how the house was run. He was given an office quite a distance from that occupied by Bing, and it was there that I met him when I was in New York in October that year. He had asked me to come and see him when he heard I was in New York, and we talked about his plans and hopes for the future, and how truly pleased he was at the prospect of working with Rafael Kubelik, who had been appointed music director of the Met from 1973, the first in the theatre's history. Then, out of the blue, he asked me whether I might be interested in coming to work with him if it could be arranged. We went on to discuss the possibility of creating the post of *dramaturg* at the Met. Early in January 1971 I received two letters; one from Gentele in which he said 'Regarding our plan, I can tell you that Mr Kubelik is very much in favour of it', and the second from Kubelik himself in which he wrote:

> 'Göran Gentele mentioned you in connection with the position of "dramaturg" at the Met. I told him how happy I am that this could be worked out with you. I know your work in the past and I cannot imagine anybody better for this job. I hope it will materialize.'

I was in seventh heaven. I told one or two of my New York friends including Dario Soria and his wife Dorle. Dario was a refugee from Mussolini's Italy, and he and his wife had set up the Cetra-Soria gramophone label in America; he then helped establish Angel Records; and finally in 1970 he was appointed managing director of the Metropolitan Opera Guild. He could not have been more enthusiastic and encouraging. Then there was Alton Peters, a lawyer who was on the Met's board, and whose wife was the daughter of Irving Berlin; he was and is one of the more progressive and informed members of the board and he too was enthusiastic about the suggestion. I do not know whether Bing was conscious of my conversations with Gentele, but I do know that he was upset by the fact that I had been invited to give a lecture to one of the Met's supporters' groups that held their meeting in one of the theatre's rehearsal rooms without anyone having told him in advance!

During the winter and spring of 1972 I discussed the possibility of going to work in New York with various friends, including of course George and Patricia★; and I also spoke about it to John Tooley. I received a lot of good advice, but everyone asked me the same question – 'Do you think Phyllis would enjoy living in New York?' Of course, Phyllis and I had spoken about this ever since the idea had first been mooted, and, in truth, Phyllis, as always, was for my doing what I thought best for my future and for my happiness. It was not until after the project had been abandoned that she told me how glad she was that we were not going to have to uproot ourselves and transfer our home across the Atlantic.

In June, we went to the States for our son Simon's wedding. We planned first to spend some time in New York to hear some performances of the summer Verdi Festival at the Metropolitan, and of course to have further conversations with Gentele. Unfortunately, while staying in our friend Ruth Uebel's apartment I gashed my arm on the frame of an old print of *Der Freischütz*. We did not know how to dial the equivalent of '999' – but managed to get the occupants of the next-door apartment to contact the police and ambulance. I was rushed to the nearest hospital with flashing lights and blaring sirens but before they embarked on patching me up they asked Phyllis whether she would be able to pay for any subsequent treatment! The accident and the fact that one of the operatic scenes depicted in that fateful frame was of the Wolf's Glen from *Der Freischütz* was surely an omen.

I spoke with Gentele on 19 June, a few days before he left New York for a holiday in Europe; four weeks later he was killed in a car crash in Sardinia. Kubelik resigned as music director after only one season, and the question of a *dramaturg* at the Met was never again mentioned.

During a second visit to the States in 1972, as well as hearing opera in New York and New Orleans, I spent ten days in San

---

★George and Marion had separated in the early 1960s and were divorced in 1967. George married Patricia (Tuckwell) in July that year.

Francisco where the Opera Company was celebrating its fiftieth anniversary. The season included three cycles of the *Ring*, the first US performance of Einem's *The Visit of the Old Lady*, and a Symposium with the less than inspiring title 'Opera Today', which I thought would be a wonderful opportunity for me to trot out some of my King Charles's Heads to an assembly that included most of the directors of the world's leading opera houses. The 'keynote' address was to have been given by George, but at the last moment he had to cancel his visit. His absence meant that there was no one to put the British point of view which I thought would have proved interesting if not exactly invaluable to the other participants. I offered to say a few words from the floor, but the offer was refused. One session was given over to a panel of American critics, the original idea of an international 'Critics' Forum' having been foolishly shelved. Although I enjoyed the social side of the conference and some of the performances, I could not help feeling frustrated. I did manage, however, at a dinner party attended by several important backers of the season, to express my feelings about the version of the *Ring* that the San Francisco public was hearing. Not only was it given as the programme informed us in very small print, in the reduced orchestration of one Gotthold Lessing, but there were savage cuts. The fact that the War Memorial Opera House in San Francisco is half as large again as Covent Garden meant that the authentic Wagnerian sound was seldom heard. When I mentioned this to a member of the Opera House's administration I was told that the local patrons could not be expected to sit through an uncut *Ring* as would their European counterparts. The cuts were made, presumably, because had they not been, the management would have had to pay orchestra and stage staff overtime. And those cuts were unbelievable, including as they did a large part of the Fricka-Wotan scene in *Die Walküre*, part of Wotan's Narration and of the wonderful confrontation between Siegfried and the Wanderer in the first scene of the last act of *Siegfried*; then, in *Götterdämmerung*, the Waltraute scene was sadly mutilated. I could not believe that this was possible, and I said as much and wrote even more strongly about it in *Opera*. I pointed out also that the claim that the company was giving three 'complete' *Ring* cycles was hardly true and that local audiences were being short-changed. The distressing thing about it all was that most of that audience thought they were hearing the real thing, and that Otmar Suitner was the greatest Wagnerian conductor since Furtwängler! Kurt Adler, like David Webster and Rudolf Bing, became yet another opera house administrator for whom the editor of *Opera* was no longer *persona grata*.

Although not strictly one of my King Charles's Heads, in that it was not a cause which I had championed over a long period, was my successful campaign against the 'no applause' rule for *Parsifal* at Covent Garden. Like many people, I had never seriously questioned the announcement that appeared in the Covent Garden programme when *Parsifal* was revived in 1951, which stated: 'In accordance with the composer's wishes there will be no curtain calls and the audience is requested to refrain from applause.' Then I read Angelo Neumann's *Personal Recollections of Wagner*; Neumann was director of the Leipzig Opera in the late 1870s and the early 1880s, and with Wagner's approval he formed a touring company to perform the *Ring* in London, Paris, Rome, St Petersburg and elsewhere in Europe. In his memoirs he gave a detailed account of the seven performances of *Parsifal* he heard at Bayreuth in 1882:

> 'It was at the close of the first when Wagner, amid the thunders of applause from the audience, appeared on the stage surrounded by his artists, that he asked the public not to applaud again during the course of the performance. So the second performance passed with a calm and reverent hush. This called forth another speech from the Master. He must explain, he said, that it was only *during* the performance (i.e. in the middle of scenes) that he objected to applause; but the appreciation due to the singers at the fall of curtain was quite a different matter. So, at the next performance the people expressed their enthusiasm at the end of each act.'

The mystique of no applause for *Parsifal* most certainly developed after Wagner's death in 1883, beginning that summer when the work was again heard at Bayreuth, and Cosima, Wagner's widow, certainly encouraged it. However, in Italy, that most Catholic of countries, *Parsifal* was always applauded at La Scala and elsewhere, and there were curtain calls. At the Metropolitan, New York, Act II was always applauded and the conductor and orchestra acclaimed before the beginning of the final act, as indeed were Fritz Reiner and Weingartner at Covent Garden in 1937 and 1939. At Bayreuth in the late 1950s and early 1960s Wieland Wagner advocated applause, but the Bayreuth audience remained fiercely divided on the subject, and attempts to applaud were shushed by a large part of the public. Eventually the *Parsifal* programmes included a notice published by the management before the war and printed in German, French and English, which stated quite clearly that

> 'Many complaints had been made that a part of the audience had attempted by hissing to prevent applause after the acts of *Parsifal*. The Committee thinks it advisable to publish the wishes of the Master himself in this respect: "The quiet finish to the first Act precludes, of course, any applause; but the Master himself wished that after the 2nd and 3rd acts the audience might express their thanks to the Artists by applause. The re-opening of the curtain at the end has been arranged by the Master's desire and it will therefore be continued."'

And that was what happened at Bayreuth; but gradually during the 1970s curtain calls became the custom after Acts II and III. That Bayreuth notice was reproduced in the Covent Garden programme for the 1971 revival, but it was not until the new production under Solti in 1979 that the work was treated by the audience as an opera and applauded without any inhibitions.

To return to my 1966 campaign. An editorial in the February *Opera* (the Covent Garden revival of *Parsifal* was scheduled for the end of that month) and a letter to *The Times* included much of what I have quoted above; I asked whether it was any more profane to applaud *Parsifal* than a performance of the Verdi *Requiem*, the *Messiah* or the *B Minor Mass*. Surely, I argued, it is just as profane to treat a work performed in a theatre as if it were a religious rite in church; and I asked whether those upholders of the 'no applause' tradition denied themselves food and drink (often alcoholic) during the long intervals.

Not unexpectedly *The Times* correspondence columns reflected views from both sides; and there were comments from my colleagues, mostly in support of applause, except from Peter Heyworth, who wrote that as a result of my campaign 'The Royal Opera House, not in the normal course of events a *Kulturbolschewismus*, has rashly cut across the tradition of 80 years inviting us to applaud the revival' – for Covent Garden issued a press release saying that they were going to remove the 'no applause' paragraph from the programme, or, as *The Times* put it, 'You may clap *Parsifal*.'

And that was the end of the story as far as *Parsifal* at Covent Garden was concerned. But Herbert von Karajan, who presides over the Salzburg Festival and who is revered by many people as if he were God himself, is not of Wagner's opinion about the applause question. In an interview that appeared in January 1981, at the time his recording of *Parsifal* was released, he denied that he 'was more papist than the pope', but rather that it was as a musician that he asked for contemplative silence at the end of *Parsifal*, a work for which he has a special love; and that, he maintains, is only possible if the deeply spiritual mood that ought to prevail in every member of the audience at the end of the work, is not destroyed 'in a loud, worldly and almost brutal manner'. I suppose that is why Karajan allows his Berlin Philharmonic Orchestra to remain visible with the pit raised rather higher than it need be, with the individual faces of the players brightly lit up from the music stands, and with the conductor himself just as much in evidence, and even signalling a prohibition of applause with a magisterial wave of the arm! As my colleague Max Loppert wrote in *Opera*, 'Pious shushing of the audience did the same at the final curtain', and he asked 'Is it not time that this ludicrous custom was at last laid to rest?'

19

Conferences, Lectures and other Exercises

———

Conferences, or what the Americans call conventions, serve a variety of purposes. They offer an opportunity to meet one's colleagues from all over the world, to hear experts hold forth on their specialist subjects, to join in a round of social engagements, and to travel to interesting parts of the world. Of course, they also have their disadvantages: they are time-consuming and tiring, and they often achieve little as they offer a political platform for those who want one. In the 1960s I rarely refused an invitation to participate in these overseas junketings, but as I grew older and wiser, I became more selective and refused more invitations than I accepted.

In 1966 I had been asked to take part in the first international conference organized by the Verdi Institute of Parma. The Verdi Institute was founded in 1959 by the distinguished Italian musicologist Mario Medici, who remained its director until 1980; he edited its splendid bulletins (which were translated into French, German and English) and organized its conferences which initially took place every third year. The first, in 1966, which I could not attend, was held in the lovely Giorgio Cini Foundation on the Isola di San Giorgio Maggiore, in Venice, and the delegates were mostly Italian. The second conference, in 1969, was devoted to the different aspects of *Don Carlos* and lasted a week; it was far more international in character and its participants, including some of the leading Verdi scholars of the day, came from all over the world. It began in Verona, where performances of *Don Carlos* were being given in the famous open-air Arena whose artistic director at that time happened to be Medici; continued in Parma at the home of the Institute, and concluded at Bussetto, Verdi's birthplace. It remains one of my most pleasant memories of the last twelve years.

The Verona summer season is the most famous open-air opera festival in the world; it takes place in the magnificent Roman Arena built during the first century AD, and was obviously the scene of more bloody events than any depicted in the operas now performed there. There is room for more than 20,000 people in the Arena, and it is invariably packed to capacity. Its very size cries out for spectacular productions of works with large choruses. The orchestra is nearly 150 strong, the chorus over 200, and in operas like *Aida* up to 800 'extras' are engaged. The favourite works over the years have been *Aida*, *Turandot*, *Mefistofele* and *La Gioconda*, and it was in the last-named opera that Callas made her European debut in 1947, the same year that her 'rival', Renata Tebaldi, sang in the Arena for the first time, as Marguerite in *Faust*.

Although the Arena audience includes opera fans from all over the world it remains predominantly Italian. The audience can be as cruel in its shouted comments as is the one in Parma, not so many miles away. One's first visit to a performance in the Arena is breathtaking; and as the lights are dimmed each one of the thousands of spectators on the stone tiers of the amphitheatre lights a candle, applauded by those sitting in relative comfort in the body of the Arena.

As well as *Don Carlos*, the two other operas given in 1969 were *Turandot* and *Aida*. The first I heard, the second I decided to miss. The entertainment on the *Turandot* evening began long before the music, with jugglers, acrobats, fire-eaters and the like arriving in ancient Peking and delighting the huge audience; later, those extras participated in the opera itself. Peking, as designed by Pier Luigi Pizzi, looked very splendid, and Princess Turandot herself made her first appearance high up in the Palace balcony seemingly hundreds of yards away; and the Old Emperor was enthroned even higher.

The Turandot at the first few performances that summer had been Birgit Nilsson, but by the time of the Conference she had forsaken ancient China in favour of legendary Cornwall, as she had departed for Bayreuth to sing Isolde. Her replacement was the Czechoslovak soprano, Hana Janku, a worthy substitute. The part of the unknown Prince was sung by a Rumanian tenor called Ludovic Spies – large and impressive as to figure, rather less so as a voice. His publicity agents had plastered Verona with his picture in an obvious attempt to influence the audience, who, like myself, did not approve of the way he tried to compensate for his small voice by bawling out his top notes with disastrous results. I was reminded of what Ernest Newman had written about Giovanni Martinelli's singing of Calaf at Covent Garden in 1937, when he remarked that although Martinelli's voice might not have had the volume and brilliance that some parts of the score demanded,

> 'his phrasing and nuances were full of exquisite subtleties; and for once "Nessun norma" was sung in the musing half-tone that Puccini has prescribed for it, and not bellowed at us fortissimo for the sole glorification of the tenor. Above all Martinelli made Calaf not only a prince, but also a gentleman.'

It was during that 1937 season that Newman, bemoaning the generally poor standard of singing in the Italian operas, suggested that perhaps it was the combination of *verismo* opera and open-air performances that had contributed to the general decline of singing, adding that 'Italy had ceased to be the land of *bel canto* and become the land of *mal aria!*'

To return, however, to the Verona of 1969. *Don Carlos* was staged by the great French producer Jean Vilar with stark evocative settings designed by Luciano Damiani. Although the beautiful Fontainebleau act was unfortunately omitted, a fact on which I commented in my lecture to the Verdi Conference a few days later, the performance certainly did justice to one of Verdi's greatest operas. There was fine singing from Montserrat Caballé as Elisabeth de Valois, Placido Domingo as Carlos, and Piero Cappuccilli as Posa. Caballé, who had suffered a bad fall a few weeks earlier, had the help of two walking sticks to support her not inconsiderable weight. Yet, by means of a few well-chosen gestures, facial expression, and vocal acting, she managed to convey the full gamut of Elisabeth's emotions. Rarely have I heard the Queen's farewell to her lady-in-waiting, the Countess of Aremberg (both verses fortunately allowed on that occasion), so movingly delivered; and her singing of her two duets with Carlos, in which one hears the beautiful themes of the Fontainebleau act, made one regret more than ever its exclusion. Caballé's performances at that time promised much; indeed I was so impressed by what I heard from her on that occasion that I wrote in *Opera* 'Caballé is a natural singer, her phrasing is like that of an instrumentalist. Not since Callas in her hey-day has there been such an interpreter of Italian opera.' Would that she had continued that way.

Domingo was a revelation as Carlos, possessing as he did, and still does, one of the most beautifully produced tenor voices and one that is used with taste; and has indeed surpassed the promise that he then showed. The Italian mezzo-soprano, Fiorenza Cossotto, sang the Princess Eboli with little finesse, but she delighted most of the audience with her superb voice and uninhibited use of it. Cappuccilli's career was then some twelve years old, and he had already become something of a Verdi specialist. Without having the imagination and personality of Tito Gobbi, he continued to be the leading Italian Verdi baritone until the emergence a few years ago of Renato Bruson.

The Verdi Conference opened on 30 July but as I was unable to arrive in Verona until August, I missed the first few sessions; none the less, there was more than enough to digest during the remaining few days. In fact, too much was attempted, something in the region of sixty papers being read; and since there had been little attempt at preliminary co-ordination there was a great deal of overlapping of subject matter. In the absence of simultaneous translation, the poorer linguists among us had a rather thin time, and there were large gaps in the audience when papers were being read in languages not understood by large sections of those attending.

Despite some rather dull papers from a number of German and Italian contributors, there was still a great deal of both enjoyment and instruction to be had from the congress; and the Anglo-Saxon contingent, including Andrew Porter, Desmond Shawe-Taylor, Charles Osborne and Julian Budden, made some distinguished contributions. The subject of my own paper was *The Rediscovery of Don Carlos in our Day*; in it I suggested that it was the famous Covent Garden production of 1958 that had done more than any other revival to reveal what a great opera *Don Carlos* is. I described the magic of the Fontainebleau act in Visconti's production,

'A model of scenic perspective, colour and lighting; with the castle in the distance, and the lights in its windows appearing as if by magic as autumnal night fell and we heard the extraordinarily beautiful music unfold as Carlos and Elisabeth declared their love for one another – music that returns again and again during the course of the opera whenever Carlos and Elisabeth meet, and which is so nostalgically recalled by Elisabeth in her great scene and aria "Tu che la vanità" in the last act. To cut the Fontainebleau act has the same effect as cutting the Otello–Desdemona love duet from Verdi's *Otello* – and who would think of doing that?'

I spoke about Giulini's position in Italian musical life, prefacing my remarks by making an apology for criticizing my hosts, something I had always considered to be bad manners. I told the audience that in England we regarded Giulini as the greatest conductor to have emerged from Italy since Toscanini, and that we found it increasingly difficult to understand just why he was all but neglected in his native country by the musical establishment. 'That he was not appearing regularly at La Scala was a scandal,' I continued, 'and that he was not acknowledged by his compatriots as one of the greatest Verdi interpreters of all times, seemed very strange.' It was Giulini, I stressed, who as far as British opera-goers were concerned, had rediscovered *Don Carlos*.

My discourse was given on the penultimate day of the conference which by then had moved to Parma, to the home of the Verdi Institute itself. I recollect it was a very, very hot afternoon, and during the rather boring paper that preceded my own, I was amused to see my colleague Desmond Shawe-Taylor, who had removed his shoes, fast asleep. But my most vivid memory of the whole conference had nothing to do with *Don Carlos* at all; it was of Sir Isaiah Berlin, who although attending some of the sessions in Verona did not actually read a paper himself, leading a group of us, including Charles Osborne, his friend Ken Thompson, Phyllis and myself to one of Verona's most famous restaurants, the *Dodici Apostoli*. He walked as quickly as he talked, that is at almost break-neck speed, which was hardly the sensible thing to do in the mid-day heat of Verona. But it was worth it, for we had an unforgettable meal.

The conference had been preceded by a five-week stay at the Villa Schifanoia, a Medici villa half-way between Florence and Fiesole; it was formerly the home of Myron Taylor, the American Ambassador to the Vatican, who had made it over to the Vatican to house the Department of Fine Arts of Rosary College, a Catholic postgraduate school, whose main home was in Chicago. Each year a summer school for music students was held in the beautiful villa under the direction of the pianist Orazio Frugoni, one of those cultured Italo–American musicians who was a great opera enthusiast and was related by marriage to the famous mezzo-soprano Giulietta Simionato. He had made himself known to Phyllis and myself when we were in Florence in 1968 and suggested that I might like to come and teach a course on the history of opera the following year. I agreed, for it was an opportunity too tempting to refuse; and, although it meant a great deal of preparatory work, including the putting of countless music examples on tape, it was worth the effort.

The students on this summer course included several non-Catholics, nearly all Americans. There were a number of young nuns, presided over by Sister Michele of the Dominican order; they all wore modern dress, and could not have been nicer. The main aim of all concerned was to gain extra credits for their degrees, and therefore they had to submit a couple or more essays, and undergo a *viva voce* examination at the end of the five weeks, so that I could grade them.

Part of the time while I was at the Villa coincided with two other musical events in Florence: the Cassado cello competition and a UNESCO conference on 'Opera and Ballet on Television' organized by my friend Jack Bornoff. One of the adjudicators of the cello competition was Slava Rostropovich who also had one of his pupils playing – they both came to lunch at the Villa as also did Yehudi Menuhin – I believe one of the pupils from his school was also participating in the competition. I remember an hilarious evening with Yehudi, Frugoni and some of the students in a local *trattoria*, when we all let our hair down and imitated well-known singers and conductors.

I am always amazed how educational standards differ in England and America; most of these post-graduate students, some in their early twenties, had only reached the equivalent of 'A' levels, certainly as far as their ability to express themselves in writing was concerned; and their knowledge of their chosen subject, music and opera, was often elementary. To be fair, I had found the same situation existing when I used to lecture to the students at the London Opera Centre. I assumed, for example, that young singers embarking on an operatic career would have heard of Gluck's reforms, of the change in orchestral pitch that took place last century, of what *bel canto* meant; but it was rare to find a student who did, and that often meant the simplification of the syllabus I had prepared.

The weeks at Schifanoia and the conference in Verona were the climax of a particularly exhausting six months which had included a winter visit to Munich for the new production of *The Ring*, a spring trip to Milan to hear Beverly Sills make her European debut at La Scala in Rossini's *L'Assedio di Corinto*, and a short stop in Geneva on the way home from Italy to hear Michael Langdon as Osmin in *Die Entführung aus dem Serail*, followed by hours of frustration at Geneva Airport after the cancellation of a BEA flight back to London that resulted in my missing the première of Humphrey Searle's new opera *Hamlet* at Covent Garden. As that piece apparently turned out to be rather less than a world-shattering event, it probably did not matter all that much. The year ended with a visit to Paris to hear the Bolshoi Opera in performances of *Boris Godunov*, *Prince Igor* and *Eugene Onegin*.

I had to refuse invitations to participate in the Verdi Conference of 1972 in Milan and the following year in Turin, the latter with reluctance as it coincided with the opening of the rebuilt Teatro Regio with *Vespri Siciliani*. But I gladly agreed to participate in the 1974 conference in Chicago which was organized in collaboration with that city's Lyric Opera and whose main themes were 'Verdi in America', *Simon Boccanegra*, and 'Verdi in the World' (an odd title). It was a splendid affair with the number of social functions, organized with that generous hospitality that only the Americans seem to display, almost outnumbering the purely cultural events. Lee Freeman, a wealthy Chicago lawyer, and his wife contributed a very large sum of money which made the conference possible.

The British contingent was even stronger than it had been at Verona, including as it did George Harewood, Julian Budden, Charles Osborne, Andrew Porter, Desmond Shawe-Taylor and myself. There were more than sixty delegates from all over the world, and the participation of such distinguished figures as Saul Bellow, Luciano Berio, Roman Vlad and Joseph Kerman, to say nothing of Maria Callas, whom Carol Fox, the Lyric Opera's director, had persuaded to talk at one of the sessions about 'Singing Verdi', ensured the success of the conference, at least as far as attendances and public interest were concerned. Some of the 'round table' discussions and papers read also contributed a good deal to

Verdi scholarship. But as at Verona, the week was really heavy going. Even when at university I had never attended so many lectures in so short a period, and many of the contributors blithely ignored the official directive which requested that papers should be between twenty and thirty minutes long – some of the delegates spoke for nearly an hour, and one afternoon session lasted from 1.30 p.m. until nearly 6.00 p.m. All this, coupled with the fact that several papers were given in Italian, which necessitated close concentration by means of headphones to the simultaneous translation, meant that many of us left Chicago somewhat battered and suffering from an excess of verbiage. It was very noticeable that the British and American participants, to a man, kept to the required time limit.

The Callas afternoon deserves chronicling as it was one of the very few occasions when she talked in public about opera, if only in the vaguest and most general terms. It had been announced that she was going to talk on 'Some considerations on singing Verdi', but as she had come to Chicago quite unprepared to do this, she announced, or rather Bill Weaver who introduced her and chaired the session did on her behalf, that she would answer questions put to her by Congress participants and members of the public. What happened was that she answered those questions she approved of and turned others into the kind of questions she wanted to be asked. She astounded us all by saying that she thought all operas were far too long and that therefore she approved of cuts. 'What would you cut from *La traviata*?' she was asked. 'Most certainly the baritone aria in Act 2 [the famous 'Di Provenza'],' she replied in all seriousness; a remark that could hardly have endeared her to any baritone worth his salt! Taking courage into both hands I stood up and asked her whether she approved of the practice of singing *Don Carlos* and *Vêpres Siciliennes* in Italian translations rather than in the original French. 'Of course,' she replied, 'Italian is the only possible language in which to sing opera, anyway.' (I was so taken aback by that reply that I failed to follow it up by reminding her that when we had discussed the subject in London a few years earlier she was of the opposite point of view.) Callas also suggested that artists, singers and conductors often know better than the composer; and she suggested that Serafin, to whom she owed so much, was 'gospel' as far as tradition was concerned. This brought Charles Osborne to his feet to remind Maria that the artist is, after all, the servant of the composer, and not vice versa.

It was Andrew Porter who raised what was probably the most important question of the week in the introductory remarks to his paper, suggesting that if these conferences were to be of any practical use then there should be some kind of co-operation between the musicologists on the one hand and those responsible for putting on opera on the other. 'What for example is the use of finding out what Verdi intended in his two versions of *Boccanegra*,' he asked, 'if producers, singers and conductors either ignore the composer's intentions and continue to perpetuate bad traditions?' Loud applause from the audience, and a large 'boo' from Carol Fox, director of the Lyric Opera who had been sitting at the back of the hall and who, accompanied by her assistant, then walked out. But Andrew was right as he so often is. The answers to his questions were there for all to see and hear in the Lyric Opera's performance of *Boccanegra*, in which it was obvious that the Italian producer, Giorgio De Lullo, had signally failed to imbue his cast with much insight into the various relationships and tensions inherent in the opera, and so the cast was left mostly to its own resources, which in the far too large Civil Auditorium meant singing and acting in an old-fashioned and big-gesture manner, while the chorus, standing in serried ranks, never became involved in the action. The conductor, Bruno Bartoletti, a sensitive and cultured musician, but without the strong personality that makes it possible for him to communicate or impose his ideas on the forces under his command, was unable to persuade his cast to observe musical niceties; and there was far too much stopping for applause which American audiences are generally indiscriminate in bestowing on singers, good, bad, or indifferent.

Far more exciting was the performance and production of Verdi's *Vespri Siciliani* that I heard at the Metropolitan in New York, just over a week later, even though it was sung, much to Andrew's chagrin, in Italian rather than the original French. It was excitingly conducted by James Levine and produced by John Dexter who, unlike De Lullo, concentrated on relationships between characters, making them behave like real people rather than the cardboard figures they so often are in what I and my colleagues have come to call 'instant opera' – i.e. performances in which stars fly in and then with the minimum of rehearsal proceed to give the same individual performances as they do on half a dozen international stages.

I decided after the Chicago Conference that I would not, in the future, allow myself to be tempted to accept invitations to participate in similar events. Instead I would confine myself to taking part in 'round table' discussions, sitting on juries at International Singing Competitions – though those could take me away from my desk for anything up to a week. As far as lectures were concerned, I had, over the years, built up a considerable repertory; and I have no scruples at all about repeating them.

20

Anniversaries and Celebrations in the Seventies

———

During the 1970s there was a plethora of operatic anniversaries; post-war Covent Garden celebrated its Silver Jubilee in 1970, and this coincided with David Webster's twenty-five years as general administrator; *Opera* and its editor celebrated their Silver Jubilees in 1975 and 1978 respectively; Bayreuth had its hundredth birthday in 1976; and I had my sixtieth the following year.

David Webster had decided to retire at the end of the 1969–70 season; his health had been failing for several months and as Solti was to end his ten-year period as music director the following year, 1970, David thought it a fitting time to retire. His own and Covent Garden's post-war achievements were to be marked by an exhibition at the Victoria and Albert Museum, organized by the museum, the Opera House, the Friends of Covent Garden and the Arts Council, which was planned to open in mid-August 1971, and to last for two months. Sadly, David was never to see it, for he died three months before the exhibition opened; however, he had sat in on some of the early planning meetings of the Exhibition Committee, on which he had invited me to serve. I was asked to advise on, and contribute to, the splendid Exhibition Catalogue which sold for a pound, and which I see from recent specialist booksellers' catalogues has become something of a collector's item. As well as writing the 'Introduction to the Royal Opera' for the catalogue, I contributed short essays on 'British Singers Abroad', '*Tosca* and Puccini' and '*Aida* and Verdi' and gave a lecture at the museum during the course of the exhibition on 'The Emergence of the British Singer'.

Some twenty pages of the July 1970 *Opera* were devoted to David, including a splendid article by George, and tributes from Boris

Christoff, Tito Gobbi, Geraint Evans and several other artists. I selected twenty-five photographs to illustrate my own personal choice of that number of memorable evenings at Covent Garden during D. W.'s tenure of office; these included the return of Flagstad as Isolde in 1948, the first *Wozzeck* under Kleiber in 1952 and Callas's debut as Norma the same year, the opening night of the Kubelik régime (*Otello*) in 1955, *The Trojans* in 1957, the famous *Don Carlos* the following year, the return of Callas in *Tosca* in 1964, and *Moses and Aaron* in 1965; a truly representative cross-section of the operatic achievements of David's period as general administrator, and one of which any opera house might be proud.

On 30 June, that year, there was a Gala Performance at Covent Garden attended by the Queen Mother and Prince Charles. Three dozen or more singers, seven conductors, the orchestra and chorus all participated. The programme included items sung by artists who had begun in the chorus in the 1940s and had since become international stars, like Charles Craig, Michael Langdon and Josephine Veasey; by artists who had begun their careers in small rôles and had been nurtured by D. W. to become stars in their own right, like Joan Sutherland and Geraint Evans. Other participants included those singers whom David had himself engaged, such as Jon Vickers, and several non-British singers who had been regular visitors to Covent Garden and had become part of the Royal Opera's family; Regina Resnik and Tito Gobbi were among these. It was a memorable evening and was followed by speeches and, of course, a splendid party.

Five years later, *Opera* celebrated its twenty-fifth anniversary. We had purposely refrained from having a twenty-first birthday party in 1971 because we thought it would sound much more impressive to say that the magazine had survived for a quarter of a century than merely to have attained its majority! Of course, we had a special anniversary number with only the second colour cover in our history – a montage of twenty of our best covers. The issue ran to 128 pages of which about forty were advertising, and we charged our normal cover price, which then was 35p. I managed to assemble an impressive list of contributors for the number including George, Isaiah Berlin, Sir Adrian Boult, Antonia Fraser, Hans Werner Henze, Peter Hall and Gunther Rennert; and there were eight pages of birthday greetings from singers, conductors and opera house directors.

Splashing out, I arranged for a lunch-time birthday party for nearly two hundred people to be given in the Crush Bar of the Royal Opera House on 6 February. It was a splendid occasion, with Sergeant Martin, Covent Garden's famous 'linkman', announcing the guests, and Phyllis and I greeting them at the top of the staircase. There were singers from both the London houses; some international celebrities too, like Placido Domingo, Janet Baker, Reri Grist, and Georg Solti who, with his wife, had flown in that morning from Chicago and driven straight to the Opera House from Heathrow. We very nearly did not have any copies of the anniversary issue to distribute to our guests, for the printers in Scarborough, whose ideas of keeping to a schedule were erratic to say the least, had not delivered the copies on time; one of the firm's directors whom I had invited to the party, arrived shortly before the first guests were due with just enough copies to go round. (A few months later we changed to new printers in Bournemouth!) The BBC also did me proud, and as well as talking about the twenty-five years of the magazine's life with John Amis on a Sunday morning music programme, I was invited to take part in Woman's Hour.

I was touched and surprised to read an editorial devoted to our birthday in the American *Opera News* a few weeks later, in which the editor, Robert Jacobson, paid handsome tribute to its English counterpart, saying that the magazine's 'Coming Events' section was 'indispensable as a source of information, and its review coverage impressive in scope'. Like several American readers, Bob Jacobson noticed 'from time to time a chauvinism for anything English emerging, building up reputations of certain UK singers who, when venturing out into the international world, have not always lived up to their advance billing'. He concluded '*Opera* sought to promote and to build the foundations of opera at home. That so much is now flourishing [in Great Britain] must be a source of pride to the editor and his staff.' It certainly was – and, more important, still is.

I don't know why I decided to have a party for my sixtieth birthday; I suppose I regarded it as some kind of watershed; and as I had missed out on my fiftieth, being in New York at the time, I welcomed an excuse for having a celebration at home. Phyllis and I thought it would be a good idea to mix our guests so as to have a cross-section of friends from the world of opera as well as family friends and relations. One of the best-kept family secrets was that Simon was flying over from Boston specially for the occasion.

In order to include several operatic artists it was necessary to find a date as near as possible to my actual birthday on which they were not singing – and that, as anyone who had to plan a series of performances knows, is not easy. After several false starts we found that 6 October, a Saturday night, was the most convenient for nearly everybody; and on that evening Woodland Rise took on a decidedly operatic flavour with Janet Baker, Josephine Barstow, Ande Anderson, Charles Mackerras (who came on in full evening dress after conducting *La Bohème* at the Coliseum), George and Patricia, and several of my colleagues joining in the celebrations. My diaries reveal that my next two birthdays were just as operatic, for in 1978 I was in San Francisco and in 1979 on the way home from Tokyo where I had been with the Royal Opera.

In the San Francisco company in 1978, as so often before during Kurt Adler's régime, there was a strong British contingent, and Richard Lewis and his wife arranged a surprise birthday party for me at one of those splendid restaurants on Fisherman's Walk, to which he had invited several artists including David Atherton, Raimund Herincx, Forbes Robinson, Paul Hudson and Francis Egerton. A nice and much appreciated gesture towards a critic!

Between the magazine's Silver Jubilee in 1975 and my sixtieth birthday in 1977, a far more important and impressive celebration had taken place: the centenary of the Bayreuth Festival, for which a new production of the *Ring* had been planned. I had seen each of the four previous new Bayreuth *Rings* of the post-war period – two each by Wieland and Wolfgang Wagner – and was just as eager to see the fifth, which would mark the first *Ring* to be staged there by someone outside the Bayreuth family. It was to be a completely French team that was to undertake the mammoth task, for Wolfgang had invited Pierre Boulez to conduct, and Boulez had specially asked for Patrice Chéreau as his producer – and that meant him being accompanied by his team of designers and assistants. In other words, that most German of all music festivals was to be taken over by a French artistic team for its centenary production. As I jokingly said to some friends, the new *Ring* was France's revenge for the Franco-Prussian war; and certainly in the upper parts of the house, there were, on several evenings, an exchange of blows between young French and German members of the audience, and arguments were heatedly carried on until the small hours in the Bayreuth restaurants, with members of the Chéreau team being booed on their entrance. But that was nothing like the booing that broke out in the theatre after each performance; but I suppose Wagner would have enjoyed the furore himself, for he was, after all, one of the arch-revolutionaries of all time.

In recent years booing has become as common at Bayreuth as in most other opera houses, a fact partly explained by the change in the make-up of audiences and partly by the decision made towards the end of the 1960s to allow curtain calls after each act and solo calls at the end of the evening rather than just raising the curtain two or three times on the final tableau. The conductor, who in the famous Bayreuth covered pit can sit, as do the orchestra, in shirt-sleeves and without a tie, now has to dash from the pit at the end of the performance to put on a dark suit or dinner jacket in order to take his curtain call.

The changes in the whole atmosphere at Bayreuth that followed the death of Wieland Wagner in 1966 were certainly noticeable when I returned there in 1971 after an absence of six years. The audiences were more fashionable, resembling the smart Karajan-set of Salzburg, with the women bejewelled and be-minked, and the men often pomaded and as heavily-scented as their female companions. The average age of the audience also seemed to have fallen, and it is often the younger elements among them who give voice at the end of the evening – many obviously basing their standards of criticism on gramophone recordings. Although the audience is predominantly a German one, far more French, English, Italian and especially Japanese can now be heard during the intervals. The Japanese also seem to have introduced the habit of bringing their infuriating little tape-recorders with them, and on more than one occasion the quieter moments in a performance have been spoiled for me by the gentle whirring of their machines, even though they are often concealed beneath the kimonos of the ladies who operate them for their husbands!

A characteristic sound of the old Bayreuth was the noise made by the audience lowering the cane-chairs, which had probably been there since the theatre opened, and then lowering themselves into them. There was little or no give in the seats, so that changing one's position to get more comfortable was not a silent operation and was generally met with loud shushes from one's neighbours. The new wooden seats have even less give than their predecessors, and although cushions are not hired out as they are at Verona or Savonlinna in Finland, they are to be recommended.

That 1971 summer was one of the hottest of post-war summers; but everything at Bayreuth is measured by or related to a previous Bayreuth Festival. So I was told that the excessive heat was the worst anyone could remember since the year before Siegfried Wagner's death, which was a very convoluted way of saying that it was the hottest Bayreuth summer since 1929. The timing of *Parsifal*, be it conducted by Knappertsbusch or Horst Stein, is always compared with the timings of Toscanini in 1930 and 1931, and so on. Applause and curtain calls, being a more recent phenomenon, do not have records going back very far; but their length is chronicled and timed; and the length of applause after the third performance of *Götterdämmerung* in the fifth and final year of the Chéreau *Ring* in 1980 has gone down as the longest kind of public demonstration in Bayreuth's history, lasting more than an hour – which is longer than the last act of the opera itself. That will doubtless become the yardstick against which all future ovations for a Bayreuth *Ring* will be measured.

When the Chéreau-Boulez *Ring* was first disclosed in 1976 it seemed to some like a bad dream, to others a stimulating and thought-provoking experience, and to yet others, including myself, an error of judgement on the part of Wolfgang Wagner and his colleagues. Yet during its successive repetitions until 1980 it gradually came to be accepted by more and more Wagnerians who made their pilgrimage to Bayreuth. The publicity it initially received, mostly because of the adverse reviews, obviously helped the Bayreuth box office, for although many of the 'old guard' refused to return, the French contingent increased in numbers to compensate.

Not all the singers were happy with it initially either, and one, Karl Ridderbusch, refused to sing Hunding and Hagen again in the production; others, like Gwyneth Jones, Donald McIntyre and Peter Hofmann, found much to praise in the new approach, and were enthusiastic about working with Chéreau. Quite a number of the

Bayreuth Orchestra were unhappy with Boulez's rehearsing methods and conducting, and encouraged, it is said, by Horst Stein, who had conducted several *Rings* in the previous production, refused to return the following year.

Chereau's experience at producing opera was, until Bayreuth in 1976, limited to *Les Contes d'Hoffmann* in Paris and *L'Italiana in Algeri* at the Spoleto Festival, hardly the most suitable preparation one would have thought to face the challenge of a *Ring* cycle anywhere, least of all at Bayreuth in its centenary year. It was, as I have said, Boulez who insisted that Chéreau should be engaged, but that was after attempts to get Ingmar Bergman and Peter Stein had failed! Perhaps it was just as well that Peter Stein did not accept Bayreuth's invitation, for he said he would like to produce the *Ring* without music, letting the words speak for themselves! That Chéreau and his team approached their task seriously has never been denied, it was the method they employed that upset so many people.

It would take a whole book to analyse in detail the Chéreau *Ring* and to illustrate how he staged each of the Tetralogy's seventeen scenes – indeed two such books were published in 1981 to coincide with the release of the complete recording and the filming for television of this *Ring*, which for better or worse has now been preserved for posterity. In a short phrase Chéreau staged the *Ring* as a black comedy, cutting the Wagnerian gods and goddesses down to size, and placing the action and costumes at the time of the first production of the *Ring*. This idea worked well enough for the first two operas, but far less so for *Siegfried* and *Götterdämmerung* where the time-scale went all awry. Chéreau's idea of uniting the work's mythological elements with the Industrial Revolution on the one hand and the power politics of the twentieth century on the other just did not work.

In a way I was sorry that I did not return to Bayreuth in the intervening years to see how Chéreau had modified his conception, or to hear how, or if, Boulez's dry, analytical approach to the music had changed. Each of them spoke of both interpreters and public alike not being able to see the wood for the trees,

'One would like at times to discover a work without knowing anything about it all [said Boulez] like those archaeologists who have only a piece of broken pottery to go on in their researches and are thus forced to discover the intrinsic qualities of creation on the evidence of one simple object.'

Chéreau and Boulez certainly scored a joint success with both critics and public in 1979 when they joined forces again for the first performance of the complete *Lulu* at the Paris Opéra, one of those institutions that Boulez had once said he would like to see blown up.

My lengthy review of the Bayreuth *Ring* in our autumn festival number brought forth a tribute from an unexpected quarter. By then, Walter Legge and I were on the friendliest of terms and his long letters, nearly always hand-written, arrived with amazing regularity; they were as witty and perceptive as his conversation. In our November 1976 issue we published a ten-page article by him on Lotte Lehmann, who had died in August that year; and Walter wrote to thank me for the way it was presented and for the choice of illustrations:

'Dear Rosevale [he began – he always chose a ridiculous nickname for me] What should I do first, thank you or congratulate you? In all modesty I find the Lehmann piece as it stands excellent although I says it as shouldn't. I hope you have no complaints. My congratulations too on two of your pieces. Bayreuth – yours is the only sensibly balanced essay on the fracas I've read and I've savoured the major part of the German, Austrian, Italian, French and English criticisms. The other on Baker.'

(I had reproduced a transcript of a conversation I had had with Janet Baker about her work in opera and her artistic *credo* in the same issue as Legge's Lehmann piece had appeared.)

I wish it were possible to publish a selection of extracts from the letters that Walter wrote to me between 1970 and his death nine years later; they were full of nuggets of information about artists past and present – often I am sure libellous – but amusing and knowledgeable. I cannot refrain from quoting from one letter he wrote me in the summer of 1975, when in replying to one of his regular requests for information about a famous singer's activities – in this case the German soprano Meta Seinemeyer in pre-war Dresden – I said how much I envied him having heard her at Covent

Garden in 1929, and also, a few years previously, what I had always regarded as a legendary performance of *Don Giovanni* under Bruno Walter. In his next letter Walter wrote:

'Don't bemoan the *Don Giovannis* with that, on paper, enviable cast. Stabile wobbled and ogled, Lehmann and Leider behaved like tetchy and avaricious Berlin Boarding-House proprietresses, and Krauss, known to the frequenters of the gallery and amphitheatre as 'lavatory Krauss' because the sounds he made belonged there. Aquistapace (Leporello) was a ridiculous choice when Pasero was about. I heard all the performances and left each one disillusioned. Don't tell a soul, but although Schumann sang exquisitely she was too damned ladylike for Zerlina or for Susanna.'

The last anniversary of the 1970s I would like to mention briefly was my own silver jubilee as editor in the summer of 1978. I do not consciously remember thinking that the event should be celebrated in any way whatsoever, but my colleagues obviously did. During the 1970s there had been a number of changes in the composition of the magazine's editorial board. In the summer of 1970 Philip Hope-Wallace, who had joined the board in 1954, decided to cut down his activities, having reached the age of sixty; and although he continued to contribute to the pages of *Opera* until a few months before his death in September 1979, his presence at our occasional editorial meetings was greatly missed. Charles Osborne, an operamaniac who had studied singing and worked in literary and musical journalism before coming to England from Australia in 1953, replaced him. In 1966 he joined the Arts Council and later became its Literature Director. His passion is Verdi, and he has proved a valuable board member. In January 1973 Rodney Milnes joined our ranks, and in 1975 Elizabeth Forbes.

Rodney, whom I first met, as he has reminded me more than once, when I went to give a lecture to the *Opera Club* in Oxford, was and is essentially a shy person. I believe I have played an important rôle in drawing him out of his shell and helping him develop his career; I know I was largely instrumental in getting him invited to contribute a record review to the BBC's regular Saturday morning programme. Anyway, Rodney has proved not only an invaluable member of the board, becoming associate editor with

Alan Blyth in 1976, but also has become a loyal friend. Elizabeth, who forsook the safe haven of an antiquarian book shop in Mayfair for the more risky and exciting life of a freelance journalist, has also proved her worth as a member of *Opera*'s team. There is no operatic fringe event throughout the length and breadth of the country that she will not dash off to hear, and more recently she has ferreted out performances of rare works in the German and Swiss opera houses to attend.

It was Rodney, I believe, who set in motion the various events that surrounded my twenty-fifth anniversary as editor. These included a blush-making 'tribute' in the June issue of *Opera* in 1978 entitled 'The Boss' which I did not see until the magazine was printed because, as Rodney wrote, 'It is the first issue of the magazine for 25 years in which its editor does not know – in broad detail if not down to the last comma, inserted in page-proof – what is going to appear.' My other associate editor, Alan Blyth, was responsible for a short feature headed 'Singing his Praises' that appeared in the *Daily Telegraph* during the week that the June issue of *Opera* was published; the final paragraph read:

> 'The opera world is vying with itself to pay him tribute. Lord Harewood, his predecessor as editor of *Opera*, gives a lunch for him next Tuesday, Colin Davis a party on the Wednesday, John Tooley a lunch later in the month and Scottish Opera, due to the pressure of invitations, a party at the Aix-en-Provence Festival in July.'

It was Alan and Rodney who helped organize the memorable lunch that George and Patricia gave for me at their London home; all the editorial board, except Andrew who was in New York, were present and, except for Phyllis and Patricia, no wives or other partners were invited. Andrew sent a letter which was read out at the lunch: 'Please count me there in spirit, in affection, and appreciation of a "force for good" – for taking opera seriously over a long cumulative span,' he wrote.

Colin Davis's party was held at Covent Garden in 'Room 37', one of the three rooms where the music director works high up in the opera house on the level with the 'flies'. It took place after the penultimate performance of *Tristan und Isolde* which Colin was conducting that season with Jon Vickers and the American soprano

Roberta Knie in the title-rôles; they, together with the rest of the cast, had been invited to the party as had also several of my Covent Garden 'friends' and some of Colin's colleagues. Colin put his box at the disposal of Phyllis and myself that evening. I had been to the first *Tristan* of the season some two weeks earlier and my review for the July *Opera* had already been written:

> 'This was one of the truly great operatic evenings in Covent Garden's post-war history; it certainly was one of the finest *Tristan und Isolde* performances I have ever attended. As far as Jon Vickers was concerned, his acting and singing throughout the long evening, culminating in a last act of searing intensity, made him the best Tristan I have ever seen and heard – and that includes the legendary Lauritz Melchior, who was never much of an actor anyway! Except for Callas's Violetta, Vickers's Tristan was the greatest piece of operatic acting I have experienced. ... Sharing the evening's triumph were the magnificent Covent Garden Orchestra and Colin Davis whose fiery, committed, and exciting account of this wonderful score would alone have made this an evening to remember.'

I wonder what I would have done about that party had the *Tristan* performance been a bad one and I had been forced to write an unfavourable review. In any case, Colin's invitation had come to me at least two full weeks before the first night! Unfortunately, the performance on the night of the party ran into difficulties. It was obvious that Vickers was not in his best voice, and by the end of the second act he was clearly in vocal trouble. The second interval dragged on and on, and Paul Findlay, John Tooley's assistant, came up to us in the Crush Bar to tell us that Vickers could not finish the opera and that Colin would make an announcement from the stage. The interval bells rang, the audience, in ignorance of what was in store for them, filtered back, and, as there was a further delay, the gallery started a slow hand-clap. Then Colin appeared and announced that Vickers was unable to continue and that they would begin Act III with Isolde's entrance. After a few seconds of astonished silence, there were shouts from the audience of 'Give us our money back!' An understandable demand from those who had paid up to £18 for their tickets; they had not, however, read the small print on the back of them, which states among the 'conditions of sale' that 'If the performance has to be interrupted money is not refunded if more than half of it has taken place'.

Of course, Jon Vickers went straight home to bed, and I was sad that he could not come to the party, which reached its climax when the lights were suddenly switched off and Colin, who had momentarily disappeared, emerged from his inner office, carrying an enormous birthday cake suitably inscribed, with twenty-five candles alight. Roberta Knie, the Isolde of the evening, helped me blow them out.

The celebratory lunch arranged by John Tooley was held in the retiring room behind the royal box in the Opera House, and in addition to Phyllis and myself the guests included Garrett Drogheda, Claus and Mary Moser, John Tooley, Colin Davis and his wife, and Ken Davison. It was a relaxed and enjoyable occasion, with all of us letting our hair down.

I was touched and delighted by the many letters and telegrams I received, and cannot forbear from quoting two of them: one from Peter Pears (a telegram) and the other from Sir Robert Mayer (a letter). Peter's telegram read: 'Dear Harold, many jubilatory congratulations and much love from Peter Grimes, Quint, Herring, Vere, Aschenbach Pears'. While Sir Robert's letter began:

> 'By chance I spent today at home. Thus I learned of your celebration [this was because on 7 June I was guest of the week on the BBC's Woman's Hour programme] in which I wish to participate. The world in general lacks faith. But not you who has displayed plenty of it coupled with admirable courage. May the next 25 years be equally or probably even more successful.'

Despite Robert being not far short of his own hundredth birthday the letter was hand-written.

Perhaps the most unexpected event and one that gave me very great pleasure was being awarded a decoration by the Italian Government. A telephone call from the cultural attaché at the Italian Embassy was followed by an official letter from the Ambassador, Roberto Ducci, inviting Phyllis and myself to the Embassy to receive the decoration, of 'Cavaliere Ufficiale' of the Order 'Al merito della Repubblica Italiana'. When the citation was read out I learned that the award had been made for my services over a quarter of a century to opera in general and to promoting the cause of Italian music drama. As 'Peterborough' commented in his column in the *Daily Telegraph*, 'Harold in Italy, as Berlioz would have said'.

21

Memorable and not so Memorable Performances during the Seventies

———

Inevitably in a book of memoirs it is not possible (nor indeed was it my intention) to chronicle year by year all the performances I attended which for one reason or another I can still recall. Some of the post-war peaks like Callas's *Traviata*, the Giulini-Visconti *Don Carlos*, the Bayreuth Centenary *Ring* have quite easily fallen into place in the different sections of this book; and others, which made a youthful impression on me and helped to lay the foundations of my critical faculties have been described earlier on. However, there were some performances during the 1970s which I have been unable to bring into the main narrative and which I feel should be included. I make no apologies for gathering them all together now, except to say that, for me, they stand out as evenings I cannot forget. Of course, it is just as possible to recall performances that were so awful and which should be best forgotten, but because of their awfulness have remained in the memory, as it is to remember superlatively good ones.

One of those latter was Hans Hotter's operatic farewell in June 1972. Hotter was then sixty-two and had been singing in opera for more than forty years. He sang his first Wotan in 1934 in Hamburg and it is as a Wagner *Heldenbariton* that he will be remembered. He chose to make his last appearance in Act III of *Die Walküre*, the act in which Wotan bids a last farewell to his beloved daughter Brünnhilde; on this occasion Hotter was also bidding farewell to his public and the operatic stage. This event took place not, as one might have expected in Munich or Vienna, Covent Garden or Bayreuth, where

Hotter had reigned supreme as Wotan for so many years, but at the Paris Opéra; and as Bernard Lefort, the director of the Opéra, said in his speech from the stage, it was Hotter who was honouring the Paris Opéra by having chosen that house for his last performance.

It was a very moving occasion, and it was sad to have to realize that for the very last time one had seen that giant among Wagnerian gods stride onto the Valkyries' rock and then proceed to dominate the stage as no other Wotan had done during the preceding quarter of a century. Naturally time had not stood still, and Hotter's voice in 1972 was not what it had been in 1948 when we first heard him in London with Flagstad. But, aided by one's aural memory, we heard again those grandly-shaped phrases and that dark, resonant, slightly nasal, but very personal voice. And when Wotan, as he gazed fondly on his beloved Brünnhilde for the last time, came to the passage beginning with the words 'Der Augen leuchtendes Paar' the voice again became meltingly beautiful and his tender singing infinitely moving. It was one of those great moments in an opera house that those lucky and honoured enough to be present would always treasure.

After the final curtain, and in the presence of the whole cast and various officials of the Opéra, Hotter was presented with two medals, one from the Paris Opéra and the other from the Paris Wagner Society. Wisely Hotter made no verbal reply, he had let Wotan's final words be the last sounds we would hear from him on the operatic stage. And how touched he was at the small reception held after the performance when he was greeted by old friends and admirers from London.

At the Edinburgh Festival two months later, the Teatro Massimo of Palermo performed three operas at the King's Theatre: Bellini's *La straniera*, Rossini's *Elisabetta, Regina d'Inghilterra*, and Verdi's *Attila* – the performances were memorable for quite another reason. What looked most exciting on paper proved to be disappointing in the extreme, and for the first time at an Edinburgh Festival I saw ticket-holders in front of the theatre holding up tickets for sale rather than brandishing bank notes in the vain hope of buying one. Words like 'disaster', 'disgrace' and 'fiasco' were being bandied about Edinburgh that summer. *La straniera* just got by, despite Renata Scotto not being in good voice, but at least she displayed some knowledge of the *bel canto* style, which the other singers did not. *Attila* was given an unsubtle, provincial performance quite out of place at a festival; but it was in Rossini's opera that the nadir was reached. As I wrote: 'This had to be heard and seen to be believed.' It was one of the most depressing evenings I have ever spent in an opera house, and I had to keep asking myself whether this was an intentional travesty of Italian opera cleverly put on by Pierre Boulez, who had said that all opera houses should be blown up, or whether it really was as bad as I thought it was. 'Visually ugly and misconceived, non-produced, badly played, inadequately sung, except for a moment or two from the tenor, Pietro Bottazzo, it is best to draw a veil over the evening's proceedings.' The BBC obviously thought the same, for it cancelled a broadcast of a recording it had made of one of the performances to be put out two weeks later, and instead substituted a tape of the same opera which the Italian Radio had made for the BBC as its own special Coronation tribute to Queen Elizabeth II in 1953.

The Italians were put to shame that summer at Edinburgh; they were routed by the Scots' own company, Scottish Opera, whose production of Berlioz's *The Trojans* was a striking example of a musically-prepared opera. That alone would have made a journey to Edinburgh worth while for the opera-goer, and as so often happens when Janet Baker is singing in an opera, it was her evening. 'Her Dido remains one of the great interpretations in present-day opera,' I wrote. Fortunately, London was also able to hear it at Covent Garden shortly afterwards when she shared the rôle of Dido with Josephine Veasey. It had wisely been decided for those series of performances to sing the work in English, rather than in the assorted French accents that had marred the previous revival in 1969 when, because the work was going to be recorded, Philips Records and Covent Garden agreed to record the opera in Franglais obviously with the international market in mind. The decision to sing the work in English three years later was more than justified. Janet Baker was in inspired form and her performance cast a spell over the house. Dido's Farewell to Carthage and the death scene became one of those rare experiences in an opera house which was something to treasure.

It was Janet Baker's year in more senses than one, for at Glyndebourne, in Peter Hall's production of Monteverdi's *Il ritorno d'Ulisse in patria*, she sang the rôle of Penelope. In her hands and throat

Penelope emerged as one of the great figures in operatic literature. The stage pictures created by Peter Hall and his designer John Bury turned the scenes on earth into a Renaissance-like court, looking like reproductions by old masters. One rarely experiences such visual pleasure in an opera house, which was an added reason for the Glyndebourne *Ulisse* remaining vividly in my memory.

War and Peace is one of the great literary masterpieces and although Prokofiev's opera based on it may not count as one of the great musical achievements of the century, it is none the less a compelling piece of music theatre; and when performed as it was in 1972 by the English National Opera it is difficult to resist. It has certainly become one of my favourite operas, and, because its performances coincided with the BBC's excellent television serial of Tolstoy's novel, it drew large and enthusiastic audiences to the London Coliseum. Colin Graham, one of England's best operatic stage directors, is never so happy as when handling large crowds, and *War and Peace* with its ballroom scenes and battle scenes, brought out the best in him. There were some excellent individual performances as well: Josephine Barstow affecting and entirely credible as Natasha, Norman Bailey completely convincing as Marshal Kutuzov and Raymond Myers hardly less so as Napoleon. They, and indeed every single member of the enormous cast, looked as if they were really living their parts and not just behaving as opera-singers dressed up.

The following year (1973) brought yet another fine performance by Janet Baker: Mary Stuart in Donizetti's eponymous opera which she sang in the English National Opera's production in December. It is a strange opera in that the audience has to wait for nearly an hour after the curtain has risen (including in this case an interval) before the protagonist makes her first appearance. Then, when at the beginning of the second act, Janet Baker began to sing, walking in the gardens of Chatsworth and remembering her early life in France, the magic began to work. The mood engendered reminded me very much of that scene in Verdi's *Don Carlos* when Elisabeth de Valois recalls her happy youth at Fontainebleau. Janet Baker has, as had Callas, the gift of being able to make the listener believe that we are hearing the music she is singing for the very first time and that the ink is scarcely dry on the pages of the orchestral parts; and, again like Callas, has that rare ability to make the music she is singing seem much greater than it really is – this was especially the case in a work like *Maria Stuarda*.

Just as memorable that autumn were the performances of Peter Pears as Aschenbach in Britten's last opera, *Death in Venice*, of which the English Opera Group gave the first London performances at Covent Garden. It was a *tour-de-force*, for Pears, then aged sixty-three, was virtually on stage the whole evening; and although the rôle, which seemed far longer than Peter Grimes, was specially written for him by Britten, it is most demanding. Britten, already mortally ill by then, was sitting in a box, and, because the effort of getting down onto the stage to take a curtain call would have been physically too exhausting, he acknowledged the audience's acclamation from where he was sitting – a most moving moment.

Covent Garden had contributed one of those 'not so memorable' occasions a few weeks earlier when it staged a new production of *Tannhäuser*. That it got on to the stage at all was a miracle, for serious differences of opinion had developed between the producer, the Czech Vaclav Kaslík, and the conductor, Colin Davis. Charges and counter-charges were made and lurid accounts of tantrums and of various people storming off stage during rehearsals were current. Kaslík insisted on working with the designers Josef Svoboda and Jan Skálicky, the same team which had been responsible for a misbegotten attempt at Verdi's *Nabucco*, also conducted by Colin Davis, two years previously. One never ceases to wonder at the way opera house managements come to make decisions. After the fiasco of *Nabucco* it should have been perfectly obvious that a Kaslík–Svoboda–Skálicky *Tannhäuser* would likewise flounder – I sometimes think managements collectively have no visual sense at all! Mr Kaslík departed for home before the first night and the programme informed us that what we were seeing was a production 'conceived' by Mr Kaslík. Hidden away in small print elsewhere in the programme was the information that the assistant to the producer was one Elijah Moshinsky. It was his salvage operation that saved the evening from complete disaster and launched him on his successful career as an opera producer; in recent years his productions have included Covent Garden's excellent *Peter Grimes*, *Lohengrin*, *The Rake's Progress*, *Macbeth* and *Samson and Delilah*.

I will not easily forget my first visit to a Salzburg Easter Festival in early April 1974. It was Karajan's eighth 'Osterfestspiele' and it left me with mixed feelings. It was enjoyable to be in Salzburg when the weather was not unbearably hot and without being jostled off the pavements by crowds of tourists as one is at the summer festival; but one had to pay for it by mixing with the predominantly French and German smart Karajan jet-set audience – the exorbitant seat prices successfully ruled out a large British contingent from being there, though I did spot Edward Heath in the audience! It is ridiculous enough to put on evening dress for Glyndebourne after lunch and travel down by train from Victoria Station in the early afternoon, but at least the performances there continue into the evening; but to see an audience dressed up to the nines at four o'clock on Good Friday afternoon for a performance of Bach's B Minor Mass which was over before seven seemed ludicrous! All attempts at applause were quickly suppressed by Karajan looking like a shocked school-master at an unruly lower-fourth. The conductor's own sartorial effort was interesting; he was wearing a polo-necked shirt and the Berlin Philharmonic was in day clothes.

Of course, I did not go to Salzburg to hear the B Minor Mass but for a performance of *Die Meistersinger* for which I had inexplicably been invited, with Karajan's approval, to provide an essay in the programme. As so often before, I found that Karajan's conducting lacked heart and compassion, everything being so carefully calculated. Karajan was, as usual, his own producer, and the result was realistic and traditional. The huge stage of the new Festspielhaus had a rather empty look about it, especially in the great Act III finale; and by using the areas in front of the proscenium arch for sections of the extra chorus, a curious stereophonic effect was achieved, and on reflection, perhaps, that was exactly what Karajan wanted.

After Salzburg, we went to Vienna where we heard an outstanding performance of *Katya Kabanova* produced by Joachim Herz at the State Opera. This was the first production by Herz I had seen and, with his designer, Rudolf Heinrich, he built up on stage a stark, unromantic and very working-class looking small town, Kalinov, on the swamps of the Volga. The outdoor scenes were played on duck-boards or cat-walks, and the feeling of water and sky and of virtual isolation was intensified by the use of blacks and whites and brilliantly cold lighting. There was a feeling of complete desolation and hopelessness. We were greatly impressed, and in my review in *Opera* I said that the sooner Herz was invited to stage an opera in London, the better. He was invited a few years later by George to stage *Salome* for the English National Opera, and he naturally brought with him his designer Rudolf Heinrich, who died suddenly in a London hotel shortly before the first night.

The *Katya* cast included that great singing actress Astrid Varnay, whom I had known since the time of her Covent Garden debut in 1948 and with whom I had never lost contact. She gave a superb performance as Kabanicha, severe and dominating and she could hardly be faulted. She invited Phyllis and myself to lunch at the Hotel Sacher where we sampled the famous *Tafel-spitz*. It was also at the Sacher that Leonie Rysanek, whom we heard in glorious voice in the title-rôle of *Medea*, entertained us.

Paris is near enough to London to make a long week-end there a pleasant experience – travel is easy and our friend Charles Pitt, who is also the magazine's Paris correspondent, has a lovely apartment just off the bustling Rue de Lévis, where we always stay. Charles is an antique dealer by profession, but he has a history degree and is musically trained. In recent years, he has become something of a Britten specialist and it was entirely due to his efforts that the splendid Britten Exhibition was organized to coincide with the Paris production of *Peter Grimes* in 1981, and then subsequently taken on tour to Geneva, Cologne and London.

Our visit to Paris in June 1975 was to see two new productions which were part of the Opéra's centenary celebrations – *Faust* and *La forza del destino*. The week-end we were there coincided with a strike by the stage-hands and property men of the Opéra; so when the curtain rose on *Faust* we saw a virtually bare stage, and Faust's opening words, 'Rien! En vain j'interroge' were greeted with gales of laughter from the audience. The banners of the striking stage-hands were clearly visible hanging from the 'flies' and bore such devices as 'Solidarité aux Reviendications Machinistes Accessoiristes GRÈVE'. There were a few cat-calls at the end of Act I, either from sympathizers of the strikers who thought everyone taking part in the performance was a 'fascist pig' or from those who had arrived late and not heard the announcement made before the performance and so thought they were witnessing a very modern production of Gounod's opera. Despite the difficulties, the evening was a success, mostly because of the fine performances by Mirella Freni as

Marguerite and Nicolai Gedda as Faust. Freni in the prison scene appeared with cropped hair and in a strait-jacket and moved several of the audience to tears. *La forza del destino*, given 'Sans décor mais en costume' was a rather muted affair.

La Scala's famous production of *Simon Boccanegra* staged by Giorgio Strehler and conducted by Claudio Abbado, which the Milanese brought with them to Covent Garden in 1976, remains one of the greatest Verdi productions of our time. La Scala has a certain magic about it; admittedly that magic does not always work, but it did on that occasion and one felt that the audience had fallen completely under the spell of Verdi's music and Strehler's production; so much so, that when the final curtain fell there were fifteen to twenty seconds of complete silence before the applause began.

Two nights later I was in Milan where Moshinsky's production of *Peter Grimes* completely bowled over the audience, as it was later to do in Korea, Japan and Paris. Berlioz's *Benvenuto Cellini*, hardly a popular opera, was also a success, and within a short week Colin Davis had become the darling of the Milanese – his dashing performance of the overture being greeted with cries of 'bis'.

One experiences few truly memorable performances in New York, but John Dexter's staging of Britten's *Billy Budd*, which I heard in October 1978, fell into that category. Although Britten's opera had been seen in a shortened version on American television in 1952 and had also been staged in Chicago and San Francisco, it had never been seen in New York. Dexter had staged it at the Hamburg State Opera during Rolf Liebermann's régime there, and the New York production visually duplicated the Hamburg production. William Dudley's exciting and realistic setting for the man o' war, seen on the enormous Met stage from prow to stern rather than as is more usual in *Billy Budd* productions prow-on, was nothing short of magnificent. The Met's wonderfully-equipped stage enabled the whole structure to be raised or lowered without any difficulty or noise; and so we were transferred from the bridge to quarter-deck, to the berth and gun decks, and finally to the hold, deep in the bowels of the ship, where Billy Budd in irons awaits his execution. Dexter made the battle scenes far more realistic and convincing than ever before.

America has produced many fine baritones, and there have been three who have distinguished themselves as Billy Budd: Theodor

Uppman whom Britten chose to create the rôle at Covent Garden in 1951, Robert Kerns who sang the part in several revivals, and Richard Stilwell who sang it in Dexter's production both in Hamburg and New York. Peter Pears, who was the first Captain Vere, was on hand to sing the part again at the Met and showed yet again how fine the English language is to sing in.

On several of my previous visits to the Met I had been annoyed by the behaviour of the audience, and I have related how what I had written on that subject had upset Rudolf Bing. But since James Levine has become music director and Anthony Bliss general manager, there has been a subtle change in the make-up of the Met audience. It is true that it still continues to applaud a new stage picture as it is revealed, to greet the entrance of a favourite singer with more applause, and to obliterate the ends of arias and acts by premature applause; but they have become younger, better informed and less formal in their dress. So it was not entirely unexpected that they should fill the house for Britten's opera and display great enthusiasm at the end.

The last memorable production of the 1970s was the English National Opera's *Julius Caesar* in December 1979 which I was unable to see until its fifth performance, by which time, as a result of the enthusiasm with which it had been greeted by the critics (with one notable exception, but this review did not appear until much later), tickets were at a premium. Janet Baker in the title-rôle, a part originally sung by a *castrato*, provided some of the most exciting Handel singing heard on the London operatic stage for many years. Magnificent as was her performance of the bravura arias, it was with her quiet, subtle singing of the 'Hunting aria', 'How silently, how slyly', with its horn obbligato, that she reached the greatest heights. She was ably partnered by the seductively beautiful Cleopatra of Valerie Masterson; each lady seemed to spark off the other, so the atmosphere positively sizzled. Nor did they have it all their own way, for the cast included three more fine ENO singers, Della Jones as an ardent Sextus, and Sarah Walker as a warm, matronly Cornelia and John Tomlinson as Achillas; Charles Mackerras conducted, making Handel really come to life in the opera house – no easy task when one remembers those countless 'scholarly' performances under other batons which have made a Handel evening in the theatre long and tedious. Mackerras provided the vocal decorations and it was those in addition to the ENO's whole approach to Handel that had furious Handelians breathing fire and brimstone. None the less this did not prevent the production winning the *Evening Standard* Opera Award for 1979.

When the opera was revived in the spring of 1981 I asked the Handel scholar, Winton Dean, to review it for the magazine. Winton had been a regular contributor to *Opera* since its earliest days and had been a personal friend for as many years. Winton, like so many musicologists, is strong on scholarship but rather weak on judging whether performances are theatrically viable. He had not seen *Julius Caesar* in its first season at the Coliseum, and had only heard the broadcast. He wrote,

> 'I was anxious to reconcile my unfavourable impression of the broadcast with the obvious enthusiasm of the public.... As both an advocate of the assumption of Handel's operas by our professional companies and an admirer of the artists engaged I wish I could share their enthusiasm.'

And then there followed what I can only describe as a vituperative attack on Charles Mackerras and the ENO, which ended with the following sentence: 'Sir Charles Mackerras is a magnificent conductor in many areas, but I wish he would leave Handel's operas to someone who has given more study to his style.' At least that is how Winton's final sentence appeared in *Opera*, for I felt that what he had originally written, which I am not prepared to reproduce here, was libellous!

It was hardly surprising that Charles Mackerras immediately reacted, and he managed to get a letter to me in time to be published in the July issue. In it he suggested that Winton had taken umbrage because the ENO had decided not to use his (Winton's) edition of the opera that he had prepared for the production by the Barber Institute in Birmingham. Winton was furious, and behaving rather like a schoolboy, sent me to Coventry, pointedly choosing not to notice me when I was sitting close to him at a performance at Glyndebourne! He replied to Charles in a letter that we published in the August issue of *Opera* which also included several letters from readers joining in the controversy; the first batch of letters supported the Mackerras camp, then the Handelians sprung to Winton's defence and the correspondence, one of the liveliest and most controversial to have appeared in the pages of the magazine, continued for two more months after which I had to bring it to a close with the time-honoured phrase, seldom used in *Opera*, that 'This correspondence is now closed'.

22

Rewards and Punishments

———

Since I became actively involved in the world of opera, in other words since the late 1940s, there have been many rewards and not a few punishments. Some of these have already been related, especially those performances that have given me so much pleasure and the confrontations that have sometimes caused me pain. There have also been what I referred to earlier as fringe benefits; but against these must be set those frustrations, and annoyances that confront anyone in a position of some importance and has, willy nilly, come to be regarded as an authority in his field.

In order to end these memoirs on a relatively happy note, perhaps it would be best to deal with some of the 'punishments' first. Regular readers of *Opera* will know that in each issue the following notice is prominently displayed in the body of the magazine:

IMPORTANT NOTICE
The Editor of OPERA requests readers to respect his privacy and NOT to telephone for information about performances, casts, etc. after office hours or during the weekend.

There was a time, several years ago, when readers and, I am sure, quite a few non-readers of the magazine, would telephone me at all hours of the day and night to ask for information about operatic activities abroad, the dates when their favourite singer was appearing, or for the programme of several German or Italian houses for two or more weeks ahead. The calls often came during meals or when we were entertaining guests, playing Scrabble or watching television. Readers would phone from abroad – even from America – often forgetting the time difference; and someone once phoned from Australia in the early hours of the morning asking where they could get tickets for a Sutherland performance that was announced for Holland. Office hours seem to mean different things to different people.

The telephone is, on the whole, a nuisance; and the installation of an answering machine, after the frustrations of having calls transferred to an answering service which did not always function efficiently, partly solved my problems. I sometimes wonder whether I should take a firm line and say that enquiries by telephone cannot be answered and that those seeking information must write, enclosing a stamped-addressed envelope or an international reply coupon, plus a 'search fee'; and some kind of proof that they are regular readers of the magazine. It might make life easier.

Perhaps the most annoying telephone call I received came at 2 o'clock one morning when we were awakened from a sound sleep and a voice said 'So you didn't like Rita Hunter's Brünnhilde the other week,' referring to a less than enthusiastic review about that singer's performance in *The Twilight of the Gods* at the London Coliseum.

'I could not believe in this Brünnhilde [I had written] Now this may be my fault, but Rita Hunter's homely figure and lack of an heroic stage presence was for me a handicap, for which her very beautiful and often deeply moving singing could not compensate. I could *not* believe that this Brünnhilde was the figure through whom the world was going to be redeemed.'

I have also learned that it is not only what one writes that can upset people but what one says in broadcasts, lectures, or even conversations when a remark about a singer, conductor or even a colleague can either be misconstrued or reported to the person in question in a distorted version. I remember, after having downed a couple of powerful cocktails that Americans are so adept in concocting, making an admittedly foolish remark at a dinner party in New York about a colleague in England – I believe the word 'fascist' was used. Some weeks later I was telephoned by a very angry and seemingly hurt colleague who opened the conversation by saying 'I understand you accused me of having fascist sympathies, at a party in New York the other week.'

Strained relationships are not only unpleasant and wearing, but generally quite unnecessary and although I learned to live with them they have often caused me deep distress while they lasted. Perhaps I am too easy going and too ready to forgive; but life would certainly have been easier had I not gone through those unhappy times with David Webster and Garrett Drogheda. More recently, there were a series of misunderstandings between myself and Colin Davis which reached their climax when I accompanied Covent Garden on its tour to the Far East. Colin said some things to me in public which he immediately regretted, and he wrote to me to apologize and to invite me to have breakfast with him on his birthday. I certainly have never held that unfortunate episode against him, and have remained one of his most fervent supporters, sometimes to the surprise and even to the annoyance of some of my colleagues.

Those kinds of episodes were emotionally draining and added to the responsibility of running the magazine, writing books, and generally undertaking more than was physically good for me. This resulted in a slight heart attack in November 1979 shortly after I had returned from my trip to South Korea and Japan.

The consultant who came to see me was called Cecil Symons. He arrived at my bedside with his team, and the first question he asked me was whether I was the Harold Rosenthal connected with opera; when I replied that I was, instead of asking me how I was feeling, he enquired whether I had heard Carlos Kleiber conduct *La Bohème* at Covent Garden. There was a look of complete astonishment, if not disbelief, on the face of the ward sister, and Dr Symons continued 'They don't know what we're talking about I'm afraid,' and proceeded to explain to his team that Carlos Kleiber was a great conductor, son of the famous Erich Kleiber. That established a perfect relationship between my consultant and myself. We talked operatic shop on his every visit. I had with me in hospital an interleaved copy of the second edition of the *Concise Oxford Dictionary of Opera* which I was revising for the book's first reprint and I positively purred with pleasure when he told me he had my Dictionary on his bookshelf.

I continue to see Dr Symons at regular intervals, and learned from him that he had spent some time in his younger days in New York, and that the doctor with whom he was working was one of the regular medical advisers to the Metropolitan Opera; when he learned that young Cecil Symons was an opera fan he often sent him to the Met to be on duty, and he was present in the house at the performance of *La forza del destino* when Leonard Warren collapsed and died on stage. I suppose I could say that punishment though that heart attack was, meeting Cecil Symons and still having him as my medical adviser has been one of my rewards.

There have, of course, been many others and those have included the three occasions on which I was invited to accompany Covent Garden for part of their three visits abroad; to Berlin in 1970, to Milan in 1976, and to Korea and Japan in 1979. The company's visit to Germany (they also performed in Munich) was, in its way, the culmination of Solti's musical directorship. In an interview I published in the magazine in July 1968, I had asked Solti what else he would like to achieve before he left Covent Garden, and he replied that he would be sad and disappointed if he could not take the opera company abroad, complete with orchestra and chorus, 'so that either Europe, or America, or better both, could hear and see for themselves what our standards are'. I believe that Solti also wanted to demonstrate to Munich, where he had been music director in the immediate post-war period, just what *he* had achieved! The company took three operas to Germany, Verdi's *Don Carlos* and *Falstaff*, and Richard Rodney Bennett's then new opera *Victory*, which was greeted with a mixture of laughs, where none were intended, and with boos at the end of the evening. Geraint Evans scored a real personal triumph as Falstaff and he and Solti were called before the curtain countless times. *Don Carlos* was in the Berlin company's own repertory, but the inclusion of the Fontainebleau scene was something of a novelty for German audiences.

Solti had not conducted many performances of *Don Carlos* at Covent Garden but when he walked into the pit at the Deutsche Oper in Berlin, he was rewarded with an ovation such as one never hears *before* a performance in London – an ovation which necessitated his bringing the orchestra to its feet three times, and the success of the evening hardly seemed in doubt. The Fontainebleau scene was a revelation to the Berlin audience – at the dress rehearsal one photographer who did not know his Verdi particularly well, asked whether it was the last act of *Falstaff* that was being rehearsed – or perhaps *Victory*! Josephine Veasey's singing of the 'Veil Song' stopped the show and clinched the evening's success – and the cast, except for Carlo Cossutta as Carlos, was a British one, including, as well as Veasey, Gwyneth Jones, David Ward and Peter Glossop. During the intervals, one heard such comments as 'Ja, die Veasey ist die

Fricka in Karajan's *Ring*; Gwinet Yones (*sic*) ist sehr schön'; 'Aber der Ward ist ein Mensch'. My favourite overheard remark, however, occurred before the curtain rose on the first act of *Victory*, when my neighbour in the stalls opened her programme and turned in consternation to her friend with the words 'Oper in Englische Sprache. Mein Gott!' – and during the first interval, 'Einmal ist genug.' At the party after the first *Don Carlos*, at which the British and American diplomatic and military establishment was well represented, I was asked by one high-ranking military gentleman why Covent Garden had bothered to bring over its own scenery and costumes at what must have been great expense when there was a perfectly good *Don Carlos* production in Berlin that could have been used; and another asked, somewhat incredulously, whether the orchestra really was British, adding that it had played so well that he thought it must have been German! 'The conductor belongs here [i.e. in Berlin] though doesn't he?' I was asked. I hastened to point out that Solti had been at Covent Garden since 1961 and that he lived in London. Despite these amusing idiocies which, by contrast, did not occur when the company was in Milan, where audiences seemed much better informed and knowledgeable, one feels a sense of pride on such occasions, even if one is accused, from time to time, of being chauvinistic.

In 1974 Garrett Drogheda retired as chairman of Covent Garden, and I was asked by the music section of the Critics' Circle to arrange a farewell lunch for him. This took place, appropriately enough, at the restaurant not far from the Opera House, called L'Opéra. In the little speech I was called upon to make I teased Garrett about his famous 'Droghedagrams' – the messages he sent to all and sundry after a performance or after reading a less than favourable review. I reminded him how on one occasion he had sent me a note during a performance – when I was standing in for Andrew and doing a stint on the *Financial Times*, which was of course Garrett's own paper – which began, 'I don't in the least wish to influence you, but I should like to suggest that in whatever tribute you pay to Amy Shuard you should, if you agree with me, praise her for her German diction which seems to me outstandingly good and to put rings round the others.' Garrett took it all in good part, and when I presented him with a couple of old programmes from my own collection he was visibly moved.

Another reward, though one I would much rather had not come my way when it did, was a summons from the BBC late one Friday afternoon, to come to the studio as quickly as I could to record a tribute to Maria Callas who had died a few hours earlier. I had two hours in which to write my script, choose the recordings with which to illustrate Maria's art, and then record an hour's programme which was to be transmitted on the following morning. I listened to that broadcast and made a cassette of it which I have played from time to time. Whenever I hear it I am close to tears, especially the closing minutes in which I recalled that unhappy last concert she gave at the Festival Hall in 1973, when she was but a shadow of her former self.

'I was reminded [I said] of the graphic and very moving description by the famous nineteenth-century critic, Chorley, of Giuditta Pasta's ill-advised return to the London stage as Donizetti's Anna Bolena nearly a hundred years earlier. It was witnessed by the great French actress, Rachel, who turned to an acquaintance and said, "It's like Da Vinci's Last Supper – a wreck of a picture but that picture is the greatest in the world."'

But I wanted to end that tribute with a happy memory, and I reminded listeners that twenty-five years earlier I had been one of the first, if not the first person, to play a Callas record in a Sunday operatic programme on the BBC, Elvira's 'Qui la voce' from *I Puritani*. In it we heard Callas phrasing the music like a great instrumentalist and declaiming the text as if singing were just as natural a means of expression as the spoken word. That is what made her unique. I certainly still find it impossible to listen to another Norma, Violetta or Tosca, for Callas's voice and the inflections she gave to certain phrases remain indelibly in my memory.

Another 'sad' reward was being invited to deliver the address at the Service of Thanksgiving and Remembrance for Norman Tucker, who had been so successful a director of Sadler's Wells Opera in the 1960s and whose living memorial is the English National Opera today.

I suppose that all critics have something of the performer in their make-up, and I certainly have always enjoyed standing in front of an audience. In recent years I have 'appeared' with Tito Gobbi on several occasions, in London at the Queen Elizabeth Hall in the Adrian Boult Lecture which was organized by the British Institute of Recorded Sound, discussing with him 'The Baritone and his Rôles'. It was Tito who specially asked for me to do this, and so pleased was he with our partnership that we have repeated the evening in Liverpool at the Philharmonic Hall, again in London for the Friends of English National Opera at St Martin-in-the-Fields, and we recorded a shortened version of it for the BBC's 'In Repertory' series. That is the kind of thing that has made it all worth while; as has being invited to serve for several years on the *Evening Standard*'s Opera Panel which decides on the annual opera award. During the last few years it has gone to Colin Davis, Charles Mackerras, the English National Opera, Jon Vickers, and Carlos Kleiber.

Why do I continue in my world of opera? I suppose because, although as a critic I might be seeing my 250th *Tosca* or 500th *Figaro*, I know that there is always someone in the audience who is seeing it for the very first time, and that I have to try and recapture the excitement for them. And then, of course, there is always the prospect that at any performance, that magic spark that joins orchestra, stage and audience will ignite and we will all be caught up in one of those rare experiences that make a great operatic performance. But that can only happen two or three times a year, if that; should it happen more often then one would get operatic indigestion.

It was in 1970 that Peter Hall wrote to me saying how he had 'adored his visit to Bayreuth that year'. 'It was splendid,' he continued, 'to see the genuine article rather than all the imitations which litter Europe. Also I was sitting in the front row and I could see what the singers were thinking.' Ten years later it was announced that Peter had been invited by Wolfgang Wagner to stage the new *Ring* at Bayreuth in 1983 with Solti conducting. Because I have yet to be disappointed with one of Peter's operatic productions I cannot wait for that event. I am sure it will be quite different from the Chéreau-Boulez *Ring* – perhaps it will even be traditional. But it is the anticipation of such events that prevents me from giving up my job; and on the day that I begin to be bored with opera, should it ever come, then I will stop writing about it. But I hope that day will be a long time in arriving.

Index

—

Index

Index

Index

Index

Index

Index

Index

Index

Index

Index

233